# Studs, Tools, and the Family Jewels

# Studs, Tools, and the Family Jewels

## Metaphors Men Live By

Peter F. Murphy

The University of Wisconsin Press

The University of Wisconsin Press
2537 Daniels Street
Madison, Wisconsin 53718

3 Henrietta Street
London WC2E 8LU, England

5     4     3     2     1

Printed in the United States of America

Library of Congress Cataloging-in-Publication Data
Murphy, Peter Francis.
    Studs, tools, and the family jewels: metaphors men live by / Peter F.
    Murphy.
    182 pp.        cm.
    Includes bibliographical references and index.
    ISBN 0-299-17130-2 (cloth: alk. paper)
    ISBN 0-299-17134-5 (pbk.: alk. paper)
        1. Men—United States—Language—Psychological aspects.   2. Sexism
in  language—United States.   3. Masculinity—United States.   4. English
language—United States—Sex differences.   I. Title.
HQ1090.3 .M87        2001
305.31—dc21            00-010619

Dedicated to Shere Hite, Leslie Fiedler,
and Roland Barthes (1915–1980)—those with whom
I share a profound interest in the everyday

# Contents

# Preface

I realize that writing this book makes me vulnerable. By revealing something of my own sexual experiences and reactions to this discourse in a less than heroic light, and in proposing alternative metaphors that are "unhard," I open myself up to mockery. Men need to take these kinds of risks, however, risks that women in the feminist movement have been taking for decades (even centuries) as a way to confront what is touted as natural and normal. If men are to participate authentically in the struggle to change the way we think about masculinity and femininity, to move the discourse beyond the oppressive and the demeaning, we too must take some risks.

Writing this book has been emotionally difficult. As I worked my way through each of these metaphors/tropes of male heterosexuality, I became more and more disturbed by the alienated descriptions of what was purported to be my sexuality. Although I found some relief in the realization that somehow I had managed to resist adopting much of this identity, and that I was not alone among my male friends in this survival, I remained saddened that most men have nonetheless been crippled by this discourse (and to a great extent my friends and I are not exempt). The power of language to create our identities and to teach us how to construct interpersonal relationships is so overwhelming that even those of us who have reflected critically upon who we are as men will never be able to transcend completely the effect this discourse has upon us.

Some figures of speech were individually more poignant to me than others, but collectively they proved to be quite disturbing. "Blow job," for example, gave me the most trouble emotionally; I realized that even though I was quite well aware of this trope, I initially failed to incorporate it in the list of metaphors I planned to analyze. Although I eventually made the decision to include it, it was not an easy choice. The reification in this phrase, its reduction of one particular form of sexual pleasure to an experience that is both external and mechanical, affected me profoundly.

"Gang bang" was another extremely troublesome phrase to think about. The immediacy of the gang rape case in Gouverneur, New York, a village in northern New York near where I grew up, made vivid my own near-miss with this experience when I was a young boy. A gang bang, while not gang rape, was one experience that many boys believed proved their manhood. How that assumption resonates with the socialization of male heterosexuality in general was an insistent reminder of how depressing (and ultimately crippling) men's maturation can be.

The project brought humorous moments as well, and I should mention a couple. While writing the book, I realized that if I had been researching Twain or Faulkner when a friend asked what I was working on, I would have answered, "*Huck Finn*" or "*The Sound and the Fury.*" With this book I had to respond by saying, "Getting laid." Or, when I described the overall project to a friend and I came to a phrase like "jerking off," he said, "That's one you better keep at arm's length."

The title of the book elicits laughter too, probably in part because the topic tends to embarrass people. When I presented an early version of its thesis at a small liberal arts college, I became aware of the absolute necessity to add a separate chapter on humor. As should become clear from the text, the discourse of masculinity can be very funny in a tragic sort of way. Male heterosexuality can be understood as a tragicomic experience. Frequently, though, the actors apprehend neither the humor nor the misery.

I wrote this book to help reveal the insidiousness of language in the tragedy of contemporary manhood. By unearthing the multiplicity of masculine discourse, how it works against us while appearing to empower us, I hope men will better understand who they have been forced to become in American society. Out of this knowledge we may be empowered to re-envision, indeed re-imagine, and re-construct ourselves as men.

# Acknowledgments

Sarah Gutwirth deserves the strongest acknowledgment and the deepest thanks for her contributions to this book. It is customary to acknowledge one's wife, lover, soul mate, partner, and/or significant other at the end of this particular section and frequently to talk about love, friendship, emotional support, and patience. While Sarah provided all these invaluable qualities, she is also an excellent editor, critical reader, and demanding audience. She read this book almost as many times as I wrote it, and she always brought to her engagement new insights, new phrasings, new questions. Without her suggestions the book would not be written as well as it is, thought through as thoroughly as it has been, nor articulated as clearly. Where it fails in these areas, the responsibility is solely mine; Sarah's recommendations only improved it.

Few people have the good fortune to marry into a family of editors, critics, and creative geniuses. I count myself one of those lucky few. Thus with the warmest, most sincere sentiment I thank Madelyn, Marcel, and Nathanael Gutwirth for their inestimable contributions to, and their unremitting support of, this project. For those of us who have been raised with the myth of the meddling, inimical mother-in-law, any man whose mother-in-law could read this book cover to cover without rejecting her son-in-law as a pervert should be honored—and I gratefully take this opportunity to honor Madelyn Gutwirth. Her own feminist work provided me with a more than worthy goal to which I could only aspire. Her editorial suggestions improved immensely the quality of this book. Marcel Gutwirth, a funny man in his own right, and a highly sophisticated, even brilliant, commentator on laughter, strengthened the chapter on humor in particular and provided countless technical corrections to the entire text. In addition to his numerous grammatical revisions, he made sure I included the *l* in "public." Nathanael Gutwirth, one of the great original minds in the world of advertising, gave me the title. What more need be said?

Neil Schmitz and Bruce Jackson read the earliest draft of the manuscript, and for that torturous experience I owe them both a great debt. Neil's suggestions for reorganization and emphasis gave me some much-needed direction at a time when my own doubts about the project were emerging. Bruce's observation at the end of the section entitled "Blow

Job"—that if this is really "your take on the term," I should get counsel-
ing—convinced me that I was on to something after all. For their support
at an early stage in the project I thank them both wholeheartedly.

Michael Kimmel also read a very early draft and a subsequent version
of the manuscript. His observations at each stage in the project provided
useful guidance. His belief in the importance of the book and his suggestions for improvement warrant an enthusiastic thank you.

Nancy Walker read and commented on the humor chapter, and John
Massaro responded to the chapter on sports. Their remarks helped
strengthen these sections.

My agent, Anne Edelstein, provided support for the project when I
needed it most. I thank her for her suggestions and for her belief in the
book.

Two readers, James Armstrong and Leonard Duroche, deserve warm
thanks for their advice and suggestions. Professor Armstrong, in particular, provided copious notes, minute observations, and difficult questions.
His observations forced me to be more clear and precise.

The people with whom I have worked at the University of Wisconsin
Press have made the production of the book painless and enlightening.
My editor, Raphael Kadushin, was always reassuring, helpful, and astute.
Polly Kummel, copy editor extraordinaire, made both my writing and my
thinking more precise. In addition, she contributed many kind words and
humorous anecdotes.

I want to acknowledge the undergraduate students at the State University of New York at Potsdam who attended the very first presentation I
gave of this work. Their responses inspired the chapter on humor and
helped me to understand much better the audience to whom the book is
addressed. David Brown, professor emeritus of politics at SUNY–Potsdam,
who invited me to deliver the paper that gave rise to this book and who
has followed the maturation of the manuscript through its several incarna-
tions, deserves a heartfelt thank you. I want also to thank the Women's
Studies Program at SUNY–Potsdam, which invited me back to present
the chapter on humor and in that way provided coherence to a work that
sometimes seemed on a track of its own.

My dear friend Victor Chaltain, with whom I grew up in the north
country of New York State, helped me think through the meanings of a
discourse we were both raised with. As always, Victor kept me honest
about who I am in this discourse, my ambivalence, and my lack of
immunity.

Another dear friend, Susan Pearles, suffered through the earliest stages
of this project. For her support and critical observations I thank her
deeply.

I must acknowledge Goddard College for awarding me the John Dewey

Fellowship, which gave me a year off from my responsibilities as dean for academic affairs to finish the book. In this context I should also thank Scott Cameron, my attorney from Montpelier, Vermont, whose hard work and perseverance guaranteed a remuneration that allowed me to work on the book full time. I hope my project is the first in a long line of scholarly undertakings supported by this fellowship; I hope also that subsequent awardees do not need the services of an attorney.

On a related note I want to acknowledge some members of the Goddard College faculty, and especially of the administration, for providing some invaluable clarification about the nature of the discourse I have examined here. Contrary to popular belief, men do not have a monopoly on the authoritarian, competitive, self-serving mentality that informs the discourse of male bonding. If I learned anything at Goddard during my rather brief tenure, it is that the struggle for liberation requires a subtle, critical, and constant vigil. This engagement is in no way the exclusive purview of women.

In closing, then, I want to acknowledge the male friends I gained at Goddard who, I believe, are committed to a feminist future. I want to thank Tom Arner, Bobby Buchanan, Steve Shapiro, Richard Schramm, David Boyce, and Ken Bergstrom for the work they are doing as teachers, as husbands, as fathers, and as friends.

A revised version of the chapter on humor, chapter 6, ran in a special international issue of *Mattoid* as "Examining/Experiencing Masculinities" (vol. 54 [1999]: 61–73).

I used *The Oxford English Dictionary* to locate many of the epigraphs I cite throughout the book and credit to their original authors; I want to acknowledge the work the *OED*'s researchers have done to identify specific examples of usage.

# Studs, Tools, and the Family Jewels

# Introduction

Language orders life through concrete utterances . . . and life enters
language through concrete utterances as well.
—M. M. Bakhtin, *Speech Genres and Other Late Essays*

We can assume that there is a set of discourses of femininity and masculinity, because women and men behave within a certain range of
parameters when defining themselves as gendered subjects.
—Sara Mills, *Discourse*

Institutional practices people draw upon without thinking often embody assumptions which directly or indirectly legitimize existing
power relations.
—Norman Fairclough, *Language and Power*

The metaphors of gender reflect ways of constructing the world, and
ways of coping with it.
—Helen Haste, *The Sexual Metaphor*

Men bond around issues of sexuality, and when they speak about themselves, about other men, and about women, their discourse tends to concentrate on a few recurrent themes. Clearly, their primary focus is on the
penis. From that central preoccupation men create a discourse of masculinity that in turn engenders a sexuality of war and conquest, whether the
battle takes place at work, on the playing field, in the bedroom, or on an
actual battleground. For most men all relationships are tactical encounters
that have to be won, lest they risk the loss of manhood. The language men
use to describe the way they interact with other people, women especially
but other men as well, evokes a conception of manhood imbued with a
sense of alienation, distrust, fear, and confusion. When men speak of their
lives as men, they hide behind a discourse that protects them from close,
personal, caring relationships with others; they cower, ironically, behind a
language whose meaning even they do not fully comprehend.
   The main purpose of this book, then, is to reveal the insidiousness of

3

language used by men to speak of manhood and heterosexuality and in this way begin to undermine the discourse of male bonding. By making public the meanings of these disparaging terms, I hope that fewer men will feel they have permission to use them against women and other men.

The dominant perspective I use assumes that language shapes us, constructs our reality, and creates our identities. The book analyzes metaphors in order to reveal the shared assumptions they reflect about masculinity.[1] This book is less about rigorous scholarship and ironclad categories than it is about accessibility to words and phrases, and new ways to look at the discourse of male bonding. Rather than see the book as another contribution to linguistics or to academic cultural studies, it should be seen as a critical, even feminist, glossary. Ideally, people should be able to open this book to any one of the terms, read about it independently of the rest of the book, and gain something from that brief section. If a person should become interested from that serendipitous encounter, she or he may want to read further—another section in the same chapter, one from a different chapter, or even one of the introductory pieces to a theme. This book should be read from the middle out, not just from the beginning to the end.

In fact, the first organizational structure I tried was an alphabetical list without thematic chapters. The eminent scholar Michael Kimmel, an activist in the U.S. men's movement, suggested the current organization, and I agree that it strengthens the book. I still believe, though, that an argument can be made to include the metaphors in alphabetical order, in the way Roland Barthes does in *A Lover's Discourse*. The themes provide coherence, of course, and they elucidate the violence of the masculine experience. A list, on the other hand, points to the randomness of it all. For this reason the organization is alphabetical within the thematic chapters.

This analysis of metaphors of manhood is intended to reveal the assumptions about masculinity that American men take to be normal. Ironically, this discourse reflects an objectification of self and sexuality, a phallocentric sexuality, a disembodied sexuality, and a great deal of ambivalence about sexuality.

Metaphors emerge from conversation, not just from novels and poetry, and inform the speech of the most fundamental section of our society, the common folk, our friends, who are not intellectuals or authors or academics. Speech is fundamentally metaphorical, and folk language embodies a speech that is poetic in nature. Indeed, this metaphorical language is a part of the ordinary discourse many of us frequently rely on to make our points in conversations.

Aristotle acknowledged and the Romantics emphasized—especially Wordsworth and Coleridge, who recognized the poetic nature of everyday conversation—the predominance of metaphors in popular discourse. Coleridge, for example, denounces the artificial distinction between language and reality, asserting, according to Terence Hawkes, that "metaphor provides the means by which words are 'elevated' into 'living Things'" (53). The metaphors I examine are metaphors for men and by men. They are the metaphors men have created, have imagined, have imposed upon themselves. These tropes are not literary metaphors but rather the poetic language of regular people. These "conventional metaphors," to use Lakoff and Johnson's phrase, reflect the values of a society and are not independent of the metaphorical concepts used by that society.

I do not intend, however, "a discourse of discourse determinism."[2] Analyzing language allows us to explore the underlying assumptions of reality. In this way it interacts with other behavior to constrain the ways we understand ourselves and how we construct our identities. Language reinforces social roles, and, while it may not construct them, discourse both gives us permission to perpetuate certain behaviors and restricts the parameters in which our assumptions can change. We objectify women in our language because our behavior objectifies them. Metaphors that reify women are imaginable because they make sense from what we experience in life. We could not use objectifying language if we did not engage in objectifying. It would not make sense. Language reinforces this alienation and makes it difficult to imagine other ways of behaving. Although language does not determine this reification, it describes it in a way that gives it legitimacy.

While it is true that men can imagine certain metaphors only because they make sense in the cultural contexts with which they interact, changing the language can provide an alternative vision for masculinity; it can suggest another way to talk about and thus conceive of heterosexual male behavior. The conclusion to this book posits some alternative metaphors that I hope will initiate a broader conversation about how we conceive of ourselves as men and how we describe those different conceptions in the language we use.

The suggestion that metaphors have to be understood within the larger cultural context in which they are articulated, and that they mean more than their literal interpretations might suggest, is not self-evident for all theorists. Donald Davidson's now famous (or infamous) assertion that "metaphors mean what the words, in their most literal interpretations mean, and nothing more" (29–30) notwithstanding, we cannot deny the importance to a metaphor of the unusualness of the idea as well as the originality of how that particular concept is conveyed. The uniqueness of the language used, the connections between images of two unrelated ideas or concepts captured by two dissimilar words, make a trope metaphorical. The metaphors interpreted in this book have a much more dynamic meaning than each word used separately or together. "Blue balls," for example, if interpreted literally, brings to mind the small rubber ball used in the game of racquetball, whereas "pussy whipped" might conjure up a cat-o'-nine-tails made by weaving several cats together, or a woman's pubic hairs fastened to a wooden handle to make a horse whip. Although literal interpretations of these metaphors are inadequate, they do inform many of the interpretations I suggest. Literal meanings interact with the figurative and in that way enrich the associative meanings.

Recent work on metaphor, certainly most relevant to this book, examines metaphor as a cultural phenomenon that permeates popular discourse. Although Hawkes's primer on metaphor allows for an appreciation of the broad historical context in which our thinking about metaphor has evolved, his concluding remarks focus on the contribution anthropologists have made to the examination of metaphor. Central to his concern is the significance of the social context for a clear understanding of how effective metaphor can be within a culture.

Conceptions of how metaphor works as discourse and not just as language stress the importance of a cultural environment to the understanding of how metaphors function and give meaning. These observations underscore ways in which language exerts power to suggest that it is not neutral; rather, it contains within it constructions of everyday life that have ramifications across a spectrum of behaviors and values.

In this realm discourse theory offers important insights into the power of language to reinforce social roles, especially in the broader context of ideology. Although, as Sara Mills observes, no single or even clear definition of "discourse" exists, understandings of discourse gain clarity within the context of linguistic theories and analyses of language. Discourse theory comprehends language usage in its broad social context. Thus language can no longer be conceived of as "simply expressive, as transparent, as a vehicle of communication, as a form of representation . . . [but rather] as a system with its own rules and constraints, and with its own determining effect on the way that individuals think and express themselves" (S. Mills, 8). That is, a discourse can be seen as "a set of sanctioned statements which have some institutionalised force" (62). This use of language influences the way people act as individuals and the way they think. Discourses structure our notions of identity and restrict the way we can imagine ourselves as gendered beings. Discourse organizes social relations and in that way polices personal relationships.

The discourses of work, sports, war, and heterosexuality, for example, reinforce culturally constituted social roles. The construction of heterosexuality depends upon "the norm of marriage, the family and procreation, which provide the particular 'regime of truth' for the classification of 'other' sexual and moral practices" (Mort, 44). Although homosexuals constitute the most aggrieved victims of this particular regime of "normality," this official standard also torments single or celibate people, whether straight or gay. The norm of heterosexuality pervades our everyday lives and determines in a variety of oppressive ways who we are as social beings.

In his book on the relationship between language and power Norman Fairclough examines the connections among discourse, power, and ideology. Fairclough distinguishes between coercion and consent as the basis of power and focuses his analysis on the role of ideology. As the primary means of manufacturing consent, ideology relies on acquiescence, frequently based on the notion of common sense, or the assumptions of knowledge held by a community or group. The discourse of male bonding, grounded as it is in the institution of heterosexuality, depends on a series of assumptions widely believed to be natural, normal, and truthful. These premises represent what Fairclough calls an "ideological common sense . . . in the service of sustaining unequal relations of power" (84). Fairclough goes on to suggest that commonsense assumptions establish and consolidate "solidarity relations among members of a particular social grouping" (84). The social grouping whose relations of domination the discourse of male bonding perpetuates is, of course, that of heterosexual men. When heterosexuality is seen as "a set of discursive constructs with which subjects interact, refusing certain elements and accepting others" (S. Mills, 96), the extent to which many of our choices are next to nonexistent becomes apparent. Common sense, in the guise of seemingly innocuous metaphors, perpetuates the myth of a transhistorical human nature that represents a normal and appropriate social order.

Cultural anthropology provides another broad theoretical framework for comprehending the social nature of language. James Fernandez, and David Sapir and J. Christopher Crocker, for example, focus on the social context in which metaphors occur, whereas Herbert Landar suggests that language is not an isolated creation of individuals but rather a product of a collective elaboration.[3] Fernandez, for one, speaks directly about the contribution anthropology can make to metaphor theory: "First in its insistence upon the role of culture in the formation of metaphoric models with which various peoples reason . . . and second in its concern to avoid over concentration on metaphor as the uniquely interesting trope, but rather to see metaphors in their natural context in dynamic relation to all other tropes" (9–10). For the metaphors examined here, this characterization underlines two crucial points: the discourse of male bonding is not only cultural but exists in direct relationship to the ways in which men think or reason about their sexuality, and these metaphors should not be seen as isolated examples of male oppression of women but as part of a larger linguistic framework in which men conceptualize and describe their relationships with women and with other men.

Anthropology focuses on the politics of everyday speech as a cultural phenomenon and regards language as a broad-based discourse within a larger social and historical context. For Sapir, "the metaphoric . . . process is not a simple game of substitution, but rather a creative game where the pregnant . . . interplay of two disparate terms provides insight that, although it might at times be trivial . . . can also be . . . profound and revealing of important and deep cultural understandings" (32). Some work in literary theory echoes this notion of a dialectical relationship between the two dimensions of metaphorical meaning. Hugh Holman and William Harmon, for example, in their handbook of literature, point out that the identification of one object with another invests that first object "with emotional or imaginative qualities associated with the second" (298).

The transference of emotional qualities in the metaphors I examine enhances the power of these tropes. "Gang bang," for example, combines the brutality of a gang with the violence of a bullet being fired. Together, taken literally, these words exemplify the power men have over women, while as a metaphor they allude to the male myth that women are over-sexed, craving intercourse with several men. As a metaphor, "gang bang" becomes a means to control this mythical sexual need of women by providing an implicit threat that if women do not behave, men will control them with as many men as it takes to do so. This metaphor, like all the others on my list, is not neutral. It is specific to a particular society and acquires meaning only within the broad context of its culture.

Thus a more precise title for this book might be *Analogies, Similes, Synecdoches, Metaphors, Metonymies, Ironies, and Allusions Men (and Women) Live by in the North Country of New York State.* That is a long title, to be sure, and nowhere near as poetic as *Studs, Tools, and the Family Jewels: Metaphors Men Live By.* It captures, though, some of the challenges inherent in this work, as well as the regional specificity of speech.

To begin with, the phrases I examine here are not just metaphors but qualify as a variety of tropes. Some terms I analyze might be more accurately referred to as metonymies, especially if we understand a metonymy as that which uses "one entity to refer to another that is related to it" (Lakoff and Johnson, 35). "Pussy whipped" might be a good example: "pussy" becomes a metonymy for female genitals and a synecdoche for woman. Similarly, to say, "He doesn't have the balls," makes "balls" refer to strength or bravado or manhood in general. Indeed, throughout the discourse of male bonding examined here, synonyms for the penis represent a metonymy for the man. To make the case for each of these tropes as constituting either a metaphor, a metonymy, or a synecdoche would detract significantly from a consideration of what these phrases mean as ways in which men describe their heterosexuality. My objective here is to comprehend the language we use in order to envision changing that discourse, not to compartmentalize words or phrases.

Second, these tropes affect women as well as men. These metaphors

men live by are experienced equally by women. The stress on the word
"men" might suggest that the masculine experience is somehow a universal, unrelated in any way to the experience of women. But these metaphors
profoundly affect the lives of women. They specify, define, and structure
the experiences men have with women in our society. The recurrent characterization of male sexuality as hard, dominant, powerful (e.g., "having
the balls," "gang bang"), and mechanical (e.g., "jerking off," "lead in your
pencil," "wet dreams," "piece of tail") structures the kinds of relationships
men can conceive of having with women (and with other men, for that
matter). Women are not merely victims of these metaphors as men are;
ironically, women frequently perpetuate their oppressive structures when
they talk about their own interpersonal relationships (e.g., "shooting
blanks" and "studmuffin").[4]

Although many women are privy to such metaphors and indeed also
live by them, as part of masculine discourse the metaphors provide a language of oppression in which men may speak secretly about their relationships with women. These metaphors that men live by propose to exclude
women from the conversation and in this way control the dynamics of the
heterosexual relationship.

Third, popular speech is regional. Although metaphors represent a
way in which people understand their language and their experience,
metaphors differ significantly from culture to culture and region to region.
Discourses of gender in particular vary over time and by race, class, eth-
nicity, location, sexuality, nationality, age, and other factors.[5] From items
on my list "cock" demonstrates this difference best. In the northern United
States "cock" refers to the penis, whereas in the South it refers to female
genitalia.[6]

The metaphors examined in this book are predominantly heteronormative, and they are the ones with which I am most familiar.[7] As a male who
was raised in the northeastern United States and, even more specifically,
in the north country of New York State, the metaphors I am familiar with
may not be the same ones a young boy growing up in the Southwest or in
an urban ghetto or in Hawaii may know. These metaphors are also different from those used by gay men, no doubt, but just how much gay male
discourse differs from the dominant male heterosexual discourse is an area
still in need of examination.[8]

The tropes examined in this book voice commonly held assumptions
about masculinity and femininity. They describe, at times poetically, the
beliefs men and women share about sexuality and gender. Language is not
neutral, and discourse frequently articulates unfounded presumptions and
opinions that people take to be true. These metaphors convey, at times
subtly, at times vociferously, traditionally sanctioned assumptions of difference: of male superiority and female inferiority, of male prowess and

female sexual availability, of male fear and female deceit. This discourse of male heterosexuality, in the form of metaphor and allusion, elucidates the dynamics of male–female relationships.

Discourse is by nature metaphorical, and this book examines the metaphorical character of everyday speech. My concern is with the politics of language, with how we can change the way we talk about and describe ourselves as men. I focus here on the metaphors of daily conversation more than on literary metaphors,[9] although literature, as Leslie Fielder has made abundantly clear, reinforces many of our conceptions of manhood.[10]

How the more than forty tropes I examine operate as descriptions of behavior and interpersonal relationships, and how they fall into a few central themes of masculinity, focus my inquiry. Each domain is cognitively intertwined in the conceptual structures involved, however, thus creating the potential for overlap. Courage as a male ideal, for example, is needed both in war and in competitive sports, and courage and sexual prowess are supposed to go together in the ideal male (impotence is a sign of being a "sissy"). This intertwining can lead to overlapping discussions in the different chapters suggesting the relatedness of several metaphors.

Clearly, then, these themes of manhood are not mutually exclusive, nor are the metaphors themselves. While a characterization of masculinity as machinelike and mechanical constitutes a separate theme in this book, the mechanistic metaphor also infiltrates motifs of work, conquest, and sport. The chapter on war and conquest might also have been called "Sex as Violence," but war is the broad ideological framework in which men are socialized to believe in violence. War endorses rape, murder, and conquest, but, more important, war teaches men to be warriors and through that identity to trust violence as a solution. Other themes might also be appropriate: for example, "Sex as Objectification," though it should become clear that this theme could serve as an overarching rubric, and "Sex as Animalism and/or Strength," under which "cojones" and "stud" might be discussed.[11] I decided on the five themes I use because they seemed the most general and the most helpful as categories. The themes are fluid; they provide a loose organizational structure that, I believe, suggests connections and relationships.

Several metaphors will overlap the individual categories: for example, "wimp" is discussed under sport but could also go under heterosexuality; "having the balls" and "pussy whipped" are examined in the section on war but could be discussed equally under sport; "faggot" and "stud-muffin" are analyzed under heterosexuality but also relate to men as machines.

With the few exceptions of "bottom line," "husband," and "jock," the rest of the metaphors under consideration relate directly to sex (though the case can be made that "jock" has at least an implicit sexual connotation). This almost singular focus on various aspects of sexual acts underscores men's fixation with size, power, performance, and control and how they always imagine sex through sexual conquest.

Men's confusion, or even ambivalence, about masculinity emerges in several metaphors examined here, especially those that are synonyms for the penis. Take, for example, the term "dick." While it represents a personification of the penis and signifies the phallocentric aspect of male sexuality, "dick" is also a term used to denigrate other males, those who are mean, domineering, and spiteful. This confusion reflects a degree of ambivalence about sexuality that should strike men as absurd. We love our dicks enough to give them names, while we use the terms we apply to them as the central insult we bestow on those we do not like. When the phrase "jerking off" refers to a person, a "jerk-off" who resists doing any work, this synonym for male masturbation—potentially a pleasurable experience—becomes derisive and demeaning.

The language of male heterosexuality allows men to hide their vulnerability and in the process cripples them as human beings. Ultimately, men translate their fear of being seen as weak or nurturing into violence against women and gay men; language expresses this violence, sometimes covertly but always effectively. Lucy Komisar, in her work on violence and masculinity, stresses this effect when she points out that sexual violence provides the ultimate proof of manhood and that "even the language of sex is a lexicon that describes the power of men over women. Men are aggressive as they 'take' or 'make' women, showing their potency ('power') in the 'conquest.' Women, on the other hand, 'submit' and 'surrender,' allowing themselves to be 'violated' and 'possessed'" (134–35). The not-so-subtle difference between the words "take" or "make" to describe men's behavior versus "submit" or "surrender" to describe women's makes clear the power of the phrases examined in this book. Metaphors of masculinity, tropes of male heterosexual behavior, discourses of manhood—all contribute to the ways in which men keep women in their place and men maintain their position of power over them.

As an instance of backlash against feminism, a subject about which much has been written over the past few years, the popularity of many of these phrases during the 1960s attests to men's fear of women's demand for equality.[12] The phrases "blow job" and "gang bang," for example, spread from the United States to Britain in the 1960s. Helen Haste, in her book on the dominant sexual metaphor of duality, observes the magnitude of "the violent rhetoric produced in response to early manifestations of feminism," which she sees as motivated by a "deep terror" on the part of some men threatened by "the idea of women defining sex in their own terms" (181). As women gain some power in contemporary society, men fear for the continuity of their privilege. Their response has often been one of anger and contempt, and these feelings of doubt and animosity are manifested in the way men talk about women, the way men bond together to keep women down. Men wield the language of masculinity as a weapon against women in the ongoing attempt to remain in power.

The discourse of male bonding embodies what Bob Connell and others have come to call "hegemonic masculinity." Harry Christian, for example, in his work on ways to become an antisexist man, suggests that the omnipotence of heteromasculinity occurs in relationship to subordinated masculinities and to women; quoting Connell, Christian maintains that "most men benefit from the subordination of women, and hegemonic masculinity is the cultural expression of this ascendancy" (8). The metaphors I have identified for analysis contribute to men's power over women and over other men. Men learn this discourse of masculinity at an early age as it is passed down from one generation of men to the next. For little boys, according to Victor Seidler, language offers a means to conceal themselves. Men learn to "master" language as a mode of control over the world around them. Language becomes a way for men to assert their independence and their power (strength), but as Seidler makes clear, "as we learn to deny and estrange our individual and collective needs and wants so that we can live up to these ideals of ourselves we form and shape the kind of personal and sexual relationships we can have with others" (142). A critical engagement with this language, this discourse of male bonding, can contribute to our ability to transcend and even replace a form of communication and a structure of behavior that cripples us all, women and men.

My approach to examining these metaphors has been informed by the work of Roland Barthes and Raymond Williams, most notably, *A Lover's Discourse* and *Keywords*, respectively. Barthes's fascination with the language of everyday life, coupled with his particular focus on the discourse of love, which is derived from his personal experience, inspired me to embark on this project. In *Keywords* Williams analyzes the historical development of significant political terms, such as "class," "culture," "democracy," and "work." He began his research with the *Oxford English Dictionary*, which gave him the etymology of each word and the evolution of its use. In many cases I choose to examine phrases, not singular words, and thus my formal research begins with a variety of dictionaries of slang.[13] After recalling these metaphors from my years of growing up male, I used the information contained in the slang dictionaries to reflect upon my own experience with this discourse. That is, my interpretation relies on both etymological research and impressions derived from growing up male in northern New York.

These are not the only metaphors that can be examined, of course; they are just the ones I can recall from my maturation into manhood. The list is not exhaustive, the categories are not exact, the interpretations are subjective and personal. None of this is an exact science and it is not intended to be. The primary objective of the book is to introduce a new way to think about how we construct ourselves as American men in the immediate context of the language we use to talk about ourselves as men and in the process at least to rethink that identity.

To a great extent, then, my interpretation relies as much on my imagination as it does on a set of defined interpretive criteria. It should be clear that my methodology, as loose as it may be, synthesizes insights from cultural anthropology, literary theory with an emphasis on discourse theory, and the politics of language vis-à-vis ideology and concerns about power. The broader theoretical context relies on feminism as an interpretive framework to examine representations of gender and sexuality and to appreciate the subtleties of power in all interpersonal relationships.

In addition to the thematic chapters I used to organize the individual tropes, I have included a chapter on humor as a means to focus attention on the form of male discourse, not just its content. Chapter 6 examines the means by which insidious humor enhances the power of the discourse of male bonding in subtle and even perfidious ways and focuses on humor's ability to mitigate the actual intent of this discourse, thereby sanctioning a control of interpersonal relationships.

The concluding chapter, chapter 7, attempts to provide some alternative metaphors as a way to re-envision masculinity. While in no way comprehensive, this chapter is meant to initiate the development of a different discourse of masculinity. Very much a work in progress, the last chapter should be seen as initiating a conversation, certainly not as the last word.

Literature, popular culture, and discourse in general reinforce our beliefs about gender, but as powerful as they may be they are not omnipotent. Of course, one school of thought would disagree with my contention that changing the language will change behavior. This group maintains that only with the transformation of cultural behavior can a new language emerge. I believe that the relationship between language and behavior is more dialectical, however, and that if we can introduce new verbal descriptors, we can affect the way we think about ourselves as cultural beings. If, as I believe, masculinity is largely a social and cultural construction, we can affect its meaning. How we talk about ourselves as men can alter the way we live as men.

# I    The Language of Male Bonding

# 1   Sex as Machine

> By renouncing a large part of his humanity, a man could achieve godhood: he dawned on this second chaos and created the machine in his own image: the image of power, but power ripped loose from his flesh and isolated from his humanity.
>
> —Lewis Mumford, *Technics and Civilization*

The most powerful cultural metaphor for masculinity is the machine, a cold, disembodied, efficacious piece of equipment. It encompasses, and is far more omnipotent than, the metaphors of businessman, athlete, warrior, hunter, and husband/father. True masculinity as a finely tuned, well-oiled, unemotional, hard, and cost-effective apparatus deeply informs the way we conceive of manhood, a manhood that, according to Elisabeth Badinter, the French feminist, "is not bestowed from the outset; it must be constructed, or let us say 'manufactured.' A man is therefore a sort of artifact, and as such he always runs the risk of being found defective. There may be a defect in the manufacture, a breakdown in the machinery or virility, in short, a failed man" (2).

The *Oxford English Dictionary*'s definition of machine can be read in a way that develops this instrumental view of manhood: "a combination of parts moving mechanically . . . from habit or obedience to rule, without intelligence, or . . . one whose actions have the undeviating precision and uniformity of a machine" (1687). Male sexuality as involuntary, dumb even, and a product of rote memorization counters the contrasting cultural assumption that real men are independent, in control of their own destinies, and of superior intelligence. Lewis Mumford distinguishes between a machine and a tool and suggests that the difference "lies in the degree of independence in the operation from the skill and motive power of the operator: the tool lends itself to manipulation, the machine to automatic action" (10). Metaphors abound that characterize the penis as both a tool and a machine, even according to Mumford's differentiation. The penis as an object for manipulation informs such terms as "jerking off," whereas the penis as an instrument subject to automatic action inspires such

17

phrases as "getting a nut off," "hard-on," and "letting his little head rule his big head."

The language of masculinity examined in this book suggests that there exists an uncritical conception of masculinity reducible to a half-dozen general themes, all of which rely on a mechanical vision of manhood. This insight is not new, of course, but it remains relatively unexamined. In 1975, in what might be seen as the early years of the contemporary American men's movement, Marc Feigen Fasteau published a book called, quite simply, *The Male Machine*.[1] Here Fasteau describes at great length this stereotype of masculinity:

> The male machine is a special kind of being, different from women, children, and men who don't measure up. He is functional, designed mainly for work. He is programmed to tackle jobs, override obstacles, attack problems, overcome difficulties, and always seize the offensive. He will take on any task that can be presented to him in a competitive framework, and his most important positive reinforcement is victory. (1)

Fasteau goes on to develop the metaphor of the machine by referring to men's impenetrable armor, their internal circuits, their clashing gears, and their absence of intimacy. Men as automatons, men as executives, men as super athletes, men as invincible soldiers, and men as sexual performers— these are the mechanical roles males must assume or be labeled faggot, queer, wimp, or wussy.

Although the association between masculinity and the machine may be a recent one for the American men's movement, the mechanistic conception of masculinity began at least as early as Plato and Aristotle.[2] Helen Haste examines the development of the mechanistic metaphor through Descartes and Bacon and finds that this conception of masculinity reinforced the belief that nature could be brought under control; with "Nature cast in a stereotyped feminine role, and Man cast in a stereotyped masculine role of activity and control" (76), man as rational machine becomes a means to master the organic and the natural (i.e., the feminine). Mumford carries this point forward when he suggests that "in attempting to seize power man tended to reduce himself to an abstraction, or, what comes to almost the same thing, to eliminate every part of himself except that which was bent on seizing power" (31).

Although the clock, considered to be the first real machine, represents best this desire to control nature, Mumford sees the "iron discipline of rule" (13), which occurred in both the monastery and on the drill field, as introducing the kind of structure and mentality Western civilization needed to build machines of production and conquest. Mumford demonstrates this in an illustration of a fortified camp from 1573: "Sixteenth century drill was the prelude to eighteenth century industrialism. Precision and standardization appeared at an early date in the formations, the exercises, and the tactics of the army. The mechanization of men is the first step toward the mechanization of things" (fig. 3, after p. 84). As the instrument that keeps track of time, the clock helps realize the bourgeois ideal that time is money. The earliest machines, then, reinforced the ideals of a society fixated on efficient production, market value, armaments, and competition, ideals that reverberate throughout the Western conception of masculinity.

In contrast to the introduction of mechanization into the mine and onto the battlefield, the machine "came most slowly into agriculture with its life-conserving, life-maintaining functions" (Mumford, 36). Despite this positive aspect to mechanization, the epigraph to this chapter emphasizes the alienation of the machine from man's humanity and his obsession with power and control. Men as machines identify with death, their own and others'.

The mechanical model of masculinity fixated on control manifests itself today in a variety of ways. Many men still believe, for example, that if they can just master the right technique, they can satisfy women sexually and bring them to orgasm. Men project upon women their limited view of their own sexuality and assume that with a sufficient number of mechanical strokes anyone can "come." This assumption reduces women's sexuality to passive nature while envisaging men's sexuality as instrumental and active.

Ironically, the discourse of masculinity examined in this book demonstrates men's ambivalence about power and control. The phrase "getting a nut off" exemplifies this confusion. A man who "gets his nut off" participates in a passive occurrence delivered upon him by a woman whom he watches as if from afar or who performs a sexually satisfying act upon him. The man is not in control of this activity, nor is he in control of her sexual pleasure. The contrast between men's socialized need to dominate and their desire to relinquish control haunts many metaphors examined in this book.

Indeed, the discourse of masculinity resonates with this instrumental conception of manhood, and the metaphors examined in this section refer explicitly to male sexuality as mechanical. This allusion informs several other sections as well: men at work, men at war, men on the playing field, and men in intimate relationships all reflect a vision of manhood as operational, technical, and perfunctory. A man as a machine, with his tool, his prick, his hard-on getting a nut off provides the dominant metaphor of masculinity.

## COCK

As a "spout or tap, such as in a barrel" (Spears, 86), a cock functions as a spigot that allows for the flow of wine or cider out of a wooden keg. The first cocks were made completely of wood and consisted of only two parts, the screwing device that turned on and closed off the flow of liquid, and the tube through which the liquid flowed. This "faucet . . . by which the flow of a liquid or gas can be regulated" (*American Heritage College Dictionary,* hereafter *AHCD,* 268) constitutes one of the earliest machines and certainly one of the simplest. As a machine made only of wood, "cock" has an organic origin, not just a mechanistic one, but the mechanical quality of this particular apparatus has eclipsed the natural.

In suggesting that the origin of the term "cock of the walk" (discussed separately in chapter 4, "Sex as War and Conquest") may derive from "the image of the male member . . . as . . . resembling a chicken's neck or water-valve" (102), Tony Thorne makes explicit the characterization of the penis as a mechanical apparatus, something that is turned on and off indifferently to pour water or other liquids. The penis as an unconscious machine resonates with the notion of the male body as an instrument or a device engineered to perform a particular task.

In northern New York State and, as it turns out, throughout the Northeast as well, "cock" refers to the penis. This association has been around for a long time, at least three hundred years. A synonym for the penis, especially the erect penis, this term, according to Thorne, is "used all over the English-speaking world," dating in Britain from the seventeenth century (102). Harold Wentworth and Stuart Berg Flexner cite Shakespeare's *Henry IV,* part II, written in 1599: "And Pistol's cock is up" (112).

Any assumption of universal meaning is, however, incorrect. Richard Spears points out, for example, that "in much of the Southern United States and Caribbean, 'cock' refers to the female [genitals] exclusively. Possibly related to cockles. . . . Women considered solely as sexual objects" (87). Frederic Cassidy offers as his first definition of "cock" "the female genitalia" and cites several specific references to its use in that way from the 1940s to the 1970s (707).

I had always assumed "cock" to be a generic term for the penis used everywhere in the United States with exactly the same meaning. I also inferred that "cock" came from "rooster" and had to do with "cock of the walk" as the strident, erect male member. The realization that "cock" invokes both male and female genitalia depending upon what region of the country you are from suggests, minimally, that the discourse of masculinity is ambiguous about sexuality. This ambiguity is evident throughout many terms examined in this book, especially those that have the dual meaning that conflates the penis with a bad person (e.g., hard-on, prick, dick, etc.).

Although as an early machine made only of wood, a "cock" has an organic origin, not merely a mechanistic one, the use of the word as a synonym for penis emphasizes a screwing mechanism that characterizes the penis as a insentient tool. A focus on the historical origins of the term could help to underscore the natural, the malleable, and the unassuming.

### GETTING A NUT (OFF)

> He'd get his nuts just looking at her / When I'd gotten my nuts off about six times, we got hungry.
> —Claude Brown, *Manchild in the Promised Land*

This hydraulic metaphor advances a conception of manhood removed from intimacy and satisfied by a mechanical release of liquid. Although "nut" or "nuts," as a synonym for testicles, is usually understood as a reference to the fruit or seed from a tree or bush, a "nut" is also the recipient of a bolt. A nut and bolt, like a spigot, can be seen as a simple machine or device. "On" and "off," as states of a machine's either working or not working, reinforce this mechanistic conception of male sexual behavior.

As a slang term, "getting a nut off" or "getting one's rocks off" refers both to an immediate and a passive sexual endeavor. A man gets his rocks off or comes as quickly as possible and then goes on about his business. Like a machine designed to eject newly minted parts, a man gets his nut off and moves on to the next experience in his life, like having lunch.

The epigraph from Claude Brown illustrates starkly these assumptions (and others, for that matter). For the two guys conversing, the woman is the object of their gaze, the passive detached stimulus of their sexual fantasies. One man fantasizes so much he wants us to believe he comes a half-dozen times and then just wants (has enough energy left) to eat.

"Getting a nut off" exemplifies a masculinity alienated from the subject, the man (and equally the woman, its object). Women remain the object of heterosexual male fulfillment, however, so maybe what this metaphor really describes, or rests upon, is the virgin/whore dichotomy; women are either the maidens with whom we make love or the sluts who get us off.

Like many tropes examined in this book (e.g., "blow job," "blue balls," "getting laid"), this one reduces the male heterosexual experience to ejaculation and locates it in a dispassionate occurrence of which he is the recipient. The instantaneousness of this incident reflects an ideology of masculinity that characterizes male sexual pleasure as both genitally fixated and something that is visited upon him. The passivity implicit in this metaphor suggests a confusion, however, about male power and control. The common wisdom of men is that they always want to be dominant and the active participant; men want to be on top. "Getting a nut off," like many other metaphors of masculinity, suggests that there is a certain pleasure to be found for men in passivity and recipience.

## HARD-ON

> As they had the capacity and were bound to use it once in a while, people were bound to have such involuntary feelings. It was only another of those subway things. Like having a hard-on at random.
> —Saul Bellow, *Seize the Day*

According to Thorne, "to have a 'hard on' has been the most common way of expressing male sexual tumescence since the early 20th century" (233). A close look at the construction of this metaphor illuminates how it works. "Hard" refers to the stiffness of the penis when a man (not it, not the penis by itself) is sexually excited. "On" suggests "being on," being alive, maybe even vibrant. The hint of sentience in this characterization, of the penis as corporeal, does not, unfortunately, eclipse the more pronounced implication of the penis as a wrought-iron machine part ready to be turned on at the flick of a switch or the steely hardness of a weapon always prepared to inflict pain.

Ironically, though, "hard" does not describe accurately the quality of the penis even when it is erect. The penis goes through a series of stages in the course of sexual excitement, and hard is only one part of the experience. And "hard" is, of course, a relative term. How hard is the erect penis, and how long does it remain that way?

Emmanuel Reynaud stresses the significance of this term's rhetorical construction when he observes: "If one understands words in the context of prevailing ideas, their meaning becomes clear: erection is not a delicate warmth which spreads from the penis through the rest of the body, nor a pleasant swelling of the penis when the senses are receptive to voluptuousness. Man decides otherwise; erection is the symbol of his power, the assertion of his potency, and its absence is simply his impotence" (64).

The term "hard-on," when it refers to an erect penis, emphasizes the correlation between a penis that is as hard as iron and sexual pleasure for both the man and the woman. The myth engendered in this term asserts that only when the penis is erect can sexual satisfaction take place. As many of us know, I hope, sexual satisfaction can take place without the use of the penis at all—and certainly without the penis being erect.[3]

Myths abound about masculinity, and the epigraph I borrowed from *Seize the Day* highlights one of them: the belief that erections arise involuntarily and that men have no control over them. When the narrator of Bellow's novel says, "It was another of those subway things. Like having a hard-on at random," the emphasis is clearly on the spontaneity of the penis to just react without any influence from the mind.

The ubiquity of this myth pervades the female imagination as well as the male. In her collection of short stories called *Dick for a Day,* Fiona Giles asked women to respond to the question, "What would you do if, by some mysterious means, you had a penis for one day?" While several stories provide a satirical rendition of the absurdity of the penis to bequeath power and privilege, and some provide an alternative vision of the role of the penis in love making, far too many stories rely on the trite and oppressive notion of the uncontrollable hard-on in hot pursuit of a vagina to penetrate.[4] References to the penis as "a tool for women's pleasure" (used sometimes to "jerk off in the shower" [167]), the penis with "a mind of its own" (189), the penis as a weapon (220), and the penis as a machine with "hydraulics" (233) recur in several stories.

The assumption that men are not in control of their passions, that they are ruled by their penises, informs much popular culture and certainly much religious dogma. In the realm of popular culture a joke I heard on television exemplifies this belief: "A woman has to be in the mood, a man has to be in the room." This joke reinforces the view that men have perennial hard-ons, that they walk around with their penises in a constant state of erection. When the assumption that male tumescence is both natural and uncontrollable reaches its most logical conclusion, it becomes an excuse for rape, as it did for one father in the Glen Ridge, New Jersey, gang rape (Lefkowitz, 327).

As with so many metaphors examined in this book, "hard-on" assumes a derogatory meaning when made to refer to a person. At the same time that men perceive of having a "hard-on" as a positive aspect of male sexuality, to *be* a "hard-on" is an insult. Robert Chapman points out that to "have a hard-on for someone or something . . . means either to be enamored with or to dislike and make problems for" (197).

Thorne sees this term as "a piece of macho business jargon from the late 1970s. The phrase suggests an aggressive and uncompromising wish to acquire or cement relations with a business partner" (233). In light of other terms examined here (e.g., "bottom line"), a male tendency to view all relationships fundamentally as business deals becomes clear.

"Hard-on" relates also to the male view of the penis as a weapon to wield power against a foe. The foe in this equation becomes the woman in the relationship. Reynaud describes the consequences of this kind of logic: "The erect penis is the weapon man arms himself with to try and tame a woman via her vagina; and so he tries to make it threatening, and he likes it to arouse fear" (37). Ironically, this weapon, this symbol of power "is, in fact, one of the most fragile and vulnerable organs of his body" (Reynaud, 36).

This irony makes sense, though, as a compensation for vulnerability. Men exaggerate the importance of the penis for love making because they fear what will happen if its insignificance were to become known.

## IMPOTENCE

Although all the other metaphors examined in this book constitute part of the lexicon of male bonding, impotence does not fit into that vocabulary. The impotent man, one who cannot get a hard-on, is weak, a man without power or control. Such an inadequate man represents one of the great anxieties of masculinity, and as a metaphor impotence is so formidable that it can only be approached through the use of metaphor. Men cannot talk about a lack of power except by avoiding all direct reference to it. A metaphor such as "wimp" (which suggests "limp") implies an incapacity to become erect, but the explicit reference of wimp has more to do with being womanly and a coward than with the state of a man's penis.

Bob Dole's Viagra commercials notwithstanding, men rarely refer to or talk about impotence, certainly not with other men, and they do not use impotence as an insult against another man. While virility remains one of the more vulnerable points of attack against a man, impotence, as an insult, is usually only an allusion and rarely—if ever—identified directly. The emerging subgenre of Viagra jokes (and Dole's commercials) may initiate a more open discussion of impotence, allowing men to confront their deep-seated belief that without erections they are useless. Humor frequently hides shame, however, while making explicit underlying fears. Rarely, though, do we laugh about impotence or even acknowledge it, for that matter. Impotence is one of the great male fears, and men's silence about it says far more than does their loquaciousness about other concerns.

Literally, according to *Webster's,* impotence has three basic meanings: "a) a lack of physical strength; weakness; b) lack of effectiveness; helplessness; c) lack of ability to engage in sexual intercourse: said of males" (731). Without an erection a man is weak and thus helpless as a lover. Indeed, an impotent male cannot "make love" at all, which, in the ideology of masculinity, has become identified exclusively with sexual intercourse. As Susan Bordo points out, "unlike other disorders, impotence implicates the whole man, not merely the body part. He is impotent. Would we ever say about a man with a headache 'He is a headache?'" (87). When we merge impotence with the man's entire personality, we can "expect the personality to perform like a machine" (Bordo, 87).

Historically, women have been blamed for male impotence because of their lack of responsiveness to male sexual ardor. In the first decade of the twentieth century, in the midst of our country's obsession with the evils of masturbation, an enormously popular book on sexual impotence by Dr. William Robinson identified the problem of impotence as "'frigidity' in women which 'will not call out his virility.' Once again, male sexuality was woman's problem" (Kimmel, *Manhood,* 131).

Robinson's desire to blame women ignores some important distinctions between female frigidity and male impotence; the language itself illuminates a dominant confusion. "Frigid," the term used to describe a woman who "habitually [fails] to become sexually aroused," means, literally: "1) extremely cold; without heat or warmth. 2) without warmth of feeling or manner; stiff and forbidding; formal" (*Webster's,* 581). A woman's inability to become sexually aroused is an emotional problem relating to her feelings and even her social upbringing. She lacks a cordial, friendly manner, and her mien is rigid and proper.

With the application of heat something that is cold can be warmed up. With the introduction of love, that is, or kindness and understanding, the frigid woman may be aroused, may be made comfortable, and may be able to relax and experience sexual pleasure. In contrast, male impotence, as a weakness, suggests the need for vigorous exercise and implies that only athletic men, jocks or soldiers, are potent men. A man who is not concupiscent has a mechanical defect, whereas a woman who is not lascivious has an emotional problem. A defect needs a part replaced or augmented or repaired; a problem needs some kind of attention, consideration, or response.

One reaction to male impotence has been to ignore it with the hope that it will go away. This response disregards the emotional aspect of the man's predicament and confirms the belief that male impotence is a mechanical problem for which the failing part needs rest in order to recuperate. Another solution for male impotence, and one that certainly reinforces the mechanical conception of male sexuality, is the penile implant. Looking very much like a technical device with its reservoir, pump, and cylinders, the penile prosthesis has been compared favorably to the earliest remedy for the flat tire when "a desperate driver filled his tire with sawdust instead of air. Now we have the implant, and it works quite well" (Gilbaugh, 55).

In addition to the implant, drugs have been developed to facilitate male tumescence. Before the recent plethora of interest in Viagra, men relied on a drug called the "erector injector" designed to "cause a penis to become erect from one and a half to three hours, long enough to sustain intercourse" (Gilbaugh, 54). Considering that the patient himself must inject this drug directly into his penis, this seems a bit torturous just to get an erection.

With the invention of Viagra, a pill taken orally, men can now just ingest this drug and be ready for sex almost immediately. The jury is still out on the success or failure of Viagra, but men who take it get erections, and in most cases they last for several hours. Evidence also seems to suggest that for men with heart conditions, Viagra can have serious side-effects and even lead to death. As a metaphor itself, this drug as a potential source of male fatalities alludes to the tragedy of the male fixation with an erection.

Viagra has also been responsible for the demise of many long-standing relationships and marriages. Men who were not able to get an erection for several years and who now can are leaving their wives for younger women or polarizing their wives by inflicting pain on them from interminable intercourse. The belief that all women want intercourse to go on forever is a male fantasy consistent with the idea that sex is a race, a competition, a struggle for domination.

While a great deal more still needs to be said about Viagra, at least some therapists point to its potential to wreak havoc with people's emotional and sexual lives. According to a recent *New York Times* article on the subject, "James H. Pitisci, a Miami psychologist and family therapist, [stresses that] 'with or without an erection, the level of intimacy between partners often determines the level of satisfaction.'" Unfortunately, Pitisci seems to be still in the minority of male therapists. This same article, for example, quotes experts who caution "that men who have known years of anxiety and perhaps self-loathing because of inability to perform may enter the Viagra age with unrealistic expectations that an erection alone can transform them as lovers" (Nordheimer, 2). The emphasis here, unfortunately, remains on sexual performance and the crucial role of the erection in that achievement. As Bordo points out, the term "sexual dysfunction," a euphemism for impotence, "is no longer defined as 'inability to get an erection' but inability to get an erection that is adequate for 'satisfactory sexual performance.' Performance. Not pleasure. Not feeling. Performance" (90). Tellingly, with its message of men now being able to perform all night, "do their job no matter how they feel!" the hype surrounding Viagra "encourages rather than deconstructs the expectation that men perform like power tools with only one switch—on or off" (Bordo, 90).

Indeed, all the current remedies for impotence emphasize the absolute necessity for a man to have an erection in order to experience sexual pleasure. Although an erect penis can be an important component in love making, it is neither invaluable nor crucial. Indeed, when men begin "to disassociate sexuality from a sense of manliness in order to break up the identification between sexual performance and masculinity," we will realize that manhood "can be confirmed by something other than an erect penis" (Badinter, 125). Men without erections can learn about their other erogenous zones and begin to appreciate their potential as polymorphous lovers. Were the lack of an erection to become just a flaccid penis and a cause of celebration as a source of a different kind of wonderful sexual pleasure, a man would begin to conceptualize his sexuality as, partially at least, soft, gentle, and gracious.

## LEAD IN HIS PENCIL

The penis as pencil or, more accurately, as pen, dominated much feminist literary theory throughout the 1980s. Sandra M. Gilbert and Susan Gubar, for example, explore at some length the use of this "metaphor of literary paternity" in *The Mad Woman in the Attic* and suggest that "the pen has been defined not just accidentally but essentially [as] a male 'tool'" (*Mad Woman*, 6, 8).[5] Although during the 1990s many other issues emerged in feminist theory, the penis as a tool and as a weapon of sexual dominance invites additional analysis.

The phallic image of the pencil as a long, slender, erect tube with inner workings that extrude from a small opening at the tip resonates with symbolic meaning. Through the pencil men ejaculate lead as the written word and a source of power, and through their penises men ejaculate sperm, an even more profound symbol of their power.

A colloquial expression originating in the 1900s, "lead in your pencil" emerged just at a time when women were beginning to gain access to education. Considering that one who has "lead in his pencil" is, according to Spears, a "potent, virile, and vigorous" man (215), the relationship between penis and pencil suggests more than just an innocent allusion.

As a metaphor, "lead in his pencil" refers to having an erection and being ready for sexual intercourse. The pencil itself denotes, consciously or not, the power (or at least authority) men have as those who are in control of the written word (as authors and publishers). The ability to write, the opportunity to be educated well enough (or at all, for that matter), to become literate, and to have one's ideas read and considered was for centuries the nearly exclusive and now threatened prerogative of men.

Ironically, the assertion "Here, this will put lead in your pencil" frequently refers to alcohol and implies that by consuming this beverage a man will be able to get a hard-on and to perform well sexually. John Ayto and John Simpson take this interpretation one step further when they suggest that this phrase means "to be lively or up to date, to enjoy oneself; to be promiscuous, specifically to engage in group sex [or] partner-swapping" (253). Alcohol, though, tends to reduce a man's sexual ability and may indeed prohibit him from either getting an erection or maintaining it. A man who drinks too much, who tries hard to put "lead in his pencil," may entertain fantasies about being sexually active but will probably be the first one to fall asleep.[6]

Hidden behind this rhetoric of male tumescence lies a fear of sexual achievement and its concomitant, personal intimacy. Haste points out that most men never see sex as a relationship. Rather, they equate sexuality with manhood: "Making potency central to masculine identity leads to a rhetoric of prowess and performance, [and] language is permeated with metaphors of prowess" (169). "Lead in your pencil" is just one example.

"Prowess" as a synonym for "conquest" has significance. Although other metaphors examined in this book relate much more directly to the penis as a weapon, the power of the pen(cil) is significant. The allusion to pencil may be derived from the similarity in shape between a pencil and a penis, but putting lead in one's pencil possesses at least an implicit reference to adding ammunition to one's arsenal. If, indeed, the power of the pen is greater than the power of the sword, the penis as a prepared pencil may not be as pacific as the mere similarity of shape seems to suggest. Indeed, to return to Gilbert and Gubar: "The pen . . . is not only mightier than the sword, it is also like the sword in its power—its need even—to kill. And this latter attribute of the pen once again seems to be associatively linked with its metaphorical maleness" (14).

Like other metaphors examined in this chapter, "lead in his pencil" relegates the penis to the status of a mechanism separate from a man's body. The penis as pencil, especially a mechanical pencil for which one procures lead, suggests the way in which men take care of tools or instruments that they possess and maintain as something outside themselves. Embedded in this term lies the performance motif that pervades the general discourse of male heterosexuality. The erect penis as machine (or "tool") that alone can give sexual satisfaction, and can be maintained like a car's engine, permeates our conception of male sexuality with its mechanistic imagery.

### PECKER

> Otherwise you'll start to take a leak some morning and your pecker
> will come right off in your hand.
> —Larry McMurtry, *Lonesome Dove*

This Americanism, according to Thorne, "may originate as a rural shortening of woodpecker, or as a euphemism for cock, or simply as a metaphor for an importunate member" (385). Much like a jackhammer run by a construction worker, a woodpecker attacks a tree with short rapid jabs intent on a singular objective. Personified by John Henry, the steel-driving man, this conception of masculinity as highly competitive, driven, and unbeatable imbues the American conception of manhood. The insatiable penis, like the insistent pneumatic hammer, propels forward toward productivity and victory.

The irony of "pecker" as an image for the penis illustrates the significance placed on male sexual performance and the importance for the man to "get laid." On the one hand, a man is supposed to have sex with as many women as possible. Like a woodpecker with his quick strokes, he is taught to visit as many trees (women) as he can. On the other hand, as a virile lover he is expected to "last" for a long time. If premature ejaculation is the bane of male existence, why, one may ask, have men adopted as a reference to the penis an allusion to precisely the kind of activity that brings it on?

Since the penis is an importunate member, an organ that is demanding or insistent, the allusion to the woodpecker makes some sense. The myth of male sexual desire as urgent and persistent, uncontrollable and unwilling to be denied, reemerges. The penis as a pecker, as an instrument that rages forward with a singular purpose, is metaphorical, indeed.

### PIECE OF ASS (PIECE OF TAIL, POONTANG)

> Him and four buddies want a little dough to get a high class piece of tail.
>
> —George Vincent Higgins, *The Friends of Eddie Coyle*

In recent years feminists have pointed out the pervasiveness of the idea of woman as sexual object in much of our language. The inclination to reduce women to body parts and reified entities has been around for a long time. According to Thorne, "piece has been employed in a similar sexual context, invariably referring unromantically to a woman, since the 15th century" (389). A "piece" as an isolated part of one's body stresses the possibility for replacement when it becomes dysfunctional or no longer attractive. Today, in the era of plastic surgery as a panacea for failing body parts, women (and more and more men) take themselves to a form of the body shop, just as men take their cars to for repair of dented fenders and broken windshields.

Hatred of the human body, and especially woman's body, predates the 1600s, of course, resonating throughout much of the Judeo-Christian tradition.[7] This view has structured our conception of love, marriage, and intimacy. Man's need to control women finds a strong rationale in both the Old and the New Testament, and his fear of female sexuality has its origins in the earliest works of Western literature and culture.

The longevity of this particular phrase, though, highlights the extent to which men have reduced their heterosexual desire to the need for only part of the woman, not her whole person. By degrading a woman to a sexualized body part, her ass, a man disentangles himself from any emotional involvement with a woman's mind or feelings. When women become, in the male imagination, a piece of something, men gain control, because women are no longer human and thus not equals.

"Poontang," for example, seems to refer specifically to a black woman "considered as a source of sexual gratification" (Spears, 338). According to Thorne, although "poontang" originated "from Louisiana French in which it is a corruption of putain (the standard French term for whore) [and was] first applied to black women," it refers more generally to "the female pudenda [or] woman in general, seen as sexual objects" (389).

As a general reference to women, the equation of all women with prostitutes is just one more misogynist characterization of the female. As a "piece of tail," the female body becomes animalistic, even bestial, and thus an object of disgust. Animals can be domesticated, of course, and in this way controlled and exploited.

The metaphors examined in this book frequently manifest a hatred of women or of men. None is neutral about fear of and contempt for the human body. Women as prostitutes or sluts, and men as pricks and hard-ons, form the substratum with which heterosexual relationships have to contend.

The female body as a compilation of parts (or pieces) remains a powerful metaphor today. Men still refer to a woman as "that" (e.g., "Boy would I like to try that out for awhile"), and advertisements show women from the perspective of their breasts or their behinds or their legs or their lips. Rarely do we see the whole woman, and when we do the focus is still on her function in society as an object of men's pleasure. Woman as a sentient being threatens male sexuality because a thinking being rebels against control.[8]

## TOOL

He had a thing about his penis. When he was away from me, he was always referring to it as "my noble tool."
—Anna Kashfi, referring to ex-husband Marlon Brando,
*(London) Sunday Mirror*

Then, to his extreme astonishment, Louisa squatted right atop his middle and reached into his long johns and took hold of his tool. Nothing like that had happened to him, and he was stunned, even though his tool wasn't.
—Larry McMurtry, *Lonesome Dove*

The penis as a "tool" makes explicit the association between male hetero-sexuality and the machine. This "notion of the male member as an imple-ment is very ancient. The word tool itself appeared in Middle English and by the 16th century had been recorded as a sexual metaphor" (Thorne, 522). Literally, a tool is "a device . . . [or an instrument] used to perform or facilitate manual or mechanical work" (*AHCD*, 1426), or "any implement, instrument, or utensil held in the hand and used for cutting, hitting, dig-ging, rubbing, etc." (*Webster's*, 1535).

The penis as a device for performing a chore or doing a job is one metaphor that dominates the lexicon of male bonding. The idea of the penis as an instrument to accomplish something (usually penetration of a woman to allow a man to have a quick and easy orgasm), or as an imple-ment to get a particular job done, pervades the way men think about their sexuality. The suggestion of an instrument used for cutting, digging, and rubbing resonates with the heterosexual male's conception of sexual plea-sure. As Reynaud points out:

> Man has directly reproduced his imagery of man as culture and woman as nature on the sexual organs: he has located the penis on a human scale, and the woman as a force of nature against which he fights through her vagina. Following the traditional metaphor of the phallus as a ploughshare furrowing the woman, he has diversified the imagery: with the knife blade, the barrel of a gun, or the electric drill, the vagina has become either the wound he opens or the hole he bores. His morbid imagination has produced a batch of endless metaphors, which, however, come up against the anatomical and physiological reality of the two sex organs: the vagina is no more a wound than the penis is a tool or a weapon. (31)

The association between "tool" as a mechanical device and its use as a synonym for a weapon is explicit in at least two dictionaries of slang:

Thorne refers to "the standard underworld and police jargon expression 'tooled-up' [meaning] armed with fire arms" (523), and as its second definition of "tool" the *Oxford English Dictionary* cites "a weapon of war, especially a sword" (3349). Chapter 4, "Sex as War and Conquest," examines at greater length the penis as a weapon, but for now it should be clear that both as a weapon and as a tool, the penis is reduced to an impersonal machine that functions as a device to get the job done. The goal can be either victory or efficiency, but in either case the penis becomes an effective mechanism for accomplishing a task.

The penis as a tool has its own significance, and Paul Hoch elucidates this well when he observes,

> To the extent that men see woman as nothing more than a sex object, they objectify their own sexuality as well. Man degenerates down to the "cocksman," "phallus," or just another "tool." Manhood becomes "stickmanship," love becomes "screwing," and men begin to take on roles of machinery. Sex is reduced from a total mind-body intercommunication down to a mere "organ grinding." (18)

As I mentioned at the beginning of this chapter, the extent to which men view their bodies as machines in need of mechanical repair and maintenance becomes apparent when we consider that of the very few books available on men's health, two are subtitled *An Owner's Manual* (Diagram Group; Gilbaugh). Diametrically opposite to a book like *The New Our Bodies, Ourselves* (Boston Women's Health Book Collective), for example, a health book that attracts women readers with its organic fusion of body to self, the men's health books suggest a use comparable to the manual one receives with any new machinery. The difference in titles is important: women's selves are identified with their bodies, but men believe they own their bodies in the same way they own their automobiles; men persist in maintaining a complete separation between their bodies and their selves.[9] The irony, of course, is that men do not own their bodies, they do not even understand their bodies. In fact, most men deny that their bodies ever fail or hurt or need attention.[10] Consistent with the language they uncritically embrace, men accept the belief that real men never complain about their bodies, never ask questions about their discomforts, never admit when they are ill or in pain.

As with other metaphors examined in this book, "tool" takes on a derogatory meaning when it is used to refer to someone: "Like many other words designating the male member, tool has a secondary meaning of a stupid (male) person" (Thorne, 522), "a dude [or] someone easily tricked" (Spears 449). The *OED* suggests its use as "a person used by another for his own ends; one who is, or allows himself to be made a mere instrument for some purpose . . . an unskillful workman; a shiftless person" (3349). A man who sees his penis as just a tool may indeed be an unskilled lover and is certainly a fool.

Ironically, and maybe even tragically, this man (or these men) who conceives himself as handler of an instrument, never sees himself as either a purveyor or a recipient of pleasure. Once the job is done, the tool has functioned well, has repaired the damage or fixed the leak, the man can put it back in his tool box and go on about his business. The male body as a machine with the penis as a tool robs a man of the wonder he can experience when his body becomes a polymorphous organism with a variety of erogenous zones and areas of sexual experience. The machine drones on, in contrast to the body, which sings harmoniously.

### WET DREAM

Popular definitions abound for this term and are not all that different from the formal ones. *The American Heritage College Dictionary,* for example, defines "wet dream" as "an erotic dream accompanied by ejaculation" (1534). Slang dictionaries characterize a "wet dream" as "a man's erotic dream during which he has an orgasm" (Chapman, 462), or "a nocturnal seminal emission" (Spears, 473).

These definitions come as no great surprise. Indeed, a synonym for "wet dream" is "nocturnal emission." Both terms ignore the why or the how of this experience, however, and relegate it to a hydraulic metaphor that reduces a male sexual experience to the equivalent of a geyser or an automobile engine that has overheated and is spewing antifreeze all over the place. Much of the literature on this subject, as little as there is, reiterates this perspective by characterizing a wet dream as a natural release of built-up sperm not ejaculated in "normal" sexual relations. Alfred Kinsey and his colleagues, for example, echo this mechanical view of male sexuality when they suggest that wet dreams "have been looked upon as involuntary and spontaneous releases of pressure" (527).[11]

The exclusive focus on the *what* disregards the context and the dynamics of the occurrence. What happens, quite simply, is that during an erotic dream a man ejaculates semen. But what occurs before the ejaculation, how this particular kind of response takes place, and why a man orgasms in the middle of a fairly unconscious experience are questions left unresolved by the simple phrase "wet dream" or "nocturnal emission."

Both terms locate a sexual activity outside the emotional, physical, and pleasurable experience of having an orgasm during sleep, and they ignore the significance of the act as a lived experience. They describe only the fact that when a man comes he produces a liquid, but they ignore the subjective experience. As a pseudomedical term, "nocturnal emission" contributes to the understanding of male orgasm during sleep as just one of those things better relegated to science. We learn as much about men's attitudes toward their sexuality from what is not said in this term as we do from what it expresses, because all "wet dream" tells us is that sometimes when men dream they have orgasms.

Men's ambivalence about their sexuality becomes apparent when "wet dream" refers to an individual rather than to the act of coming to orgasm during sleep. As with several other metaphors examined in this book, when "wet dream" invokes a particular man, he becomes "a dull, stupid person" (Beale, 497). Ironically, this reference captures the way in which our language fails to describe the actual experience of a wet dream. The language denies the man's active participation in the experience and the erotic sensations he feels. By focusing on the outcome and its messy aftermath rather than on the context in which it occurs, the language ignores one aspect of a man's sensuality. Most men are ashamed of having wet dreams, and some women feel threatened when their lovers have one. The lack of much overt critical engagement with the experience leaves this aspect of male sexuality hidden and unspoken. What is forbidden to be expressed prevents us from going beyond the superficial. In this way, as is true of so many other male metaphors discussed here, men retain some amount of control over their desires and passions only at the sacrifice of ignoring the depth and complexity of their sexuality.

Considering how long this term has been in existence (at least since the early 1800s), coupled with the extensive outpouring of psychoanalytic and popular works on sexuality in general, the dearth of writings on wet dreams is striking. The little that has been written on wet dreams suggests that this experience is limited to male adolescents and that eventually men outgrow it. The literature also sees the wet dream as a release of pent-up sperm; a wet dream becomes a natural reflex that allows a man to discharge bottled-up semen. Wet dreams, then, according to these authorities, disappear once men get into normal sexual relationships.

I must admit that this has not been my experience with wet dreams. I am now in my midforties, and I have had wet dreams throughout my adolescent and adult life. Their occurrence seems to have very little to do with my sexual activity. In fact, I have had a wet dream soon after making love. I may, of course, be the exception. Unfortunately, the lack of many first-person discussions by men of their experiences with wet dreams makes it difficult, if not impossible, to draw conclusions or ascertain patterns.

One of the earliest analyses of wet dreams occurs in Freud's *The Interpretation of Dreams* (1899) where he discusses them under the general topics "emission" and "sexual content in dreams." A half-century after Freud, in their 1948 study of *Sexual Behavior in the Human Male,* Kinsey, Pomeroy, and Martin devoted a whole chapter to the subject, "Nocturnal Emissions." Since the publication of their work, it appears that only one article has been written on wet dreams and that by a historian, B. R. Burg. Burg summarizes a personal journal kept between 1852 and 1858 by a U.S. Marine who recorded scrupulously the occurrences of masturbation and nocturnal emissions in his life. Citing work by Havelock Ellis, G. S. Hall, and Magnus Hirschfeld that includes material on masturbation and nocturnal emission, Burg points out that the number of cases they discuss is small and that most of the information is based on anecdote. Given the nature of my book, anecdotal material would be welcome, but men seem not to talk about or refer to their experiences with wet dreams.

Hall, as it turns out, relegates wet dreams pretty much to adolescence, and Hirschfeld categorizes them as both a sexual anomaly and a sexual disorder. Considering these characterizations, adult male reticence may not be so incomprehensible.

Ellis provides one of the most provocative and radical ideas about why men have wet dreams when he suggests that, among other things, they might be due to "the existence of monthly and yearly rhythms" (117). It is striking how little has been made of this suggestion, which was posited in the early part of the twentieth century. The idea that men might have periods, or at least be affected by the moon or the seasons, is clearly far too radical to be discussed, much less acknowledged. The thought that men are not entirely in control of their sexuality, while a recurrent source of ambivalence even in their discourse about themselves, is something men can grant only on the most tacit level.

Shere Hite's comprehensive report on male sexuality, published in 1981, reaffirms men's silence about wet dreams in general. Her study lacks any discussion of wet dreams. The absence of a single reference suggests that this rather significant part of the male sexual experience either does not warrant discussion or is too shameful to acknowledge. Given the range of sexual fantasies examined by Hite with her male subjects, anything apparently too shameful to talk about rates serious consideration.

As with many sexual subjects, Freud provides some of the most valuable information about, and insights into, the topic of wet dreams. Although his work on dreams with sexual content leaves the discussion at a somewhat oblique level focusing on three general themes—stairs and staircases, flying or floating, and dental visits—Freud interprets these dreams in some provocative ways. In, for example, "A Staircase Dream" Freud (with the assistance of Otto Rank) understands this "transparent emission dream" (403) as being about copulation. Dreams about flying and floating, with their "intense feeling of vibration in the body that accompanies such dreams" (430), relate to erection and emission.

Dreams in which people go to the dentist provide the most relevant material for an analysis of wet dreams because these dreams refer to sexual desire. Specifically, according to Freud, "ejaculation in a dream accompanies the act of pulling out a tooth." Tellingly, though, "the satisfaction accompanying the emission was not, as it usually is, directed to an object, even if only to an imaginary one, but had no object, if one may say so; it was completely auto-erotic, or at the most showed a slight trace of homo-sexuality (in reference to the dentist)" (Freud, 427). Clearly, the feeling of relief and release that comes from having a tooth pulled mirrors the hy-draulic model of ejaculation that sees male orgasm as the discharge of pent-up semen. As is frequently true with Freud, though, we learn as much from what psychoanalysis does not say as we do from what it does.

Freud's interpretation of the dental dream as referring to sexual inter-course ignores the obvious reference to the mouth and thus to oral sex. The suggestion that these dreams have no object of desire and are completely autoerotic, accompanied by the observation of the latent homosexual role of the dentist, speaks volumes about the broad social and cultural context in which Freud and his contemporaries interpreted sexual experiences in general and dreams in particular. Although the sexual attractiveness of the dentist as an object of homosexual desire is implicit, the analysis of this dream fails to mention fellatio as a source of the sexual expression brought on by the dream.

In the same section on dental dreams Freud describes nocturnal emis-sion as "a masturbatory satisfaction brought about without the assistance of any mechanical stimulation" (427)—accomplished, that is, without mas-turbation. The implicit juxtaposition of a male sexuality that is autoerotic and spontaneous (the wet dream) and one that is mechanical (masturba-tion) suggests a dichotomy that anticipates some of the insights provided by the Kinsey report.

In "Nocturnal Emissions" Kinsey, Pomeroy, and Martin begin with a challenging perception about adult male sexual behavior in general: "The evidence accumulates that the physical is usually a minor element in evok-ing sexual responses among older males, and there are few of the responses of an experienced adult which would be possible without a sufficient psy-chological accompaniment" (517). Contrary to popular belief, male sexual response is not just a mechanical, instinctual reflex but a learned behavior evolving in the context of personal and social experience. Indeed, Kinsey and colleagues find a direct correspondence between the frequency of noc-turnal emissions and the amount of education a man has acquired. This correlation rests on "the imaginative capacities of an individual" (521).[12] Males learn to be men, they are not born that way; according to Kinsey, males' imaginations about their sexuality have a direct relationship to their cultural backgrounds. A study of men's experiences with wet dreams that examined their socioeconomic backgrounds and even ideological leanings, as well as their religious identifications, might yield some valuable insights into the social construction of masculinity.

The value of Kinsey's work, although it is about fifty years old (and certainly some attitudes toward sex have changed since 1948), lies in the copious data his study produced.[13] Despite this extensive data, however, Kinsey, Pomeroy, and Martin stress the lack of information available to explain, for example, the physiological origin of these emissions.[14] They struggle to debunk the pseudoscientific explanation of nocturnal emissions that rests on the idea that the testes are the sole source of semen, a theory that allows for the hydraulic interpretation of the geyser just waiting to explode. Although Kinsey and his coauthors flirt with the relationship between built-up nervous tensions that precipitate orgasm, they quickly reiterate their position that "the physiology is not understood" (528). Referring to the dearth of "objective data on the mechanical factors that may effect nocturnal emissions" (528), they conclude their remarks with the insight that no clear patterns of nocturnal emissions have been identified and that "the situation cannot be simply summarized" (529). Some men who have high rates of sexual experience have wet dreams infrequently, whereas other men who have sex infrequently rarely have wet dreams. The exact opposite is also true: men who have sex often frequently have wet dreams, and men who rarely have sex have many wet dreams.

Both Freud and Kinsey raise important considerations of the psychological context versus the physical basis of the wet dream. Yet the lack of interest in pursuing this tack is striking.

The Kinsey report's findings, however, anticipate one premise of this chapter: that male sexuality seen as a machine in need of repair pervades our consciousness of what it means to be a man in U.S. society. Concomitantly, the overriding assumption that men's sexuality is already known, and thus not in need of examination or research, undermines our ability to comprehend the complexities of male sexual behavior. As a metaphor, "wet dream" provides us with only superficial impressions, but erotic dreams that result in orgasm are an experience that almost all men have and one that needs to be analyzed much more closely than it has been. When male sexuality becomes as much of a mystery as the common characterization of female sexuality, men will begin to understand themselves better as complicated human beings, not simplistic devices with a blueprint or schematic that explains how they work.

# 2 Sex as Work and Labor

Our relationship to work activity is a fundamental determinant of the way we live . . . our use of time and leisure, the nature of our family and sexual relations, the state of our mental health.
—Fred Best, *The Future of Work*

Workers tend to be so brutalized and depleted by the experience of work, moreover, that they are largely incapable of authentic relations with others.
—Kai Erikson, *The Nature of Work: Sociological Perspectives*

Work, in both the general and the specific sense, is assumed to be a major basis of identity, and of what it means to be a man.
—David Morgan, *Discovering Men*

The machine has influenced work since its invention introduced the potential to transform work into labor. Before the onslaught of machines a man's work was his craft, not his job. The work of the artisan or the farmer, unlike that of the modern proletarian or the corporate executive, involved an intimate relationship between what was created and how it was created. As "purposeful human activity directed toward the satisfaction of human needs and desires" (Best, 2), work gave life meaning, it enhanced our existence.

With the rise of the machine, work becomes labor, and labor generates surplus value that one exchanges for money. The intimacy of the creative process is then mediated by money, a by-product that represents workers' alienation from their creative abilities. A key source of human instrumentality resides in labor: "When a person comes to see work as a means to an end, as an instrumentality, it does not nourish the worker's spirit but depletes it, and he becomes like a machine" (Erikson, 22). Male heterosexuality conceived of as instrumental, as an encounter alienated from a man's humanity, pervades the masculine experience, and labor as both alienated work and a highly disciplined regimen imbues masculinity with certain beliefs about what it means to be a man.

38

"Work" has been variously defined. In the introduction to his collection of essays, *The Social Dimensions of Work,* Clifton Bryant demarcates the main historical conceptions:

> In the Western world . . . work historically has been associated with different value assessments: as brutalizing activity and painful drudgery by the Greeks; as religious calling and path to salvation by the early Protestants; as opportunity for creativity and self-realization by the Renaissance artisans. In contemporary society, in contrast, work is conceptually defined as a sphere of social activity related to but separated from other modes of behavior.(2)[1]

In contrast to the past, when work was directly related to one's personal and social life, work today, although it remains at the center of a person's life, frequently mediates an alienated relationship to our family lives, our friendships, and our sense of ourselves as human beings. Indeed, the problematic of work and career in American society is that it is identity defining (you are what you do), but the work identity is intransitive. Because of the fragmentation of modern life our work identities (which may be central to our conceptions of self) do not transfer to other contexts, leaving us alienated from what we do.[2] The alienated man's condition is not inherent, however, but rather one structured by experience on the job, in one's career or vocation. Each form of work brings with it a particular social relationship that influences our choices, from whom we love to how we spend our leisure time.

The structure of labor, whether industrial discipline or corporate regimentation, governs our relationship to work in much the same way a machine does. In her important book *The Human Condition,* Hannah Arendt examines the relationships among work, labor, and homo faber. She observes that the machine transforms work into labor by equating the body with the tool, "both of which swing in the same repetitive movement" (146) and both of which contribute to "a rhythmically ordered performance" (145). The discipline of the modern workplace echoes the repetition of the machine and prefigures men's relationships outside the job site. A rhythmically ordered performance characterizes with some accuracy many men's conception of love making, with their frequent emphasis on execution and achievement. As Michael Kimmel points out in his extensive analysis of the American self-made man in *Manhood in America,* "Men turned sex into work, experiencing 'performance anxiety' while they worked to 'get the job done'" (283).

The hard-driving repetition of the machine structures men's connection to work, turning work into a job and influencing profoundly the way men participate in their daily lives. In his early *Economic and Philosophic Manuscripts of 1844,* Karl Marx analyzes how the quantification of work transforms labor into a commodity that alienates the worker from his product and ultimately estranges him from his humanity. Men's relationships to themselves, to women, and to other men assume a sense of urgency and estrangement. For many men love becomes a mechanical experience with a product that is created outside themselves; love remains a means to an end, not a process or a journey.

The conceptualization of men as machines gained support as early as the Middle Ages when, according to C. Wright Mills, "the Protestant sects encouraged and justified the social development of a type of man capable of ceaseless, methodical labor" (7). This attitude was reinforced by the invention of the clock (around the fourteenth century). As the first machine and the measurer of time, the clock allowed work to be more easily quantified than previously and thus more easily bought and sold. Work becomes labor and labor becomes a commodity. As a commodity, a man's work is no longer an integral part of his life. Labor, under developing urban conditions, becomes what we do for someone else.

Industrialization has reduced labor and time to wares that men sell. Kimmel sums it up: "Rapid industrialization, technological transformation, capital concentration, urbanization, and immigration—all of these created a new sense of an oppressively crowded, depersonalized, and often emasculated life. . . . More and more men were economically dependent, subject to the regime of the time clock" (*Manhood,* 83). In this context men no longer possessed whatever small sense of autonomy and self-control they might have experienced with their work before industrialization. They no longer owned their own shops, their farms, even their own labor. They found themselves much less in control of their creative work, being overseen by bosses.

In her discussion of the crisis of masculinity at the turn of the nineteenth and twentieth centuries, Elisabeth Badinter observes, "As more and more men worked in factories at mechanical and repetitive tasks, or in administrative positions with monotonous daily routines, they no longer found that their work made the most of their traditional qualities. Strength, initiative, and imagination were no longer necessary for earning their living" (14–15). In addition, mass production, which emphasizes the need to produce more faster, tended to treat men as automatons. "Time is money," went a slogan used often among modern working men, and it describes a nation obsessed with having to get things done as quickly as possible and certainly faster than the other guy.

In his 1844 manuscripts Marx reveals the power of money to make all men equal. Money, Marx observes, allows the stupid to buy intelligence and the ugly to buy beauty. Money reduces human experience to an alienated existence in which our needs and our desires have a price tag. For

Marx "money is the pimp between men's need and the object, between his life and his means of life. But that which mediates my life for me, also mediates the existence of other people for me. For me it is the other person" (165–66). Money diminishes human relationships to economic exchange with a market value. That men talk about their sexuality in terms of business deals and precious gems should come as no surprise.

As the means by which men acquire possessions, spend their leisure time, and demonstrate their manhood in a variety of ways, the value of money becomes starkly apparent when a man loses his job. According to David Morgan, a British sociologist whose work on men and masculinity explores issues of gender and the family, "The identification of work with a male sense of self is ideologically related to the wider patterns of the sexual division of labour both at home and at work. Notions of 'responsibility' and 'sacrifice' are often presented in terms of women or in contrast to women" (77). Unemployment makes men powerless, even impotent (both figuratively and literally). Without a job and the money it provides, a man loses his self-esteem; he is no longer prepared to compete in the marketplace of career and, eventually, success. The inability to be the breadwinner, to be a successful husband and father, can drive a man to depression and suicide; at the very least it is seen to emasculate him.

Clearly, our relationship with labor is not neutral or insignificant. As a profound source of socialization, work helps to determine the way we live our lives. Fred Best makes this point in the phrase I chose as an epigram to this chapter: "Our use of time and leisure, the nature of our family and sexual relations, the state of our mental health" (1), all are influenced by our work activity. This experience affects the way we behave toward others and the way we talk about those relationships.

The discourse of male bonding thrives in the workplace, where men's initiation into manhood is intensified. Consistent with this discourse, men view their relationships with women through the lens of control, discipline, regulation, and commodity. Men's reduction of their sexuality to work, business, and an economic exchange embraces their relations to women as part of the male economy. Men spend their money and they spend their seed. This economic conception of masculinity is not a new one. Kimmel's research shows that "a recurring economic metaphor marks many postbellum advice books as men were encouraged to 'save,' 'conserve,' and 'invest' their seed, the fruits of their productive bodies, and to avoid unnecessary 'expenditure' or profligate 'waste.' Masturbation would send a young man on an inevitable downward economic and social spiral" (*Manhood,* 128). The economy of male heterosexuality pervades the discourse of masculinity. When a man has a sexual relationship, he acquires something outside himself (he gets laid), and when he gives himself sexual pleasure, he doesn't work hard enough (he jerks off). For many men relationships have a bottom line, and sex is either a dry quickie or a chore. Men's ambivalence about their relationship to work influences their personal relationships.

The literature on men and work is extensive. Up until quite recently, all studies of work and labor focused on men at work to the exclusion of women. Many recent studies of masculinity include a chapter on men's relationships to their jobs and how those associations structure their roles as husbands, fathers, and even bachelors. Frequently, these relationships take on the kind of alienated social relations anticipated by Marx in his critique of capitalist labor. Men's obsession with size carries over to their concern about how much money they earn, the size of their paychecks, because they tend to see money as a way to attract women, especially through the objects they can buy (the make of their cars, the restaurants at which they dine, the good time they can show their dates).[3]

Joseph Pleck and Jack Sawyer observe, for example, that "work is the institution that most defines the majority of adult males. Many of us look to work for our basic sense of worth. . . . As men, the desire to do good work, hold a respected position, or earn good money follows from learning as boys that it is important to get ahead" (94). Men look to the "bottom line" as they evaluate their success as husbands and as breadwinners.

Marc Fasteau asserts even more categorically than do Pleck and Sawyer that "there is no set of beliefs that allows men to value themselves without regard to the marketplace" (2). In his job and in his career a man defines himself as a success or a failure. The marketplace is larger than a man's job, however. It includes his ability to buy bigger toys, go on more exotic vacations, acquire the most beautiful woman, and demonstrate his masculinity vis-à-vis a salary, a price tag, an investment portfolio.

Fasteau elaborates by identifying several aspects of a man's relationship to work: his "preoccupation with victory," the "cult of toughness," an "excessive belief in and reliance on hierarchy," and his "need to have everything rationalized, to ignore personalities" (126, 132). Tough men compete in all walks of life to conquer women and maintain a hierarchy of masculine and feminine. That is, tough men don't dance—nor do they cry or flinch or show concern. Tough men are in control. They get the job done, no matter who it hurts or what it costs.

Not all men, however, are in control. Not all men are senior vice presidents or upper-level managers. In fact, most men have subordinate roles at work; they take orders and do someone else's bidding. These men in particular (although not to the exclusion of managers) need to find other ways to assert their masculinity, other means to maintain the hierarchy of masculine and feminine, other ways to protect their sense of superiority. As Morgan points out, "A man may feel his masculinity denied in the routine subordinated work in employment and compensate for this through exerting or attempting to exert a strong patriarchal authority at home" (98).

This necessity to maintain the privilege of masculinity is obvious both inside and outside the home. Men protect their rights in the exclusive terrain of the bar, the sports stadium, and the workplace. In these arenas of male dominance, men remain in control of their lives and the lives of others partially—but powerfully—in the way they talk about themselves and others.[4] The others, in this case, are women and gay men. Heterosexual men, real men by their own definition, though frequently possessing a sense of disempowerment and alienation, maintain a sense of control by abusing those they perceive as less powerful and deserving of ridicule. One of men's greatest armaments in this struggle for power and privilege is language, and the discourse of male bonding represents a potent weapon in their arsenal. The reduction of male heterosexuality to labor, a business deal, or an economic transaction resonates with a conception of masculinity in need of measurable success and a sense of the invaluable.

### BLOW JOB

> That white chick—Jane—of yours—she ever give you a blow job?
> —James Baldwin, *Another Country*

A euphemism for fellatio, the phrase "blow job" illustrates clearly the relationship of the dominant discourse to men's sexuality. It combines the focus on sex as machine with sex as work (and even sex as sport). By referring to this sexual experience as a job, this metaphor stresses the immediacy and the disembodiment of male sexual pleasure; sexual pleasure becomes a task or a chore, much like changing a tire or mowing the lawn. For the high school athletes interviewed by Bernard Lefkowitz "hand jobs and blow jobs [are] *jobs* that girls performed at their bidding. The guys were the foremen supervising their work crew" (128). Oral sex for these guys, as is true for many men, is about control and power. It is about getting the job done: "Sex was something that was done to them, not something they actively participated in" (Lefkowitz, 128).

The notion of the job, as a transaction or a position of employment, reduces oral sex to a business deal and characterizes male sexuality as work related and thus quantifiable. As a project or an achievement, this job reinforces the notion of male sexuality as performance. Like the well-executed play, the touchdown pass, or the grand-slam home run, male sexuality becomes goal oriented and product fixated.

As a mechanical metaphor, "blow job" synthesizes the hydraulic emphasis on water and other liquids, with the pneumatic concern with compressed air. Although the modifier "blow" may seem out of place or inappropriate, Tony Thorne suggests that this phrase "may . . . be influenced by the 'there (s)he blows' of whaling cliché" (47). Like many phrases analyzed in this book, "blow job" resonates with meaning in more than one category or theme. As a job, though, and even with its allusion to the mechanistic, this metaphor emphasizes men's understanding of their sexuality as a task related to the economy and external to their bodies (and souls, for that matter).

When a man "blows his wad," at least two different things could have occurred: he either spent or lost all his money in a wager (his wad), or he spent or ejaculated his sperm (his wad).[5] Thorne goes on to suggest that since at least the 1950s "blow," in this context, is a euphemism for "ejaculate." Acknowledging, though, that this term seems to be "a puzzling misnomer," Thorne provides one other plausible source of its origin in "the black jazz musician's hip talk expression blow meaning play (an instrument)" (47).

Clearly, though, the sensual act of blowing has very little to do with this sexual experience. The pleasure felt derives from suction on the penis, not air blown on it. Blowing warm breath across the head of the penis might stimulate that highly sensitive area, but the pleasure of fellatio arises when the penis is taken into the mouth and sucked.

As with so much of male heterosexuality, though, the erogenous becomes focused on the penis, denying or ignoring the extent to which kissing, licking, sucking, caressing, and holding the entire body gives pleasure. Indeed, a man stifles the full development of his sexuality by confining it to his penis.[6] However, in contrast to the usual focus on male control, in this metaphor someone else performs on the man, yet the sexual experience remains focused and immediate.

In my own experience with oral sex, both for me and from me, fellatio and cunnilingus remained for a long time a means to an end, a technique to be mastered toward a particular goal, that of orgasm. Oral sex has always been a pleasurable experience, but for many years my focus was on where I was going with it, the finish line, not the journey or the process or the experience. I do not think I am alone in this perception. Many men in the United States never pause long enough to see how much larger the male sexual experience can be than just ejaculation.

Although I believe that for me oral sex had much more to do with pleasure (albeit my own) than it did with power, I do not want to be naive. The very posture of the act, the physical arrangement of the two bodies, the fact that one person has another person's penis in her (or his) mouth provides for a form of caress that can be overwhelmed by its reversal of traditional power relations. In this intimate embrace pleasure and power fuse. A man finds himself in a vulnerable situation with his penis in the mouth of someone who has teeth and thus the capacity to inflict significant harm. This pleasure-power dialectic confuses most men, and their ambivalence lends itself to a discourse of objectification and derision. This discourse acts as a form of compensation by men because the person with the teeth has the power. In this way men objectify their bodies as machines and insult those who give them pleasure.

The equation of ejaculation with sexual pleasure, an assumption supported by modern sexology, understands ejaculation as a synonym for the male orgasm. Ironically, though, men can ejaculate without really experiencing the intense pleasure of orgasm, and men can orgasm without ejaculation.[7] Unfortunately for most men, fixation on the end result, rather than an appreciation of the enjoyment one can have from protracted love making, stifles their ability to enjoy a more polymorphous sensuality. Oral sex, like intercourse and even foreplay, becomes one more means to an end, and that end is ejaculation. Emmanuel Reynaud sees this phenomenon in the larger context of power: "The pleasure that a man keeps for himself is precisely that of power, in particular, power over woman's pleasure. . . . He purely and simply ignores woman's pleasure and reduces his own to mere ejaculation" (44).

The connection between ejaculation and pleasure relies heavily on this relationship between male sexuality and power. For many men sexual pleasure has very little to do with sensuality. According to Reynaud, men's obsession with imposing their wishes and controlling the relationship illustrates the extent to which men are sexually inhibited: "When he 'makes love', he does not let himself get carried away by the experience of two bodies meeting, but simply gets into 'position' and lives out his fantasies" (51). For many men—and the phrase "blow job" illustrates it well—sexual pleasure is something to be done with, to get over, and to move on to what is important in their lives: the next business deal, the Giants' game, or changing the oil.

Men's denial of the sexual pleasure involved in this particular sexual act is glaringly apparent in the assertion by the president of the United States that, even though a young woman performed oral sex on him in his office, he had not had sex with her. On a slightly more mundane level, though no less absurd, a truck driver friend of mine once told me that when he is out on the road, if a woman goes down on him (another metaphor, of course), he doesn't feel that he has cheated on his wife because he hasn't really had sex with this other woman. My question to both Bill Clinton and my friend is, "So, while you're in your office (or your truck cab), and some guy is performing cunnilingus on your wife, she's not having sex either?" Their answer, although I have not been able to ask Bill this to his face, will no doubt be, "But that's different."

More to the point might be this question: "And when your wife performs fellatio on another man, that's not sex?" Given that for most men the most egregious sexual transgression of which a wife or girlfriend can be guilty is not sexual intercourse but oral sex on another man, men's denial of the significance of such an act constitutes a profound act of denial. Men are frequently in denial about their emotions and about their sexuality.

One source of their confusion comes from religion, with its demand that women remain virgins until they are married. Although one could argue that today this requirement is stressed much less, the quandary influences the dynamics between men and women. The necessity for a woman to not have intercourse in order to avoid becoming pregnant (and to be a virgin for her husband) proposes the alternative of oral sex. An additional source of turmoil emanates from this option, however: on the one hand, a young woman wants to satisfy the man (boy) she loves by giving him sexual pleasure, and in this context fellatio is seen as a sign of commitment and love; on the other hand, the young woman who performs oral sex on a boy (or boys) is seen to be a slut or a tramp.

Another aspect of this confusion resides in issues of mutuality and intimacy. If men contend that a "blow job" is not sex because it is not intimate or mutual, how do they defend the position that if their lover does it to someone else, it is intimate? The virgin–whore dichotomy reappears, confusing both women and men about who they are in this spectrum of sexual partners and whom they desire.

One constant in all this remains the need on the part of most men to be in control, and one way to maintain this dominance is to impose a double standard. The point, of course, is not just the double standard, though that seems starkly the case. Rather, men possess a profound ambivalence about their sexuality, a deep-seated confusion about what they want from women and what they want for themselves.

One source of clarity, however, is that what is good for the goose is not good for the gander. Men want to be in control of their relationships with women, be they one-hour stands or their relationships with their wives. By defining what is and what is not sex, they extract yet another level of domination.

The use of this metaphor as a derisive remark directed against women and gay men illuminates the extent of men's ambivalence about sexual pleasure. Although fellatio is pleasurable for a man, the woman who gives a man a blow job is a tramp or a slut, and men who give blow jobs are queers and faggots. Many men enjoy the sensation of having their penises sucked but can hold in contempt the people who provide that pleasure. The epigraph from Baldwin's *Another Country* illustrates this point. Rufus focuses on a blow job as symbolic of Jane's love for Vivaldo. By concentrating such importance on this one component of their love making, sex becomes a series of acts performed, each of which has some kind of symbolic significance. Rufus does not ask about love; he asks about a blow job, as if that represents something even more important than an emotional commitment or even the missionary position, for that matter.

This disgust for the source of one's pleasure may be a displacement of fear. Men may fear the loss of control they experience and resent having to rely on others to give them pleasure. As Reynaud points out, "Man does not generally like to think that a woman can use him as she pleases" (56). The woman who performs fellatio threatens the man because she exercises some control over his pleasure, whereas the man who performs fellatio threatens the heterosexual man who may indeed have some doubts about the imperviousness of his heterosexual identity. Fellatio, after all, presupposes a knowledge of that which gives a man the most pleasure, an intimate familiarity, that is, with a man's sexual organs that only another man might fully appreciate. Men fear the obvious, that one man giving another man a blow job may occasion great pleasure.

## BOTTOM LINE

We all know what "bottom line" means, of course: How much is it going to cost me, really? In business, where this now commonly used phrase began, "bottom line" means "the result of any computation or estimate, especially one showing total costs" (Chapman, 41), or "literally the bottom line of a company's annual statement: the amount of profit, after tax, available for distribution among shareholders" (Beale, 54). More loosely construed, though, this term means "the final result [or] the main point" (*AHCD*, 163).

For business this phrase may be helpful in the way it describes profit and loss and the resultant net outcome or income. Unfortunately, though, "bottom line" has become part of the discourse associated with interpersonal relationships. The "bottom line" has emerged in our discussions of love and friendship. When a woman and her lover talk about their relationship and he says, "Okay, so what's the bottom line?" the relationship becomes just one more business deal, one more experience in which the value of the relationship is reduced to net gain or loss.

Long before the 1960s feminists such as Emma Goldman and Simone de Beauvoir pointed out that for men marriage is a way to obtain more valuable resources. The beautiful talented woman attracts for the man the envy of his male friends, which gives him power over them. Today, of course, thirty years after the height of the most recent emergence of feminism, we all know that men are no longer supposed to think that way. Men value women for their intelligence, their equality, their originality, and their independence. Men are no longer threatened by smart women, and all they really want is an equal in their relationships.

Because we operate in this broad egalitarian context, why does "bottom line" still persist as a way to understand interpersonal relationships? The easy adoption of this kind of language may be completely innocent; it may just be a tidy way to refer to the desire for a succinct picture of the particular situation. As first and foremost a business metaphor, the adoption of "bottom line" to our conversations about love and intimacy may not be all that innocent, however. This particular discourse may, rather, express that part of the male consciousness that continues to see all relationships in terms of profit. Profit pervades the American capitalist worldview, and American men are victims of this *Weltanschauung.* Greed, aggression, winning, and the need for succinct clarity dominate the way American men see the world. The belief that love is a business deal (a game or a battle or, worse yet, a war—"all's fair in love and war") that one wins or loses, and that the dynamics of the situation can be summed up and articulated clearly without ambiguity, informs the way men perceive their relationships with other people. The "bottom line" of a love relationship should provide the kind of information one needs to determine whether it is time to buy or sell, to invest or divest, to "cut the losses" or to take another risk. Unfortunately, this metaphor may throw far more light on our interpersonal relationships than we want to know or accept. If your lover ever says to you, "Okay, so what's the bottom line? Do you love me or not?" that person is revealing a habit of mind that may represent values you might want to consider further.

### BREADWINNER

One of the defining metaphors for male status, "breadwinner," merges the bread of sustenance and the bread of money with the victor in the athletic match or the battle (whether an actual military battle or just the battle of the corporate world or the battle of the sexes). Nowadays this phrase is virtually synonymous with being a good husband and father, but as early as the 1800s "breadwinner" was a British prostitute's slang for "the female genitals, specifically the vagina" (Spears, 53). The *OED* defines this term as "the tool, art or craft with which any one earns his living" (1070) and cites a specific use from 1818.

For the greater part of the past century, though, "breadwinner" has referred to the man of the house, the husband and the father. In his analysis of the rise of the American "self-made man," Michael Kimmel points out that the breadwinner role brought to these men few of its anticipated rewards. Indeed, "the pressure to be a successful breadwinner was a source of strain and conflict, not pride and motivation" (*Manhood,* 265). The destructive nature of this male aspiration echoes much of Marx's concern about the alienated proletariat. The breadwinner became a middle-class euphemism for the striving competitive world in which men were supposed to establish themselves as real men but in which they led isolated, lonely, and fundamentally alienated lives.

Not much has changed for men, even with women assuming coresponsibility for family incomes. As I have already mentioned, an unemployed man views his situation as an assault on his manhood. Men without jobs, men who cannot be breadwinners, lash out at themselves and at their families. As Kimmel points out, men who are bread losers are no longer real men (*Manhood*, 118).

### DICK

> Now that I am out of women to be in love with, I visit the men's room, where, standing before the long trough, limp dick in hand, my dribbling is hot and painful.
>
> —Richard Russo, *Straight Man*

In connection with the concept of work, in contemporary America at least, a "dick" is an unpleasant person who usually has power over you and exercises it in a demeaning and frequently cruel way. "He's such a dick" refers to an unfair boss who abuses his position and privilege. Even more telling for this chapter on male heterosexuality as an economic transaction is the Wall Street phrase "big swinging dick," meaning the guy (or woman, for that matter) who sells millions of dollars' worth of stocks and bonds.[8]

A "dick" is also another synonym for the penis, and it may have originated from "an affectionate personification in the same way as Willie" or Peter or John; the use of this word "has been widespread in the English-speaking world since the end of the 19th century" (Thorne, 128). Tracing the evolution of "dick" from Middle English, Chapman focuses on its use both as an affectionate nickname for the penis and as a verb that means to have sex with a woman:

> perhaps from the nickname Dick, an instance of the widespread use of affectionate names for the genitals; perhaps from earlier British *derrick* "penis"; perhaps from a dialect survival of Middle English *dighten* "do the sex act with" in a locution like "he dight her," which would be pronounced "he dicked her." (101)

As a metonymy, then, this sense of the word sometimes extended to mean sex in general or "acquired the generic sense of the female need for sexual intercourse, as in 'She was crazy for dick'" (Beale, 123), or "sex in general, as in 'Suzy loves dick'" (Thorne, 128). The equation of the male genitalia with all sexual desire exemplifies the assumption that male heterosexuality is both the norm and universal. Why men feel compelled to give their penises names, to personify them in some way, to remove them from the rest of themselves, points to a crucial aspect of male sexuality. Certainly, one of the better-known literary examples of this kind of personification of the penis is "John Thomas," the name the caretaker gives to his penis in *Lady Chatterley's Lover* (D. H. Lawrence).

Paul Hoch maintains that "many men even speak of their penis as if it were not a part of the body, but a distinct personality apart. Often, 'it' is even given a name (Peter). The fact that Peter, but not me, does the copulating, of course, removes me from any responsibility" (68). It also objectifies the act, removing from it any emotional connections. Indeed, Badinter takes this one step further when she points out that "many men obsessed by their virility, do not really consider their sex an organ of pleasure, but a tool, an instrument in a performance, a thing separate from themselves. Many also confess to having conversations with their penis, cajoling it, asking it to stay erect" (137). By personalizing their penises, ironically enough, men objectify them; they treat them like pets they can train to do tricks, and they relegate them to a place outside their humanity.

When one recalls that Lady Chatterley names her vagina "Lady Jane," and that the children's primer characters were Dick and Jane, one cannot help but wonder about the insidiousness of this choice of appellation. Isn't Dick always on top, asserting his desires, and who is Jane in this story? How aggressive or self-assertive is she, and how often does she prevail? The discourse of masculinity is both subtle and ubiquitous.

One possible origin of this term comes from the British armed forces from the middle to late 1800s and suggests the equation of the penis with war and with a weapon (Chapman, 100–101; Beale, 123). Hoch carries his analysis one step further when he says of the named penis, "He, not me, is the animalistic one, the savage, the avenger. He represents mankind in its most carnal aspect—the beast below" (68). The penis as weapon pervades our assumptions about male sexuality, and when men name their penises, they give to them personae that can be blamed for their aggressive behavior. As Hoch points out, the penis becomes another guy, someone outside himself whose actions the man can countenance with impunity.

Like so many other "affectionate" terms for the penis, though, "dick" also connotes a derisive meaning. Like "cock," which means nonsense, as in "poppycock," and like "jerk-off," meaning an idiot or an oaf, a "dick" is "a fool (invariably male) [and] has this secondary sense in common with most slang terms for the male member, such as prick, tool, etc." (Thorne, 128). "Dick" has several other pejorative meanings: to do nothing at all, as in to "sit around all day and do dick" (Thorne, 129); to have no value, as in "not worth dick"; to cheat or deceive as in "he dicked me around" (Spears, 118); and "a despised person" (Chapman, 101).

Because of its distance from the self, the "named penis" becomes the receptacle for much fear and self-hatred; a dick, or the penis, is a foolish, lazy, worthless, and hated deceiver. Language has a tricky way of saying what it may not have been intended to state.

### DRY HUMP

> You can't dry hump good in the car. Unless you're a midget.
> —High school student to *IT* magazine

The act that precipitates "blue balls," "dry humping" refers to "a sexual activity (often performed standing up) in which the partners simulate intercourse while they (or at least their genitals) are fully clothed" (Thorne, 156). Thorne goes on to suggest that this phrase refers usually to heterosexuals. This simulation of the sexual act occurs without either person reaching orgasm, and for the man it results in "blue balls."

The word "dry" in this phrase is in opposition, of course, to the wetness of sexual activity and in that way may be fairly harmless as a descriptor; dry sex, though, is certainly not harmless to either participant. "Dry" also means unsatisfied or unfulfilled and in this phrase seems to suggest unrewarding labor. The use of the verb "hump" seems the most telling in this metaphor for male heterosexuality, "hump" being a slang term meaning "to exert (oneself)" (*Webster's,* 708). To hump for a job suggests someone who is hustling to get one or putting forth a burst of energy to secure one. In the context of the phrase "dry hump," "hump" connotes both quickness and severity, and dry humping a woman usually occurs as part of the strategy a man implements en route to actually having sex with her. Dry humping becomes part of the heterosexual male's bag of tricks for hustling a woman to have sex.

The man assumes the role of aggressor in this scenario, convinced that part of his identity as a man requires him to conquer the woman, to coerce her into having sex with him. "Dry humping" reinforces male heterosexuality as uncontrollable, unrelenting, and necessarily on top (why do men dry hump when they know it will give them that painful condition, "blue balls"?). "Dry humping," by extension, taints the man's entire sexual experience with its implication that sex with a woman can be dry (without foreplay), a quick exertion on his part, and something he hustles (like a job).

### FAMILY JEWELS

> Rudy Yellow Shirt was twelve when the black widow danced up from
> the depths of the outhouse and bit him on his gonads. The bite felt
> just like someone had speared him with a red-hot sewing needle. He
> let out a bloodcurdling shriek and grabbed his family jewels.
> —Adrian C. Louis, *Skins*

As an allusion to the economic value of a man's genitals, "family jewels"
demonstrates the extent to which men view their bodies in terms of business, property, and political economy. Referring to the testicles, this
phrase, "which may be Victorian in origin" (Thorne, 171), derives from
"their great value and their role in creating a family" (Spears, 149). The
term became common slang in the United States in the 1900s and has
maintained a jocular use to this day. Echoing the point also made by
Spears, Harold Wentworth and Stuart Berg Flexner define this phrase as
"a man's most valuable possession, and the pride of his family, since the
testicles provide progeny" (177).

A relatively harmless euphemism for a man's balls, "family jewels" does,
however, place significant value on the reproductive function of the male. I
cannot think of any comparable slang term for ovaries, although one sometimes hears an allusion to a woman's "plumbing." This reference clearly reflects men's willful ignorance of women's reproductive organs while reducing the female anatomy to a mechanical instrument. The difference between
one's "plumbing" as an apparatus or a mechanical system that can be repaired with the right technology or parts and the "family jewels," a phrase
that connotes a tradition or a heritage as well as great wealth, both of
which are irreplaceable, may indeed exemplify the differences in our out-
look on male and female sexual significance.[9] If boys joke about the value
of their genitals while listening to older men (their fathers, maybe) deride
women's reproductive organs, males begin their understanding of heterosexuality in a context that already privileges men and devalues women.

Perhaps a form of "womb envy" and men's fear of a woman's reproductive capability engender this kind of phrase. Although genetically at the
moment of conception men and women are equal, a woman's role in the
whole process of reproduction is much more intensive and concrete. Men
may refer to their gonads as jewels to compensate for their latent realization that the testicles do not hold the same significance in reproduction as
does the uterus. That is, men's value in work as in reproduction remains
in question and thus a phrase like "family jewels" is required to assert
men's worth.

## GETTING LAID

Young guys in their twenties, of course they're going to try and get laid, and even if they don't succeed it's hardly big news.
—Lenny Henry, *Time Out* magazine

The combination of the verbs "to get" and "to lay" bring to this metaphor particular meanings of some significance. The verb "to get" means to acquire or to own and implies a transaction of some kind. It suggests, at least, something outside ourselves that we obtain. The verb "to lay" includes two forms: the passive "laid," as in the verb describing what one does with an object, and the active "to lie" (lie, lay, lain), describing what one does with oneself—a subject. "To lay" or "to get laid," then, means to relate to an object in some way, to objectify the experience, in this case of intimacy.

In the passive form, "getting laid" means to acquire sexual satisfaction from something or someone that is apart from us, different from ourselves, an other. This "something that satisfies our needs" is not necessarily a part of that experience, certainly not an intimate part of it. It may, indeed, be something (someone) we buy.[10]

We "get laid" and men "get a nut off"; we "get lucky" and men "get it up." Do women "get a nut off," or do they have another phrase to describe orgasm? "Get your rocks off," maybe, but here too the verb is "to get," with its associations of acquisitiveness. Today women also use the phrase "getting laid" to describe their sexual adventures. Women may also talk about "getting lucky," but even though the clitoris may become hard from sexual excitement, do women talk about "getting it up"?

Historically—and you may be surprised to learn this, especially given the epigraph for this section—to "get layed," meaning "to have sexual intercourse [was] said originally of the female," and began as part of U.S. slang at the turn of the century (Spears, 186). The quote from *Time Out* suggests, in the first place, that it is only natural for young men to pursue having sex and implies that women are not part of this natural process. Indeed, the pursuit is so normal that the simple act of *trying to* get laid is at least as important as actually succeeding in having sex.

The original reference to women should not be all that surprising, though, when one considers that to "get laid" is a passive construction. Although now used by both sexes, this phrase was for a long time a reference applied almost exclusively to men who "got laid" while women "made love." Male sexual activity as passive seems to abrogate the myth of men as uncontrollably passionate *and* in control. As was made clear with the metaphor "blow job," though, men are in fact ambivalent about their sexuality, especially when it comes to agency.

The present, more universal usage poses a question about sexual equality that has informed other debates about gender and sexual exploitation: Does an equitable distribution of sexual objectification mean sexual equality? Does, for example, the existence of *Playgirl,* with its nude pictures of men, eradicate or equalize the sexual exploitation of women in magazines such as *Playboy* or *Penthouse?*

The present use of this term by both sexes may mean only that the lack of intimacy in the sexual relationship has now become acceptable for all of us. On the other hand, maybe there are times when what we really want is to just "get laid," not to be in love, not to share an intimate moment but to have sex, to "get a nut off," to obtain sexual satisfaction, and to move on. Maybe "getting laid" is a fine metaphor and one that should be applauded rather than criticized. Maybe, though, if all we are doing is getting laid, if love making is an unemotional businesslike transaction, and we are not capable of intimacy on any other level, we should examine more closely the language we feel comfortable using to describe our love making.

## HUSBAND

Probably the oldest and, I believe, the most insidious metaphor for the masculine role, "husband," according to the *Oxford English Dictionary,* dates from at least the year 1000 and refers to "the master of a house [or] the male head of a household" (1352). The word "husband," as a term for a married man, derives from its meaning "to use sparingly or economically, conserve," as in "to husband the resources." A good husband, then, is "a prudent thrifty manager" (*AHCD,* 664) who has evolved, all too frequently, into a stingy tyrant and master of the household.

The insidious nature of this term derives from the extent to which most of us believe that it is both transhistorical and neutral. A husband is, quite simply, the opposite of a wife; he is the man who marries the woman, while the wife is the woman who marries the man. For most, these words have no other meaning than this, and they connote only the relationship between the man and the woman in marriage. When one considers, though, that "masculine self-definition is through efficacious production of goods and services for a family economic unit; [while] feminine self-definition requires sensitive responsiveness to the family's emotional needs" (Haste, 69), one begins to understand the way language works to provide subtle distinctions and not-so-subtle characterizations.

Although, according to *Webster's,* "wife" has no meaning outside marriage and refers to "a married woman . . . specifically, a woman in her relationship to her husband" (1671), Haste gives some depth to the term "wife." In her analysis of four images of woman (wife, whore, waif, and witch) she points out that at a subtle level "woman as wife is relatively sexless; she desires children, and sex is for that purpose. She is a faithful helpmate to man, and she is also an object of adoration. . . . Her sexuality is defused and related to her fecundity" (172). Although most women might rebel against this characterization, the socially acceptable role of wife is certainly concomitant with that of mother and completely consistent with what Margaret Small refers to as "heterosexual ideology." According to Jonathan Ned Katz, who quotes Small at some length, "the unnamed, unpaid, undervalued work that women perform for men within marriage . . . is specifically the procreation and socialization of children, and the physical and emotional care—the feeding and fucking of husbands" (148). The monogamous heterosexual family seen as the basic unit of society begins, according to Jeffrey Weeks, at the middle of the eighteenth century. With this social development the wife becomes increasingly more dependent economically on her husband, and women see their sexuality defined "in terms of male sexual needs, and the intensified emotional investment in children of the family" (15).

The *OED* provides some provocative insights into the origin of the term "wife." Originally, "wife" was a general term for "woman" but "in later use restricted to a woman of humble rank or 'of low employment' . . . especially one engaged in the sale of some commodity," as in "alewife" (3775). The relationship between husband as a manager of goods and wife as the seller of goods (and, as one involved in "low employment," in need of a manager) exemplifies the institution of marriage as an unequal business arrangement. The husband becomes the overseer of the woman, the supervisor of her financial arrangements.

The catastrophic effect for men of having to be good husbands, shrewd managers of household resources, "breadwinners," has been the subject of much discussion in some areas of the early U.S. "men's movement" and has, unfortunately, identified either women in general or the feminist movement in particular as the cause of men's unhealthy or even disastrous situation.[11] Although the high rates of heart attacks and suicides in men can be linked closely to the oppressive role and expectations of the husband in our society, an appreciation of how this term, like so many others characterizing masculinity, has a specific meaning and a long history may allow us to redefine the language more positively and thoughtfully. Can a man be in a relationship that is indeed egalitarian, a relationship that does not require him to be in control and have most of the power? What would that relationship look like, how would it function, and what would we call the people involved in it? How do we get beyond the terms "husband" and "wife," and what would we want the new titles to connote?

A few men have, over the past century or so, tried to create such alternative marriages. In 1855, for example, Henry Brown Blackwell, marrying Lucy Stone, renounced all the privileges that the law conferred on him as a husband that were not conferred on her as his wife, and he insisted on absolute equality between the sexes in marriage. Together they politicized their marriage when they read the following vows:

> While acknowledging our mutual affection by publicly assuming the relationship of husband and wife, yet in justice to ourselves and a great principle, we deem it a duty to declare that this act on our part implies no sanction of, nor promise of voluntary obedience to such of the present laws of marriage, as refuse to recognize the wife as an independent, rational being, while they confer upon the husband an injurious and unnatural superiority, investing him with legal powers which no honorable man would exercise, and which no man should possess. (Kimmel and Mosmiller, 329)

Other examples of a radicalization of marriage can be found in an experiment conducted by political radicals and bohemians in Greenwich Village in the first two decades of this century. Max Eastman, Hutchins Hapgood, and Floyd Dell attempted to create egalitarian relationships with women based on the then-feminist vision of "women's sexual fulfillment . . . [being] equal to that of men's . . . [in which] heterosexual intimacy would entirely eliminate separate spheres for men and women [with] . . . women shar[ing] the public interests of men, and men shar[ing] the private domestic life that had previously been defined as predominantly female" (Trimberger, 134). Unfortunately, these relationships evolved into fairly traditional "companionate marriages" in which intimacy was redefined to focus on providing the husband with a trusting companion to whom he could confide his problems and concerns. These unions maintained the traditional division of labor, with the women remaining keepers of the domestic sphere, providers of a safe haven in which they remained the good wife and mother. Thus, although the attempts by both Blackwell and the Village radicals turned out to be weak alternatives at best and, more accurately, failures, the existence of a history of men who were trying to create egalitarian relationships is significant and provides helpful models to contemporary men also involved in such efforts.[12]

## JERKING OFF

> I went ahead as usual and jerked off into my sock.
> —Philip Roth, *Portnoy's Complaint*

According to Thorne, this "Americanism [meaning to masturbate] . . . has gained currency throughout the English-speaking world since the late

1960s when it became a hippy and student vogue term. The phrase existed in British English in the 19th century but was never widespread" (273). Other slang terms exist for male masturbation, of course: "beating your meat" or "jerkin' your gherkin," for example. All share the distancing from sexual pleasure and the reduction of the male genitals to a piece of meat or an object external to the man.

"Jerking off," and even most male masturbation, centers on an objectification of women as well. The source of many men's fantasies during this autoerotic act is pornography of some kind or another, whether magazines or films, and in these images of female sexuality, male supremacy and objectification of the woman are prevalent.[13]

Ironically, and as is true of many slang phrases examined in this book, these phrases become readily identifiable as metaphors when they refer to a person rather than to an act. When we say, "Oh, he's such a jerk-off," we mean that he is an idiot or an oaf. According to Wentworth, "jerk off" means "to waste time; to fuck off; to cause confusion; to make many mistakes. . . . One who masturbates or wastes time, a dope" (290). Thorne takes this pejorative sense one step further when he defines a "jerk-off" as "a despicable or obnoxious (male) person" (273). Here male masturbation becomes wasting time or a stupid unproductive activity, and in a world in which men are supposed to produce goods and create a profit, sexual satisfaction not connected to male sexual prowess has no value.

The fear of masturbation and the belief in the ills purportedly brought on by this form of self-pleasure dates far into Western history. The first book of the Bible warns men against spilling their seed unprocreatively. More recently, in U.S. history the nineteenth century saw a flurry of admonitions against masturbation, most of which centered on the ancient equation of sperm with money and the ejaculation of the one with the expenditure of the other. G. J. Barker-Benfield describes at great length the work of the Reverend John Todd, who saw the ejaculation of sperm, especially through masturbation but with intercourse as well, as "equivalent in some sense to the expenditure of money" (179), because "sex no less than any other function conformed to an economy of the body" (169). Kimmel presents significant evidence that W. K. Kellogg, the cereal magnate, developed Corn Flakes as a cure-all for male masturbation.[14]

Although we may not be as hung up on the evils of masturbation today, the language we use to talk about this experience still relies on a sense of disgust and alienation. Why, for example, is the gerund "jerking" used in this phrase rather than "stroking" or "caressing"? "Jerking" describes what you might do when you have hooked a fish and you want to set the hook deep into its mouth, or you might jerk the fishing line free of a snag. While masturbating, though, men do not actually jerk their penises, they stroke them, and depending upon how much in touch with their pleasure they are, they might even caress their penises. "Jerking off," then, like so many other male metaphors, becomes a way for men to remove themselves from the sensuousness of sexual pleasure. Consistent with much of the male heterosexual experience, jerking off provides relief much more than it does fulfillment. Maybe men use such a mechanical and objectifying term to describe their ability to satisfy themselves sexually in order to gain a feeling of control over the experience, but they lose enjoyment and the sense of a relatedness to their bodies. Men seem to fear masturbation or, at the very least, to be ashamed of it, and language that allows them to establish remoteness gives them a sense of safety.

# 3 Sex as Sport

The arena of sport has always been marked by class, gender, and race,
and marked as a compelling and powerful site for routine investigation
of masculinity. For the male body is the standard currency of sporting
discourse: it is on display, at work, being measured and evaluated—
in short, being objectified for the purposes of pleasure—as nowhere
else in contemporary life.
— Toby Miller, "A Short History of the Penis"

Sports arenas are America's living galleries, where we witness all the
beauty and grace and passion of which humans are capable. They
are also asylums, filled with delusional fantasies, misogyny, misplaced
loyalties, racism, homophobia, and unclear boundaries between self
and others.
— Elliott J. Gorn and Warren Goldstein, *A Brief History*
*of American Sports*

Sports synthesize the male experience of work and of the machine; sports
train men to be successful in the world of business, and sports rely on
technological innovations to improve athletic achievements. These factors,
combined with the ways in which sports are highly competitive, aggressive,
and dominated by masculine values, leave little room to doubt the significance of the influence of sports in delineating men's roles in contemporary society.

In addition to the affinities between sports and work and sports and
technology, historians of sports have recorded the direct correspondence
between sports and war, and sports and misogyny, both of which encompass a close and mutually supportive relationship.[1] Sports provide initiation into the kinds of qualities and characteristics soldiers (and business
leaders) need in order to survive and succeed, and sports furnish political reinforcement for a xenophobic political system. Sports also remind
women, children, and nonathletic men that real men, athletic men, hold
the reins of power.

Since their earliest manifestations in pre-Greek civilization, sports have
grown out of a society's need to be proficient in war. Hunting, wrestling,

running, horse racing, and fencing gave warriors a means to improve crucial components of the limited military resources they had at hand. Ideologically, sports have been used domestically to reinforce class differences and to encourage men to become soldiers. The hunt, for example, "has been a distinguishing indulgence of the ruling class in almost any settled society" (Mandell, 85) and was symbolic of aristocratic might against the peasant.

Sports have a rich history, one that has been far from neutral. Sports have reflected social and cultural norms, and they have been recruited into the causes of one rising class or another against the status quo. In his cultural history of sports Richard Mandell points to several examples of the correlation between sports and social change. As early as preindustrial society, sports adapted to particular economic and political realities, and modern sport can be seen as evolving from the same "social circumstances that fostered rationalized industrial production" (xv). In tracing the historical development of modern sports from their origin in early European history, Mandell distinguishes between gaming and sports as a major enterprise: "New recreations and games were harmonious adaptations of new classes to their leisure time and ambitions, and the techniques at their disposal . . . [while] modern sport has rather particular origins in particular places and in social and ideological conditions" (131). The social circumstances included not only the dominant political and economic situation but technological innovations as well. Sports provided men with an arena (literally) in which they could play with new toys and improve their physical fitness, all at the same time. Sports, especially blood sports in which animals are pitted against each other, gave men the opportunity to demonstrate their masculinity through a mastery of nature that could be measured and thus proved. Additionally, technology affected the dissemination of news coverage of sports events. With the growth of radio and television, men's superiority could be confirmed far and wide.[2]

Elliott S. Gorn and Warren Goldstein find an even more insidious motive behind the role of sports in early American society. Before the rise of technology, though certainly not before the ideological role of sports, the gentlemen who arranged sporting contests offered prizes and a feast as a way to secure "the loyalty of their more lowly neighbors . . . binding men together with shared identity despite the class divisions" (8). At various historical junctures, elites have advocated popular recreations "as a means of social control" (13). Mandell reinforces these observations when he points out that "in order to make clear their menacing power to the fixed population and to maintain or advance their prestige among their peers, members of the aristocracy . . . developed distinctive and distinguishable paramilitary sports: the hunt, the joust, the tournament, and the duel" (110). That is, sports are not just neutral forms of recreation. Today, in the absence of the organized hunt, professional sports, dominated by large fierce men, remind women and children (and smaller or nonaggressive men, for that matter) who holds power. Even with the growth of female participation in sports, Mandell argues cogently, sports remain a chiefly male preserve, one in which "even the poorest man who proved his grit, his valor, his ferocity, reinforced his dominance over women and children" (8).

Poor men and even middle-class men, the majority of whom are not athletcs themselves, maintain a semblance of this aura of male privilege by being active sports fans. In a society where knowledge represents power, a man's understanding of the rules of the game, his ability to remember statistics, his knowledge of a sport's particular history or an athlete's biography, represent a form of knowledge. In a world seemingly out of control, where knowledge has become more and more specialized, a man's understanding of a game's subtleties provides him with a sense of power. The discourse of sports is an exclusive language governed by men and represents power over something they believe, and need, to be significant. The language of sports allows bored, powerless, ordinary men to obtain a sense of accomplishment through control over something they see as important. Men who cannot participate in the "manchat" of professional sports, who don't know the players or the standings, are excluded from this domain of masculinity.

The sports hero embodies this sense of control for the fan who vicariously lives out his fantasy world through the superathlete who has it all: money, fame, and beautiful women. Spectatorship emerged concomitantly with the rise of a consumer society and came replete with myths of the superathlete created by a burgeoning profession of sportswriting for an audience that sought "a sentimental sense of community, not new information or good writing" (Mandell, 189). This manchat of the sports news is incorporated uncritically into the discourse of male bonding and goes hand in hand with what contemporary sports sociologists have identified as "locker-room talk": "verbal exchanges whereby male athletes celebrate heterosexual aggression against women, as a common method of oppositional self-definition" (Gorn and Goldstein, 300).[3]

The belief that we can all become a sports hero (or our son can), even if only a local one, reinforces the notion that sports are a democratizing component of society. Sports rarely have been democratic nor, for that matter, have they been aligned with democratic efforts. On the contrary, sports remain one of the last bastions of racism and sexism, and their culture stands out for its homophobia. Konrad Lorenz's belief that sports are potentially an alternative to war notwithstanding, sports have frequently been at the forefront of the preparation for war, both practically and ideologically.

As a racist institution, sports have maintained a strong tradition. Early in our nation's history labor was seen as the burden of blackness, whereas leisure was the prerogative of whites. In British society where until recently class dominated race as an index of disparity, "sports . . . aid in the reproduction of power relations by misrepresenting the nature of major inequalities in Britain" (Hargreaves, 9). In U.S. society, where race and class are closely intermingled, the black athlete has an ambiguous role in sports today. On the one hand, American society can point to the increased number of black athletes as evidence of how democratic and inclusive U.S. society is, while, on the other hand, "sport is so inextricably bound up with the ideology and structure of white male privilege that although it may appear to advantage blacks, in fact it only confirms that privilege" (Disch and Kane, 286). The ambivalence white men feel about their sexual prowess also plays out in their relationship to the black athlete, whom they fear and hate for being what Toby Miller calls "the ultimate 'penis symbol'" (10). Miller cites Franz Fanon who, in *Black Skin, White Masks* (1967), analyzes white projections regarding black male genitals and argues that "everything Negro takes place on a genital level" in white imaginings of "the Negro" (Fanon, 157). In the arena of sports the ideology of equality and team effort mitigates at least some of this ambivalence. The myth of democracy on the playing field reinforces the belief that all players, regardless of ethnic background, share the desire to win and to play to the best of their ability. Ironically, though, to celebrate the black athlete as a fearsome hitter is also to denigrate him as "the primitive other, against whom higher status men define themselves as modern and civilized" (Messner and Sabo, 105).

Racism finds a counterpoint in the sexism and misogyny of sports. Despite the impressive growth in the number of women participating in athletics, sports continue to evolve as an expression of a male culture that keeps women in their place even while on the playing field. In many ways sports provide an excellent laboratory-type environment in which women can be allowed free and active involvement within certain prescribed areas. Women run track and field, but they certainly do not play football. Although the National Hockey League tried to install a female goalie, maybe as a test of the limits of women's participation in professional sports but mainly as a publicity stunt, she didn't last long in the net.

The misogyny of men's sports is even more pernicious. Gang rapes by adolescent males are perpetrated mostly by high school athletes. Bernard Lefkowitz's study of the gang rape of a retarded girl in New Jersey exposes the extent to which high school athletes live in such a reified air of privilege and adoration that it not only gives them permission to inflict violence but also ideologically justifies the denigration of anyone they deem inferior. In most cases those who are perceived to be subordinate are young girls, female teachers, and gay or nonathletic boys. Pointing to an FBI survey done in 1986, Lefkowitz states that "football and basketball players were reported to police for sexual assault 38 percent more often than the average male college student" (241). Although there remains some disagreement among researchers about whether the force and aggressiveness required in sports "nurture a tendency toward the abuse of women who are physically weaker than the athletes . . . there isn't any argument that athletes form a special, distinct, and often protected class of adolescents and young men in high school and college, and that some of these men think their status entitles them to do whatever they want to women" (Lefkowitz, 241). Violence against women on the part of athletes is not limited to adolescents, however. Michael Tyson's sense of privilege allowed him to believe that he actually had the right to rape the woman with whom he met in his hotel room. An argument might be made that part of what it means to be a male athlete is to remain, emotionally at least, at the developmental level of many adolescent boys. In professional football, where the exemplary female role seems to be the cheerleader, the perception of women as decorative and male-pleasing reinforces a social norm that maintains the assumption that men, and in particular male athletes, are entitled to take what they want from women, who are there to provide it.

The relationship between sports and war in U.S. history illustrates the role of athletics as an instrument of oppression and animosity. Gorn and Goldstein trace the subtleties of this association, beginning with the American Civil War which "provided a well of memory, a master metaphor for the belief that conflict between individuals, classes and nations lay at the heart of human existence" (99). As a moral equivalent of war, "athletics offered an opportunity for young men to get their first taste of glory, and for older men to renew the tingle of heroic combat" (140).

Football exemplifies this arrangement, with its military metaphors and language of war: drills, training camps, strategy, and tactics. As a preparation for leadership roles, football provides each of its participants with

> the shared experience of violence . . . the risk of injury . . . dependence on his fellows to protect him, the relief at surviving danger, . . . the sense of having gone through something together that others could not share [that] gave football players the feeling of being special, distinct, and worthy. Such feelings are also perhaps the defining characteristics of the bonds between combat veterans of military units. (Gorn and Goldstein, 163)[4]

In fact, the decades just before World War I saw a rise of college athletics that was "connected to the martial, jingoistic, and exceptionally masculine spirit of that time" (Gorn and Goldstein, 168).[5]

The relationship between sports metaphors and the language of war was not limited to World War I. America's involvement in the cold war

produced a whole new discourse of masculinity, and our instigation of the
Persian Gulf War provided one more example of how sports metaphors
influence the way our political leaders conceptualize war as a sporting
event in which their prowess is at stake.[6] U.S. presidents since at least
Teddy Roosevelt have been active sportsmen and sports fans. While Richard Nixon may be the most notable presidential fan in recent history, he
is not alone in assuming the role of the armchair quarterback that so many
American men take on during football season. Nixon, however, took it all
much further than the less powerful working-class or even middle-class
male. Nixon was notorious for his calls to George Allen, then coach of
the Washington Redskins, urging him to try specific plays of presidential
invention. Mandell provides several insights into how this situation
affected U.S. foreign policy under Nixon and how it influenced other men
in high political office. Mandell's observations warrant lengthy quotation:

> Nixon's public and private life was weirdly colored with, even molded
> by, the sports page and locker room rhetoric of "team play," "playing
> the game," strategy, and, above all, winning. It is possible that some
> aspects of the recent disappointments that Americans have endured
> can be attributed to a tendency among those at the highest levels of
> American society to permit sports rhetoric, metaphors of winning and
> losing and game dramaturgy to supply patterns for dealing with issues
> that are deadly earnest, that have a logic rooted in the real world, and
> are not games at all. We know now that the high-level strategy in the
> Indo-China adventure was planned and executed on the basis of par-
> ables drawn from professional baseball and football. One campaign
> for a step-up in bombing was called "Operation Linebacker" and Nix-
> on's code name was "Quarterback." (233)

The language of sports pervades the discourse of masculinity and helps
construct the way we see the world, as well as how we relate to such serious
undertakings as war and political involvement.

The influence of sports on the definition of masculine gender identity
is not limited to politics and government, however. Sports metaphors
abound in business as well, where "men discuss their 'game plans,' or their
ability to 'take hits,' or complain about 'Monday-morning quarterback-
ing'" (Gorn and Goldstein, 208). The language of sports also intrudes on
men in their personal lives. Well-hung jocks vie to score the most women,
whom they see not as equals but as trophies that demonstrate their athletic prowess.

Language and sports share a lack of social and cultural neutrality.
Sports are not just something we do to amuse ourselves, to lose weight, to
demonstrate our superior abilities in a friendly, supportive manner. Sports
have a history and a culture as well as a political dimension. Sports are

too often racist, sexist, and homophobic. They frequently do more harm than good, reinforcing the social norms far more than they undermine them. Although sports may have the potential to reform certain social assumptions about race and gender, historically they have helped to sustain dominant social standards, not provide radical alternatives. As Mandell observes, "Surely American sport is, among other things, disruptive of some good traditions, the preserver of some bad ones, vulgar, ruinous to some lives, a diversion from the earnestness of life, expensive, and orally equivocal. But few protest" (280).

Society's unwillingness, even inability, to protest the insidious effect sports have on social roles in modern society resembles in many ways its assumptions about language. For most people sports just exist out there in some indeterminate realm, and we should not take them too seriously (though many, many fans take them quite seriously, making sports as entertainment one of America's largest industries).

Although sports, like language, make insidious contributions to maintaining the social norms, at the same time both possess the potential to expose the contradictions within society and to introduce alternatives. Indeed, sports represent a much more complicated cultural phenomenon than might seem apparent at first glance. While on the surface they appear to be fundamentally violent, aggressive, competitive, and destructive, Allen Guttmann, the eminent U.S. sports historian, emphasizes the erotic dimension of sports. In addition, even as a male preserve sports may be the only personal space where men feel entitled to be emotional, and sports is one of the few "discourses" that brings men together.[7] It is one of the only areas in which outwardly expressed emotions are permissible for men. It is one of the few culturally endorsed ways in which men are allowed to be close.

The homoerotic nature of wrestling and other contact sports introduces, however, yet one more level of male ambivalence about their heterosexuality. In these sports men touch each other a lot; though often violent contact occurs (behavior that sometimes carries over to their interaction with women), men also might slap a teammate on the behind or hug one enthusiastically after he scores a goal or pins a competitor. Although society frequently denies or hides the homoerotic aspect of male–male relationships, especially in sports, athletics frequently allow for an explicit recognition of male beauty. Early in the twentieth century in the United States, for example, a bachelor subculture emerged that "developed its own masculine aesthetic that reveled in male beauty" (Gorn and Goldstein, 74). Our contemporary society is not immune to an infatuation and glorification of male beauty either, especially by other men. Toby Miller, in his astute and charming essay on the penis, asserts that today "sport allows/requires men to watch and dissect other men's bodies in fetishistic detail. It proffers a legitimate space to gaze on and devour the male form without homosexuality being either alleged or feared" (6). The complicity of sports in homophobia emanates from this broader context in which men fear homosexuality both in themselves and in other men.[8] This fear manifests itself in violence against males, an aggressiveness frequently apparent in the language men use to talk about themselves and other men.

Sports exemplify an overtly masculine experience, one that trains boys to become successful businessmen and soldiers and one that reminds women that men are bigger, stronger, faster, and thus potentially more successful. Sports, however, expose a deep-seated male ambivalence about heterosexuality. Like much of the discourse examined already, the language of sports and male sexuality resonates with confusion and doubt.

## CIRCLE JERK

Formal definitions of "circle jerk," what few there are, explain it as either literally a group of men who sit in a circle and masturbate themselves and/or others or "a boring or time-wasting meeting or other event" (Spears, 83). Like "jerking off," a euphemism for masturbation that becomes a metaphor for an experience at work, "circle jerk" connotes wasting one's time or not accomplishing anything.

I have included "circle jerk" in the chapter on sports rather than in the chapter on labor and work because it transforms jerking off or masturbation into a sporting event that has winners and losers. The guy who ejaculates first wins the prize. A friend of mine told me a joke recently that sums up the significance of this male experience:

q:   Do you know who the most competitive man is?
a:   The guy who wants to place first and second in a circle jerk.

Competition doesn't end there, either. The boy with the largest penis wins a prize too.

Granted, circle jerks are the experience of adolescent boys and pretty much disappear from the male experience after the early stages of puberty. Frequently, this experience is a boy's introduction to receiving sexual pleasure from another male, and it provides a sexual release at a time when intercourse with a girl is forbidden. When I look back upon my own experience with circle jerks, I am embarrassed. The shame may stem from the association with masturbation in general, and it may be exacerbated by the implied (if not explicit) intimacy with other males.

In his book, *Our Guys,* a study of a gang rape in Glen Ridge, New Jersey, Lefkowitz cautions against placing too much emphasis on the homoerotic nature of this behavior when he points out that some analysts interpret such adolescent behavior not as homoerotic but as an effort to prove heterosexual dominance and to establish masculine authority within the group. The real goal is overcoming your insecurities about sex by impressing your friends with your sexual prowess. To achieve that goal, a guy needs an audience to witness his dominating performance. A group of appreciative and responsive buddies is essential to build a reputation for sexual control and domination. (243–44)

Male bonding, whether overtly physical as in a "circle jerk" or covertly mental as in the use of language, provides men with a source of power and domination. What on the surface appears to be neutral or natural frequently occasions violence against women in a variety of forms. Adolescent male behavior, whether high school athletics or circle jerks, socializes boys to become men who perceive themselves as privileged, superior, strong, and controlling. Lefkowitz's study of the gang rape in New Jersey makes clear these connections and warns of the necessity to confront all such adolescent male behavior early and often if we are to prevent the kind of adult male behavior that evolves from what we may accept as just boys being boys.

## COJONES

Frankly, this is not cojones. This is cowardice.
—Madeline K. Albright, on downing
of a plane near Cuba

The man who has the "cojones" or the "balls" to do something has the courage to win. Although this metaphor might fit just as well in chapter 4, "War and Conquest," I have placed it under sports because the desire to win, and the sense of what allows one man to win while another loses, frequently is equated with male sexual prowess. As a metaphor for the testicles and thus a metonym for manhood, "cojones" refers to a man's inherent ability to dominate another man.

"Cojones" means "bull's nuts" in Spanish and is best known as a term used by Hemingway to characterize a courageous man. Slang dictionaries record similar meanings: John Ayto and John Simpson see a direct correlation between the testicles and "courage, guts" (40), whereas Robert Chapman equates balls with "audacity" (77).

Madeline Albright's remarks in the epigraph to this section exemplify the use of this term as connoting bravery and manliness. Albright was referring to "a Cuban military pilot's exultant cry after he shot down a light plane that was alleged to be invading Cuban airspace. 'We took out his balls!' the pilot had shouted" (Mead, 9), Albright focuses on the Cuban pilot's pusillanimity in the skirmish, pointing out that what he did was cowardly, not manly, as he had claimed.

Like "cock of the walk," and the phrase "having the balls," "cojones" reduces representations of masculinity to a man's genitals. Courage is not equated with intelligence or emotional commitment but with testosterone. The larger a man's gonads (and, of course, his penis) the greater a man he is. The penis as a metaphorical cudgel, used to beat a competitor into submission or intimidate the other team, informs the way male athletes think about themselves as men.

Men who reflect upon a situation and consider the moral and ethical consequences; men with average-sized or small penises; men who nurture or care about human life; men who do not hunt or do not kill; men who think, who read, who write; and men who love in an unselfish and emotionally charged way are not really men. The man who has no cojones is a wimp or a wuss, a faggot or a queer, not really a man at all. The man who assumes the validity of this characterization, as is true for the "cock of the walk," and believes that manhood can be understood only in terms of the size of his genitals lives a diminished existence in which his wholeness as a person is negated.

Why don't men ever measure masculinity in terms of having the brains or having the heart or having the emotions? Why are men's metaphors of masculinity always reduced to size, power, aggression, and victory? Why are they so genitally located? These are the questions a close reading of a metaphor like "cojones" brings to the surface.

## JOCK

Derived from "jock strap" and meaning, in its narrow sense, an athlete, a "jock," according to Spears, is "a male athlete, especially if large and stupid" (245). Ayto and Simpson are kinder when they say only that "jock" refers to "a male athlete, especially at university" (114). The *American Heritage College Dictionary* expands the definition somewhat when it points out that this term describes "one characterized by machismo" (731).

These constitute the popular definitions of the term. The earliest uses of "jock," however, were "to copulate with a woman" (British slang from the late 1600s), and "the penis" (from the mid- to late 1700s) (Spears, 245). Ayto and Simpson concur with the latter usage when they cite one definition as "the male genitals" and suggest that it originates around 1790 (114).

Chapman furnishes some helpful etymological information by pointing out that "the basic etymon is 'jock' [meaning] penis, from 'jack,' probably the diminutive of 'John,' which from the 14th century has been applied to males . . . and male organs" (237). "John Thomas," as the nickname for the caretaker's penis in *Lady Chatterley's Lover,* is in this tradition and a John is, of course, a slang term for a prostitute's client.

The relationship between "jock" as a synonym for "penis" and "jock strap" as a penis strap provides some insights into the ways in which language evolves while remaining historically contingent. "Jack," in the phrase "jacking off," also takes on new significance. As a metaphor for male sexuality, though, "jock" reduces men's identity to that of their bodies while glorifying the athletic and physically strong. The connection between the jock with a rigid athletic body and the "hard-on" as a rigid erect penis cannot be ignored. Men are reminded over and over again of the importance for their bodies to be like armor: impenetrable, strong, and emotionless.

As potentially an athletic superhero with the persona of a stud, the jock projects a sense of power and sexual might. Ironically, though, as a stupid muscle-bound male, the "jock" exemplifies male heterosexuality with its conception of the world as split fundamentally between mind and body. For many men the body represents the source of their identity, and the penis dominates that conception. Here too a term that glorifies the masculine body resonates with contempt for that same body. Men's ambivalence about their physiology, and their doubt that their minds and their emotions have any relevance in their lives, calls out from this particular metaphor.

### SCORING

> The boys used to go to the local dance halls and stand around . . .
> until the . . . sexual urge prompted them to score a chick.
> —Germaine Greer, *The Female Eunuch*

As Don Sabo and Ross Runfola point out in their book on sports and male identity, "Sports and masculinity are virtually synonymous in American culture" (x). Not only are there specific words for referring to certain types of men (e.g., "jock") but men frequently rely on sports metaphors to discuss their personal and professional lives (e.g., "a level playing field," "crossing the finish line," "getting to the end zone," "hitting a home run"). Adolescent boys talk about "getting to first base" with a girl, and "scoring" is the ultimate goal of the adolescent male imagination. Sports dominate the lives of boys and provide a training ground in which they become men.

When sex becomes a contest, a means for domination and conquest, male–female relationships are reduced to a game in which there are "winners" and "losers."[9] The question, "Did you score last night, Steve?" represents an extension of male competitiveness in which "females are often perceived as opponents and various strategies or game plans are developed to get them to submit" (Sabo and Runfola, xiv). Men feel comfortable on the playing field, where they know the rules of the game and can maneuver a victory. This may be part of the reason many men avoid smart women. In addition to having their sense of insecurity about their own intelligence exacerbated, men may also fear losing. A woman who understands the rules of the game may be too much of an opponent, and male identity may be too invested in being the winner.

In her book on sexism and the American culture of sports, Mariah Burton Nelson points out:

> From the pinup "girls" on football players' lockers to the very language of "scoring," many men associate sports with male sexual virility and female passivity. Men are aggressors; women are things to be consumed, like food or drink. At times blatantly, at times more subtly, the manly sports culture equates athletic prowess—or even athletic enthusiasm—with not just sex, but dominance. (86)

In light of recent warnings broadcast around the time of the Super Bowl about the increase in violence against girlfriends and wives, especially when the man's favored team loses, Nelson's observations seem even more pertinent. Several reports, not isolated examples, of college football players' beating up and/or raping their girlfriends also add credibility to Nelson's observations. Men are raised not just to be athletes in their own right but to live out their fantasies of masculinity through athletic heroes. When these heroes can injure women with impunity, we can indict sports in general as a training ground for antisocial male behavior.

In a chapter on scoring in particular, Nelson describes the reprehensible activities of the Spur Posse in Lakeview, California. This group of teenage boys, mostly football players, "turned sex into a sporting contest, tallying 'points' scored for each instance of sexual intercourse" (80). Although these young men took scoring to its most extreme, even to the point of rape, the idea of sex as triumph and as victory resounds throughout the discourse examined in this book. In the concluding remarks to her chapter on scoring, Nelson reflects:

> The sex depicted in the sacred sports culture is not sensuous, playful, spontaneous, passionate, caring, mutual. The message sent in football stadiums, in sports magazines, in sports bars, and in communities "where boys are athletes and girls are cheerleaders" is not just about exaggerated gender roles or "viva [sic] la difference." It's about domination. Sex as conquest. In order for men to remain dominant, to

> remain victorious, women must be in a subservient position. Women become opponents to defeat. Or they can be trophies: rewards for success in the intramale hierarchy. (96)

The behavior of the boys of Glen Ridge High who gang-raped a retarded girl raises questions about U.S. society in general and athletics in particular. As Lefkowitz points out:

> The Jocks didn't invent the idea of mistreating young women. The ruling clique of teenagers adhered to a code of behavior that mimicked, distorted, and exaggerated the values of the adult world around them. These values extolled "winners" . . . [and] they denigrated "losers." . . . Glen Ridge placed the elite kids—the kids with masculine good looks, the kids who stood out on the playing field—on a pedestal. (424)

Indeed, "for these young men, the essence of jockdom was a practiced show of contempt for kids and teachers alike. They tried to humiliate any wimpy guy who got in their way, but they reserved their best shots for girls who ignored them or dared to stand up to them" (111).

The overarching context for all this pernicious behavior remains high school sports, with their emphasis on competition, winning, and achievement. These values are not unique to Glen Ridge, New Jersey, and the violent outcome of this socialization resonates in sex crimes across the United States. Lefkowitz concludes:

> In the community where they grew up and which celebrated their athletic achievements; in their isolation from women and their evolving attitudes toward girls; in their fascination with voyeurism and pornography and in their actual treatment of young women; and, finally, in their choice of victim—in all these respects, the Glen Ridge Jocks resembled the contemporary profile of other privileged and popular male groups that were accused of committing sexual assaults of women. (248–49)

Women as the losers to men reinforce the dynamics of the "masculinity game." Losers are reduced to humiliation and powerlessness, and thus, as Lucy Komisar makes clear, losers take on "the classic status of women" (140).

As a metaphor for male sexuality, "scoring" is used by men "who are interested in keeping track of the number of copulations they have performed" (Spears, 385), and the term measures how a man's success with a woman depends on his "being pleasing and convincing" (Wentworth and Flexner, 449). Taken together these two insights make clear the close association between scoring and seduction. Related to the Don Juan myth, in which numbers and counting become the basis of men's relationship with women (though today this is not an exclusively heterosexual phenomenon), scoring accentuates the male obsession with quantity over quality. To score points for devising a successful strategy or for winning the game exemplifies the interest of most men in the goal or the end rather than in the quality of the experience. The idea of conquest, or of gaining the trophy in which a woman becomes the prize, reduces male sexual pleasure to a race or a game or an event for which the primary objective is to win, to be the best, to score the most points.

Maybe the saying "It's not whether you win or lose, it's how you play the game" should be the coach's advice we take seriously. If sexual pleasure can become play rather than work, joy rather than conquest, wonder rather than triumph, metaphors of male sexuality can encompass the breadth of erogenous possibility, not the obsession with winning the tournament, closing the deal, buying cheap to sell dear.

## WELL HUNG

> Death takes the innocent young. And those who are very well hung.
> —W. H. Auden

Many men compete for the honor of having the biggest penis and the largest testicles because these same men equate their masculinity with the ability to do the most harm and intimidate those who do not carry around a club between their legs. In the locker room, although men are not supposed to look at other men's genitals, the most well hung is usually known and honored. This bastion of male privilege is not unproblematic, however. Although the locker-room culture celebrates male physicality, it also reveals a culture that is fragile: "Its fragility consists of the fact that in the locker room, as on the playing field, male physical superiority is not a biological given but an ideological construct that must be produced by ritual performances that promote male narcissism and exclude male vulnerability" (Disch and Kane, 299). At no time is this vulnerability more apparent then when a female sports reporter enters the locker room, as witnessed by the 1990 experience of Lisa Olson, a sportswriter for the *Boston Herald* who covered the New England Patriots. A victim of sexual harassment by several team members, Olson was castigated by the team's owner, Victor Kiam, as a "classic bitch," an epithet later emended by Mark Clayton, a wide receiver for the Miami Dolphins, to a "dick-watching bitch." As a professional journalist and a woman who rejected the traditional female spectator role of "the adoring audience who mirrors man's performance in such a way as to exaggerate his potency and overlook his inadequacies" (Scheman, 287), Olson threatened the patriarchal myth of male superiority and invincibility. The vigor of the attack on Olson by the male athletic establishment suggests the level of fear and anger these men felt from her intrusion on their privacy (and privates, for that matter) and their male preserve.

This insecurity about the penis as symbolic of male privilege is not a recent phenomenon. As a synonym for the less-well-known slang term "mentulate," which "pertains to a man with an abnormally large penis" (Spears, 286) and more precisely means "a man with large or very large genitals" (Spears, 473; Thorne, 555; Ayto and Simpson, 282; Chapman, 462), "well hung" as a term has been in use for at least two hundred years, pervading the male imagination as a concept for far longer. The size of the penis, indeed the belief that the larger the better and the smaller the less of a man one is, suffuses men's fears and insecurities. The latent desire of many men to be considered "studs" derives from this fixation but at the same time reduces a man to an animal, a horse at stud. Men ignore the significance of identifying with a part of nature the male imagination has worked hard to control, and they fail to see the connection between the horse at stud and domesticated slave. Men romanticize the stud as omnipotent and lubricious while ignoring the extent to which all domesticated animals are just that, domesticated. In this idyllic view of the world the attraction for a man to having a large penis relates to having the capacity to cause harm and destruction; that is, the penis becomes a punitive weapon of misogyny.

The larger the better informs men's ideas about weapons, of course, and about engines and boats and other male toys. This obsession with the penis as a weapon, indeed a large club to bludgeon a woman into submission, blinds men to their bodies as fragile, sensitive, and soft. The male's preoccupation with size undermines his ability to think about the broad spectrum of giving and receiving pleasure.

### WIMP/WUSS(Y)

I'm the pit bull of SDI, you Ivy League wimp!
—George Bush to Sen. J. James Exxon

As terms connoting the exact opposite of having "cojones," "wimp" and "wuss(y)" characterize the man who is afraid to take risks and probably does not care a lot about winning. In sports jargon the "wimp" is the guy who sits on the bench, acts like a "sissy," and avoids being pummeled for the sake of the home team. In many ways the "wimp" is anathema to sports in general, but as a derogatory term for a man, "wimp" exemplifies the unqualified, doubtful, even tremulous male who prefers not to be a sports hero.

In the early 1900s "wimp" referred to a young woman or a girl. By the 1970s, according to Paul Beale, the definition had changed to mean "one who is old-fashioned and behind the times, a 'square'" (503). Today "wimp" is slang for "a person who is regarded as weak or ineffectual" (*AHCD*, 1544). Chapman synthesizes these various meanings when he defines "wimp" as "an ineffectual person; a soft, silly person; a weakling; . . . unmacho" (468).

The transition from a weak person to an unmacho man suggests that men have only these two choices: men can be soft or they can be hard; men can be weak or they can be macho. Men cannot, though, under any circumstances be emotional and cry and still be men.

Although the precise origins of the word "wimp" are unknown, Chapman speculates that "wimp" might have been derived "from J. Wellington Wimpy, a relatively unaggressive character in the comic strip *Popeye* [or] from the early 20th century Cambridge University wimp [meaning] 'young woman' or perhaps from whimper" (468). No matter its exact origin, the meaning seems fairly clear. A "wimp" is unaggressive, feeble, spineless, cowardly, and emotional. A "wimp" is more like a woman than like a man, and when you elide "woman" and "whimper," you arrive at an intonation not unlike the word "wimp."

The origin of the term "wuss(y)" is also debatable. Tony Thorne believes it was "probably inspired by 'puss,' 'pussy,' or 'pussy-wussy,' used as a term of endearment to a kitten" (570), whereas Chapman sees it as "the handy combination of wimp and pussy" (475). A "wuss," not unlike a "wimp," is a "weak, feeble person, and by extension a dupe" (Thorne, 570). According to Spears, "wuss" can be seen as "a weak, wishy-washy person" (489). In most cases, though, "wuss" (or "wussy") refers to a man, even though it is derived from pejorative terms for a woman.

Like other metaphors that suggest femaleness (e.g., "faggot," "pansy," "pussy," and "sissy"), a wimp exemplifies passivity, thoughtfulness, and quiescence. As an unaggressive man, a wimp thinks first and considers others. A wimp, then, is too compassionate and emotional to be a real man.

In national security discourse, a language that frequently reduces the potential for war to a discourse of "the big game," this point is made abundantly clear. Carol Cohn points out that

> You learn that someone is being a wimp if he perceives an international crisis as very dangerous and urges caution; if he thinks it might not be important to have just as many weapons that are just as big as the other guy's; if he suggests that an attack should not necessarily be answered by an even more destructive counterattack; or, until recently, if he suggested that making unilateral arms reductions might be useful for our own security. All of these are "wimping out." (234)

In the early 1980s, with what Kimmel refers to as the "virtual Great American Wimp Hunt," "wimp" became a negative model for men to attack. This "sensitive New Age guy," who was "warm, sensitive, cuddly, and compassionate [was] . . . poised as a masculine template for the decade, despite his receding hairline, flabby biceps, and enlarging waistline" (*Manhood*, 292–93).

Kimmel's sardonic characterization of the postmodern wimp points to several intrinsic contradictions: the new man "emerged at the expense of women; he was not new enough for a truly egalitarian relationship with an equally strong woman" (*Manhood*, 293).

Today many people use the word "wimp" to refer to any weak-willed person and no longer to just men. Barbara Ehrenreich stresses this when she observes, "Already, in popular usage, the dismissive term 'wimp' is applied almost as readily to women as to men, implying that the appropriate stance for both sexes is tough and potentially battle-ready" (230).

Both "wimp" and "wuss" are particularly offensive, however, when referring to men. They are comparable to calling a woman a bitch. Ironically, though, many self-proclaimed feminists use these terms to refer to men, even though a man using the word "bitch" (or "chick") to refer to a female would instigate their wrath.

Ironically, the same people who would confront a friend on the use of "chick" to refer to a woman use "wimp" as a perfectly acceptable term. But "wimp" is a sexist reference, let there be no doubt about it. Although it is used as a universal insult for men and women, its power as an affront comes from combining two words that connote weakness, with an association with femininity. When we call someone a "wimp," we buy into the characterization of women as highly emotional, whimpering cowards and to men as aggressive and destructive. The guy who takes all the risks to help the home team win the big game is a man, whereas the guy who sits on the bench is just a wimp. Ironically, and somewhat tragically, the heroic athlete may end up doing so much damage to his body he will end up in a wheelchair or at least walking with a cane. The wimp, on the other hand, will probably go on to college (even without an athletic scholarship) and, without the scars from high school sports, will end up walking just fine.

# 4   Sex as War and Conquest

> Wars are not an interminable series of historical accidents, nor the
> product of the machinations of evil men, nor yet the result of some
> simple single cause like capitalism or overpopulation. Neither is war-
> fare merely the heritage of our evolutionary past, an outlet for our
> "natural aggressiveness." War is a central institution in human civili-
> zation, and it has a history precisely as long as civilization.
>
> —Gwynne Dyer, *War*

> Whether war is a necessary factor in the evolution of mankind may
> be disputed, but a fact which cannot be questioned is that, from the
> earliest records of man to the present age, war has been his domi-
> nant preoccupation.
>
> —J. F. C. Fuller, *A Military History of the Western World*

> Strip away all of the rhetoric, and the core remains: we expect our
> young men to sacrifice their lives for us if war comes, and they are
> willing to be asked.
>
> —Gwynne Dyer, *War*

War can be seen as the culmination of the masculine experience, and it
synthesizes the thematic structures I have examined thus far. War provides
the opportunity for men's obsession with the machine and technology to
merge with their fixation on business and economic gain, and war allows
them to realize the training they receive in athletics and sports. In war
men experience the violent, aggressive, and death-defying occurrences for
which they have prepared for most of their adolescent and adult life. That
is, war epitomizes the socially constructed masculine world.

Although the sources of war, its origin, and its role in civilization are
much debated, military historians find common agreement on some aspects of the experience. In his most recent book on the birth and death of
war, *Ride of the Second Horseman,* the distinguished American military
historian Robert O'Connell provides a helpful overview of war's pertinent
characteristics:

> There must be an element of premeditation and planning. . . . War
> implies direction by some form of governmental structure. . . . Partici-
> pants also are presumed ready to apply lethal violence and risk injury
> and death in pursuit of [certain] objectives and in accordance with the
> dictates of the command authority. Finally, some understanding can
> be attributed to the parties involved that the results of war, for good
> or ill, will be more lasting than momentary. (5)

Other writers on war have emphasized different aspects, pointing to the
necessity for there to be "some kind of political purpose" accompanied
by "weapons, strategy, order, training and discipline, . . . and rewards . . .
brought together into a single art or practice" (Gallie, 29–30). While many
of these components remain the same today, modern or contemporary
wars also stress "the ability to mobilize the entire population for war, the
resources that make that degree of mobilization possible, and the technology" (Dyer, 43).

Barbara Ehrenreich takes issue with theories such as these and suggests that in fact either no theories of war or far too many exist. In *Blood
Rites,* her thought-provoking study of war, she analyzes the origins and
history of the passions behind war and provides what she calls "a crude
summary [of] the theories of war which modern wars have left us with":
"that war is a means, however risky, by which men seek to advance their
collective interests and improve their lives. Or, alternatively, that war stems
from subrational drives not unlike those that lead individuals to commit
violent crimes" (8).[1] Ehrenreich rejects the idea of a personality type in-
herently prepared for war, the hot-tempered macho type, for example,
and points out that war "is too complex and collective an activity to be
accounted for by a single warlike instinct lurking within the individual
psyche" (9).

From Ehrenreich's perspective the amount of time spent on the preparation for battle far exceeds the actual fighting involved in war. Central to
much of the preparation for war, especially the capacity to mobilize human resources, has been the role of sports. Athletics has functioned well
as a training ground for both warlike behavior and jingoistic commitments.
As Elliott J. Gorn and Warren Goldstein observe, in the early part of this
century in the United States "for the first time, organized athletics and
physical education were linked in the minds of leaders and participants
to patriotism and military preparedness" (181). The nationalistic rhetoric
surrounding the Olympics, that supposedly neutral sports-centered ritual,
reminds us of how often athletic competition degenerates into the promo-
tion of a sense of national worth and superiority.

That there exists an intimate relationship between sports and war is
not a new insight, of course. Carl von Clausewitz himself, still considered

the most important military theorist of the modern era, begins his treatise, *On War,* by drawing an analogy between warfare and wrestling. For Clausewitz, "War is nothing but a duel on an extensive scale. If we would conceive as a unit the countless numbers of duels which make up a War, we shall do so best by supposing to ourselves two wrestlers. . . . War therefore is an act of violence intended to compel our opponent to fulfill our will" (101). Indeed, W. B. Gallie makes the point that war possesses an inherent tendency to escalate that is "rooted . . . in men's simplest acts of fighting" (66–67).

Like so many contact sports, war engenders acts of violence aimed at conquest and destruction. Men learn to be good warriors and obedient soldiers through the high school team sports they play and the ideology of masculinity geared toward winning at all cost, no matter the goal or objective.

Scholars have documented extensively early transitions from sports to war. From something as simple as the foot race, which prepared men to carry messages more quickly, to archery contests that improved their aim, sports have helped train men to be more proficient soldiers. Hunting, probably the most significant link between war and sports, provided an armed group of men with training in tactics and warfare to kill animals much larger than they. Even for Ehrenreich, whose skepticism about most theories of war makes her reluctant to endorse any of them, "hunting is an antecedent of war . . . predating it and providing it with many valuable techniques" (21).[2] The horse, initially perhaps only a means of transportation, quickly became a weapon in the hunt and subsequently in battle; the chariot was designed as a weapon, with chariot races developed as practice in effective warring techniques. The phalanx, with its emphasis on military training and men working together as a team, was one of the earliest and most effective military innovations.

One dominant theory of the origins of war sees it as "predominantly a rough male sport for underemployed hunters" (Dyer, 10). Ehrenreich echoes this conception in a chapter entitled, quite tellingly, "A Rough Male Sport," in which she makes explicit the connection between war and sports. For both writers, war making has to be understood as a means to define manhood, to establish who the "real men" really are. This, according to Ehrenreich, "is exactly what we would expect if war originated as a substitute occupation for underemployed male hunter-defenders" (127). Thus war "becomes a solution to what Margaret Mead termed 'the recurrent problem of civilization,' which is 'to define the male roles satisfactorily enough'" (Ehrenreich, 129).

Today sports such as football provide adolescent boys with a sense of who the real men are, training them to become fierce warriors and obedient soldiers (and sometimes rapists, as it turns out, which is of course not irrelevant to the practice of war). Fasteau makes this connection when he observes that "in ordinary life, the most violent pursuits are considered the most masculine—football and making war, for example" (150). As should be clear from chapter 3, in many ways football in particular resembles war. The language of football resonates with armed services training and the battlefield.

In a highly perceptive essay on the discourse of *Monday Night Football,* Nick Trujillo examines the ways in which it reduces images of the male body to machines and missiles.[3] He provides a long (one hopes exhaustive) inventory of terms used by the announcers of these games, a list so vivid it warrants quoting at length:

> During the season players were described as "weapons," "missiles," "shields," "rockets," "hitting machines," and other instruments of violence . . . [and] among the terms used . . . to describe what these . . . weapons (bodies) did on the football field were attack, blow away, break through, burst, catapult, club, crash, cripple, crunch, decapitate, decimate, destroy, dislodge, dislocate, dismantle, drill, explode, fire, fly, hammer, hit, hurdle, jackhammer, kill, launch, mortar, mug, penetrate, plug, pop, pound, push, ram, rifle, rip, shoot, shred, slam, smash, smoke, snap, spin, steamroll, tattoo, tomahawk, toss, twist, unload, upend, whack, whip, wound and wreck. (411)

Descriptions of team sports endorse violence as acceptable behavior, just as the discourse of male bonding sanctions interpersonal relationships built on fear, derision, and contempt. Men are taught it is manly to destroy the enemy, whether that enemy takes the shape of a citizen of another nation, a woman on the street, a gay man, or an opponent on the other team.

As Ehrenreich makes clear, though, "War is not simply a clash of Others made possible by an ignorant horror of difference. . . . Warriors . . . share the basic tenets of warriordom: a respect for courage, a willingness to stand by one's comrades no matter what, a bold indifference to death" (141). With its emphasis on competition, force, and honor war provides men with the ultimate experience of male bonding. Until recently, women had been all but omitted from the armed services, and men have found in war an exclusive male club.[4] John Keegan points out, in his general history of warfare, that "the best-observed ideals of regimental culture [include] total obedience, single-minded courage, self-sacrifice, honour" (16). Men are taught to obey those in positions of authority throughout their adolescent and adult lives. Their high school football coaches instill in them the necessity to be team players, to take risks, and to sacrifice their own significance to the goals (and honor) of their teams.

On the football field, as in all walks of life for men, the ability to be forceful, to be powerful, and to dominate are qualities to emulate. In war, force takes on even greater consequence than on the gridiron, allowing men to pursue technological and mechanical innovation. In war, as in interpersonal relationships, for many men "force is the ultimate argument" (Dyer, 4). Whether we are talking about Patriot missiles in the Persian Gulf War or settling an argument with a lover, whether we are concerned with the front line of the varsity football team or gang rape, force remains for far too many men the basis for settling disagreements. Although Keegan takes the essentialist position that sees as natural and inherent men's tendency "to use weapons to settle quarrels over insults, property, women and succession to position" (25), we should not ignore his point that men tend to resolve differences with the use of force.

Men learn to be violent, however; they are by no means born warriors or rapists. Certainly, a large part of men's socialization to be aggressive and violent comes from the emphasis placed throughout much of their lives  on competition. Competition, along with greed, individualism, and the necessity to win, are, of course, central components of capitalist ideology. Men learn to compete for the best job, the largest paycheck, the most beautiful woman within a broad context of religious and economic reinforcements that posit this behavior as emblematic of the human condition. Men are taught to compare the size of their muscles, their penises, and their possessions as the source of their social significance. In war the size of the weapon, its capacity to do the most harm, is a measure of strength, potency, and, alas, masculinity. When the army teaches a recruit the difference between his gun and his weapon, his penis and his rifle, the message he receives involves a comparison grounded in the power to inflict harm.

The concept of honor unifies all this macho warrior ideology and introduces an "ingrained warrior ethic that is the heritage of every young human male" (Dyer, 14); as Gwynne Dyer also quite accurately perceives, "Men will kill and die rather than lose face" (13). Honor has always grounded the poetic cult of military might, introducing the somewhat absurd notion that an honorable kind of fighting exists. Drawing a comparison between the introduction of the chariot into warfare and the introduction of the fighter plane, Dyer observes that although "warfare is a serious business, and it may seem incredible that anything so frivolous as one kind of fighting [can be seen to be] more fun and 'honorable' than another" (48), such perceptions have at times influenced the dominant military style of an entire era. In World War I, for example, members of the cavalry remained unwilling to give up their horses long after it became apparent that the introduction of tanks had made it impossible for the cavalry to be effective or even to survive, for that matter.

Honor gives men a sense of glory as they bond with other warriors to be "real men" and not cowards. Honor also provides a basis for perceived superiority over other men, less well armed or inferior in their training. Honor, then, like the rules of an athletic event, introduces parameters in which men play out their role of soldier while demonstrating to their fellows their mastery over women, children, and those males designated as lesser men—draft dodgers, for example, war resisters, and gay men, of course.[5]

The concepts of honor, competition, and force have evolved alongside the development of better, more destructive weapons and the creation of new tactics and strategies for successful warfare. Scientific research not only has improved machines for agriculture and industrialization but created more effective weapons of mass destruction. As Dyer observes so astutely:

> At the time of Ceresole [1544], the most powerful weapons in the world, the great siege cannons, were capable of killing perhaps a half a dozen people (if they stood close together) at a range of a few hundred yards. Today, less than four and a half centuries later, the modern counterparts of those weapons, the intercontinental ballistic missiles, can kill several million people at a range of seven or eight thousand miles. (54)

Although, according to Dyer, only in the modern period has this kind of destructive capacity been dominated by technology, it seems clear that men's desire to create bigger, more forceful weapons has informed strategies of warfare throughout human history. Lewis Mumford, we may recall from chapter 1, "Sex as Machine," sees the military drill as a prime example of how the technological imagination has influenced the way armies were conceived and trained.

The male fascination with technological innovation has, unfortunately, been directed toward destruction and the control of nature (especially human beings) more often than it has toward the betterment of humanity. This desire for control manifests itself in social organization and finds some of its greatest expression not only in armies but in businesses. Business, in the broadest sense of the word—not just modern corporations but earlier trading and merchant endeavors, with their drive to acquire more land and goods—motivated war efforts. The structure of these business arrangements affected society in general and influenced the way wars were fought: "The commercial unification of the world immensely enlarged the scale, the stage, the rewards and the motives of wars between industrial nations" (Gallie, 43). Indeed, warring is generally attributed to the centralization of power in society. According to Gallie, military thinking and the thinking of businessmen or of scientists "is at the heart of the war-culture we have inherited" (67).

Dyer highlights this same point in the caption to a photo of military personnel in Saigon who are viewing graphs on an overhead projector. He points out that "the temptation to believe that all the human imponderables of combat can be reduced to neat equations was especially strong in the United States and exalted the role of the manager and planner over that of the traditional fighting commander" (see figs. following p. 153). Commerce, business, and science merge in their efforts to perpetuate wars in much the same way that they influence social values and gender arrangements.

Although considerable debate over the sources of war remains, scarcity has been identified as a primary one. Whether it was scarcity of land, food, or women, men have fought wars to obtain some form of property they believed to be their inalienable right. O'Connell, for one, maintains that war began as "raiding, imperialism and enslavement" (23), along with the desire to obtain "territory, property, and labor" (29): "The inescapable nature of war's snare would eventually be predicated on nowhere else to go and its corollary, a population too high to go elsewhere" (46). J. F. C. Fuller sees the fundamental causes of war as biological and economic. "The more prolific the herds and flocks, the more frequently had new grass-lands to be sought. . . . Similarly, the more prolific the city population, the more food was needed and the more land was necessary for its cultivation" (2). Men fought for land, food, and slaves to do the work required to sustain life. In addition, men battled to obtain products unknown to their communities, and men went to war to acquire goods that served only as badges of prestige and warrior prowess: war, that is, "served not only to enrich the victorious community as a whole, but to enhance the status of a specific group within it: the men who fought or led the fighting" (Ehrenreich, 123).

Although some confusion remains about how exactly individual men came together in groups to fight battles and to undertake such a significant project as a war, anthropologists point to what is apparently "an inherent proclivity among human males to bond in pods that scrupulously exclude women" (O'Connell, 30).

On a broader scale evidence suggests that "the dominant trend in the history (and prehistory) of human culture has been the creation of larger and larger groups within which each member is defined as 'one of us': a kinsman, a fellow tribesman, a fellow citizen" (Dyer, 6). From the tribe to the battle regiment may not have been such a great leap, especially in light of the existence of small all-male hunting groups. While the regiment is really a modern invention of war, the intimate male-centered band of hunters/warriors has been around for thousands of years. Although the "hunting hypothesis," the belief that hunting has always been an exclusively male activity and that it was "the sole 'motor' of human evolution" has declined

recently to the status of myth (Ehrenreich, 39), we cannot deny the ramifications of men bonding together in exclusive control of weapons, and with
a distinct agenda in mind. Indeed, Ehrenreich focuses some attention on
how a change in hunting strategy that coincided with the first "arms revo-
lution" initiated a new sexual division of labor that demoted women. "Instead of the communal hunt undertaken by the whole band, there was now
the male hunter's sub-band, with women relegated to the less glamorous
job of processing the meat . . . brought back by men" (111). This change
to a male-only hunting strategy may have precipitated the use of violence
as the exclusive prerogative of males. Concomitant with this development
was "the practice of treating women as booty [which] may well have encouraged misogyny in the victors" (Ehrenreich, 130).

Men bonded together thousands of years ago to further their agenda
in ways not unlike (though slightly less sophisticated than) the regiments,
sports teams, business clubs, social lodges, and college fraternities in existence today. Although, initially, these "secret men's associations artifi-
cially tried to maintain the old glory and comradeship which formerly
existed during hunting expeditions" (Ehrenreich, 124), today these men-
only groups still provide networks for employment as well as a foundation
for the continuation of male privilege.[6]

This male-dominated social arrangement we find in our society is neither without historical precedent nor is it neutral in its ramifications for
women. As Dyer observes, this new form of social organization has as
"its most striking features . . . the dominance of a warrior class—and the
depoliticization of women" (8). Indeed, according to Dyer, an inherent
relationship exists between the administration of a state and patriarchy,
both of which provide the illusion of absolute power embodied in one man
or a small group of men who are "backed by the right and ability to punish
or even kill those who disobey" (Dyer, 17). While Dyer's statement may
be too extreme to apply to contemporary life, the modern state maintains
a similar effectiveness with the use of more subtle means of control, not
least of which is discourse.

The right to control social behavior and inflict harm on those who
imagine or live out alternative social roles gains legitimacy through the
appropriation of language. Discourse is, of course, a powerful weapon
in the war between the sexes, a war really directed against the female,
whether embodied as woman or as gay man. Fuller's insight that an army's
"main weapon [is] terror" (9), coupled with Gallie's observation that "all
serious wars are decided by superior strength, whether actually deployed
and demonstrated or irresistibly threatened" (59), highlights the significance of the discourse of male bonding in men's struggle against women.

Indeed, the discourse of male bonding represents a potent example of
how language polices behavior. While terror based on such overt weapons

as spears, clubs, and guns provides an even more explicit message of who controls society, discourse offers a subtle, even veiled, reminder of who has power and how that power is maintained. When that discourse takes on the form of visual representations and symbolic meaning as in pornography, slasher movies, and music videos, the war between the sexes escalates into the realm of explicit subjection and conquest.

Although the discourse of male bonding is a means of waging war against women and gay men, gang rape and pornography represent even more overt examples of male violence against women. As frequently one of the more valuable currencies of war, women are the prize men fight for, both to act as their protector against the brutality of other men and to serve as victims of men's own assaults and rape. For Genghis Khan, certainly one of the more notorious warlords, "happiness lies in conquering one's enemies . . . in outraging their wives and daughters" (Dyer, 45). Lest we dismiss this quote as outdated barbarism, the civil war in Bosnia reminds us that rape remains one of modern man's more evil wartime outrages. And rape, especially gang rape, reminds women that small "regiments" of men (frequently, in civilian life, adolescent boys on the high school football team) can and will assert their power over them at will.[7]

Men's ability to terrorize women is not limited to rape, however. Men have a significant influence over culture in its varied manifestations, and men quite literally control the streets. From the relatively innocuous billboard displaying the beautiful blond prize selling Black Velvet to the representation of rape as normal male behavior in contemporary American literature, men's control of the images of male heterosexuality continues, despite women's advancement. The "ambivalent attitude toward rape . . . [and] the use of the penis as weapon" in such literary works as *A Streetcar Named Desire* (Gilbert and Gubar, 50) continue to reinforce men's assumption of male privilege and superiority.

Recently, with the continued strength of the feminist movement, men have become even more open in their opposition to female equality. James Gibson makes the point, in his study of violence and manhood in post-Vietnam America, that the changing relations between the sexes encouraged some men to "dream [and] to fantasize about the powers and features of another kind of man who could retake and reorder the world" (11). The hero of all these dreams turns out to be a paramilitary warrior. Although this extreme level of fantasy fortunately does not infect most men, the confusion about privilege, power, and superiority preoccupies many among us. Part of men's compensation for their fears and doubts registers in the language they use to talk about women and other men, a language that reduces intimacy to warfare and implies that love is really only a battle between the sexes.

## BLUE BALLS

Sex will relieve testicular congestion, or blue balls.
—*Playboy*

Nothing for a dirty man
but soap in his bathtub, a
greasy hand, love
nut
perhaps. Or else . . .
—Robert Creeley, "All That Is Lovely in Men"

In their perceived need to inflict their sexual desire on a woman, men do violence to themselves. In this scenario unsatisfied sexual conquest of the female causes harm to the male perpetrator.

Xiao Zhou, in an essay on virginity and premarital sex in contemporary China, relies on military language when she describes the "manipulative strategies" used by Chinese men to seduce women. Her observations about how the "blue balls syndrome" works in these situations provides insights into how this particular metaphor characterizes male heterosexual behavior. Referring to the "blue balls syndrome" as a myth, Zhou points out that "while engaging in heavy petting, the young man becomes sexually aroused; he tells his girlfriend that he will become very sick if no sexual intercourse follows. Some men tell their girlfriends that they are experiencing 'terrible' physical pain" (285). In the course of her discussions with Chinese women Zhou found that many women "fell for the 'blue ball' and 'severe pain' syndromes" (285).

As a strategy designed to make a woman agree to have sex with a man, the term "blue balls" fits easily into the discourse of conquest in both war and sports. "Blue balls," as a ploy to manipulate victory or to "score," describes a conception of masculinity bent on winning the fight and enjoying the spoils, as opposed to losing the battle and suffering the "turgid and painful condition of the testicles due to sexual excitement and frustration" (Chapman, 34).

Blue balls occur when a man rubs his genitals against a woman (i.e., "dry humps" her) while both are clothed. Although neither party obtains sexual satisfaction, a commonly known phrase for the woman's condition is not in use.[8] The word "blue" in the phrase refers to bruised balls, as in black-and-blue. If you have ever had blue balls (or "lover's nuts," as this condition is also called) you would know that it is both real and painful. But what causes a man to act in such a way as to get blue balls?

Part of the impetus behind this self-infliction of pain comes from one of the basic premises of what it means to be a man: that is, to be possessed of an uncontrollable need to experience sexual release. Another influence is the belief that when a woman says no, she really means yes. When I have experienced blue balls, both assumptions were at work. In my adolescence, when this phenomenon was more prevalent than in my adult years (though, to be honest, it did not disappear upon my eighteenth or twenty-fifth or even thirtieth birthday), I got blue balls because I was committed to the necessity of penetration and unwilling (or unable) to hear what the woman was saying. It took a long time to hear what women are saying (in all areas of my life), and much of my resistance came from certain presuppositions I had about the entitlements of being male.[9]

As a metaphor for male sexuality, "blue balls" captures succinctly the social assumption that men must get laid or become damaged in some way. This metaphor identifies men's uncontrollable sexual passion in which "blue balls" can be seen as one stage on the spectrum of coercive sexuality, a spectrum that in this case may culminate in date rape. The connection of blue balls with the imperative male need for penetration masks alternative sources of sexual pleasure. Robert Creeley's poem explores this situation and suggests in its closing words the threat to which the frustrated working-class male may have to resort to gain some means of sexual satisfaction other than masturbation with his own "greasy hand." The poem has a tone of uncertainty: the "Or else" at the end of it intimates self-doubt, a sense that a shabby and thus unattractive man, the proletarian, will not find sexual satisfaction with a woman. Blue balls, or in the case of this poem, lover's nuts, may be symbolic of male sexual confusion.

Men are not the only victims of this confusion; women are also accosted as a result of this particular brand of male obsession. Many women, not only the Chinese women interviewed by Zhou but others, have succumbed to this male ploy; that women can be victims of these kinds of assumptions clearly is not an overstatement.

The denial of the woman's experience, concomitant with the emphasis on the man's condition, exemplifies our assumptions about male and female sexuality. Men's passion is out of their control, to the point of inflicting pain upon themselves, and women must be in control not only of their own passion but of the men's as well. Men also maneuver women into assuming a certain amount of responsibility for men's pain.

Zhou focuses her criticism on the devious behavior of Chinese men but says little or nothing about how repressive sexual mores and the denial of adolescent sexual desire might contribute to this unfortunate circumstance. Robert Chapman describes the outcome of this sexually frustrating situation but refers neither to the "blue" in the phrase or to the context in which the condition occurs. If a woman's desire not to have sex were to be respected, adolescent sexuality was not denied, premarital sex was not a sin, and women's sexual desire was acknowledged (and not just manipulated), "blue balls" and its unspoken female equivalent might become obsolete terms. Men and women might make love without fear of reprisal, and men might even evolve to the point where they take control of their passion.

## COCK OF THE WALK

Although not all the slang dictionaries contained a specific reference to "cock of the walk," those that did centered on the word "cock" as a synonym for the penis, especially the erect penis. The first volume of the *Dictionary of American Regional English* refers to "cock of the walk" obliquely through the term "cock-a-doodle-doo," a term for "a ranch foreman or boss," whereas "cock of the walk" means, quite simply, "one who dominates" (Cassidy, 708). Tony Thorne suggests that the origin of the term "cock of the walk" may derive from "'cock-sparrow,' or from the image of a brave fighting-cock . . . the image of the male member . . . as a strutting fighter" (102). Consistent with Thorne's suggestion of the penis as a strutting fighter, Harold Wentworth and Stuart Berg Flexner see the cock of the walk as "a swaggering boastful male" (112). J. David Sapir points out that to call a man "the cock of the walk" is to say that he is "vain and presumptuous . . . an old goat . . . [or] a dirty old man" (11).

The "walk" may be almost as important as the "cock" in this phrase. These vain, boastful, and presumptuous men don't trundle or stroll or meander, they strut and they swagger as they assert their superiority. The image of the army drill instructor, the chief executive officer, even the college professor who "struts his stuff" is a reminder to us all of those who assume a right to dominate others. These "cocks of the walk" assert their inherent privilege based on their possession of a penis.

The connection between the erect penis and authority is both obvious and crucial. The cock of the walk suggests that the man with the largest and hardest penis (cock) is the one in control of all he sees. To view the erect penis as a weapon or as a source of power is not a new insight, and the suggestion that a male's power exists in direct proportion to how many women (hens) he controls, and satisfies sexually, should come as no surprise. The expression "cock of the walk," though, makes explicit men's reduction of their importance to their genitals. As the rooster who must constantly reassert his stature as the biggest and the meanest and the most sexually proficient male in the yard, to be the cock of the walk becomes a responsibility that no man can uphold, nor should desire to assume.

## COLD COCK

They cold-cocked him, and left him unconscious.
—James T. Farrell, *Young Manhood*

Although the precise origin of this phrase is debatable, the common definition means to knock someone out, usually with one blow. Chapman suggests two possible sources for it: "perhaps from the hammering of caulking into a boat's or ship's seams; perhaps related to Canadian lumberjacks' *put the caulks to* someone, 'stamp in someone's face with spiked boots'" (77). The use of violence informs all these definitions: to "cold cock" someone means "to hit someone hard, to knock someone out" (Cassidy, 708) or "to knock someone unconscious, with the fist, a club, etc. . . . always without warning, in order to render the person completely incapable of action" (Wentworth, 114).

The word "cock," a word we know as a euphemism for the penis, here applied to a weapon used to knock someone out, suggests the experience of rape, a kind of violence wielded against women. Specifically, this term refers to an act done "quickly before the victim can resist" (Chapman, 77) and exemplifies men's confusion about the difference between making love and getting laid.

As should be clear by now in this book, the penis as a weapon creeps in everywhere in male discourse. This metaphor's suggestion that an immediate and devious assault on someone has a direct reference to the penis illuminates the deep-seated equation of male heterosexuality and violence. When the penis becomes a fist in a boxing match, its function as the great equalizer becomes explicit.

## GANG BANG

Tear the place apart, leave the owner for dead, gangbang the waitress.
—Joan Didion

As with many phrases examined in this book, "gang bang" has several meanings. The *American Heritage College Dictionary* alludes to the violence of such an act when it defines it in the following way: "Rape or sexual intercourse involving one person and several others in succession." But it also defines the term as "sexual intercourse involving several partners who change indiscriminately" (56). What strikes one almost immediately about these definitions is how nongender specific they are and how the second definition de-emphasizes the violence. To read the first definition one might infer that men are victims of gang bangs as frequently as women or, more absurdly, that a man might be gangbanged by a group of women.

The second definition holds a much different meaning than the one I am familiar with, although the suggestion that "gang bang" refers to group sex is consistent throughout many of the dictionaries I used. My own knowledge of the term is as a reference to many men having sex with one woman during a fairly short period of time. Interestingly, the "popular" definition I have acquired, and I believe this is consistent with the male imagination, has never acknowledged rape as a part of the experience but rather emphasized the woman's willingness, and even desire, for such an activity. "Gang bang" takes on an even more powerful metaphorical dynamic when one realizes that it implies not only the violence and distancing of the heterosexual male understanding of love and intimacy, but the idea that women have an uncontrollable libido.

At the risk of buying into these assumptions about female sexuality, I want to suggest a distinction between "gang bang" and "gang rape." This is a risky point to make but one worth attempting. Rape occurs when a woman who has said no to sexual intercourse is forced to have sex anyway. But what about the woman who agrees to have sex with more than one guy over the span of an hour or two? If we categorically deny this as a possibility, we reject a dimension of an active female sexuality that may scare many of us but at the same time may be real.

Certainly for the woman who says she wants to have sex with several men in a row issues of self-esteem and the desire to be popular may furnish unfortunate motivations, but we need to be careful that in our desire to characterize female passion as only the outcome of uncontrolled male desire, we do not deny the possibility that some women want to be more sexually active than others. We have only to look at "nymphomania," a term used exclusively to describe women, to encounter another example of how female sexuality is policed in our society. Men's fear of female sexual desire is most notably epitomized in the image of the "vagina dentata," expressive of the anxiety that the female genitals will literally devour them. In our haste to censure one form of group sex, we need to be careful that we do not fall to a fear of female sexuality very similar to this one, which has dominated most of Western culture.[10]

All this is not to deny the disturbing significance of "gang bang" as a metaphor for male heterosexuality, a phrase eliciting several associations, most of which focus on the injustice endemic to the experience. The language itself couples the violence of the word "bang" with the overwhelming power of a gang. Reducing the sexual encounter to a spectator sport, a gang bang makes sex both an event outside the personal intimate experience of two people and emphasizes the fleetingness, or the immediacy, of the sexual moment. During a gang bang each man has sex with a woman until he comes (as quickly as possible), and then he leaves to let another man take his place. There is no foreplay, no lingering caress, no intimacy of any kind. The gang bang is getting laid with a vengeance; it is a violent, alienated, and momentary experience and in this way may embody at least part of the myth of male heterosexuality.

The most recent application of the phrase "gang bang" to mean the activities of a street gang in, among other places, Los Angeles, is not serendipitous but rather consistent with its original meaning. Gangbanging by urban gangs describes the violent, and at times inhumane, activities of a group of young males (in many cases still boys). The development from a "gang bang" meaning "[to take part in] sex involving several males sequentially with one woman" (Thorne, 196) to a 1980s term used by and about the members of street gangs in Los Angeles in which "the bang in question is a gunshot [and] shooting a victim is often part of the initiation process" (Thorne, 196) relies on the violence of both endeavors. This connection also equates murder with sex, giving killing an erotic allure.

Let there be no doubt about it: gang bangs can be intensely violent. When a "gang bang" becomes a "gang rape," it constitutes a denigration of the woman and a crime against her humanity. My own experience with gang bangs, which was not firsthand, occurred as a young boy growing up in northern New York State. This was one way young boys became sexually initiated, and if you did not participate in this ritual, your manhood was in question; your reluctance might very well elicit the label "faggot."[11]

Where I grew up, gang bangs, getting drunk, and fighting were all part of the initiation rites of the adolescent male. Tragically, as became apparent not too long ago in Gouverneur, New York, "gang rape" remains an acceptable practice for young men as well. Gouverneur is a small, poverty-ridden, quintessentially rural community just eighteen miles from where I graduated from high school and the scene of one of the more notorious gang rapes in recent history (outside of war, of course).[12] I know Gouverneur, though, and I know the men and boys who live there.

I don't have friends or acquaintances from Gouverneur, because when I was growing up even the tough guys from Canton High School avoided socializing in Gouverneur. They avoided high school dances there for fear one of the Gouverneur guys might think they were going after "their woman." Girls were seen as property thirty years ago, and in some circles their status hasn't changed much even today. Many wives are still seen as property, but many more have rejected that role and are perspicious enough to be involved with men who honor their new status as individuals with their own rights and freedom.

An unmarried woman, however, or in the case of the woman raped by five men in a bar in Gouverneur, a divorced woman, remains fair game for the sexual exploits of men who want to see themselves as holding all the power, even if their power is relatively insignificant. Indeed, precisely because so many men in the United States have so little real power, it is so important for them to assert dominion over women, to victimize them, that is.

As it happens, violence against women, and in particular wife beating, occurs more often in Gouverneur than in any other community in the county. "For the last ten years St. Lawrence County's reports of domestic violence have been more numerous than those of the two neighboring counties. Maria Ruiz Groh, the director of the county's domestic-violence center, Renewal House, says the center sees three to four hundred victims of spousal abuse every year" (Avenoso, 106). Indeed, Gouverneur was famous where I grew up for providing more prisoners in the county jail than any other town in the county. It was seen as a lawless town populated with violent men.

The Neanderthal mentality of the men in this one-horse village, with its "real men" in the guise of hunters and long-retired high school athletes, is different from the attitude that allowed the boys in northern New Jersey to rape a defenseless young woman in another recent and well-publicized case, but the sense of male privilege and right are similar. The communities' complicity in this violence is also comparable. In Glen Ridge, New Jersey, in Gouverneur, New York, a double standard prevailed about what is considered acceptable behavior for boys and what is acceptable for girls. And both communities struggled to "reabsorb and forgive [the woman's] assailants: People say 'the boys' have suffered enough. 'They've lost jobs because of it' one woman explains. 'They've been punished'" (Avenoso, 105).

Clearly, as Lefkowitz observes in his study of the New Jersey crime, gang rape is seen to be just another "boys will be boys" prank, not an act of violence that serves to remind all women that men have the power in our society and that they will use it whenever they are inclined to do so. Indeed, according to a 1994 national sex survey, women's perception of what constitutes forced sex differs significantly from men's perception of it: "22 percent [of the women surveyed] report being forced to do something sexually at some time . . . yet only 3 percent of men say they have sexually forced a woman, indicating that the schism between how men and women define 'forced sex' is disturbingly large" (Obermiller, 36).[13] The other message implicit in gang rape is that as long as women remain passive obedient wives and mothers they do not need to be put in their place. Single women, women unprotected or not owned by a man, risk the rage of men who believe these are available for men's sexual needs and desires.

As a teenager, gang bangs were not only incomprehensible to me but frightening. Maybe I was just insecure about my sexual prowess or the size of my penis, but even at the tender age of fourteen sex was not a spectator sport for me. Sexual intimacy was not an event that included more than two people, nor was it a sport in which other boys would cheer me on. The gang bang was an experience I could not identify with, and one I put a lot of energy into avoiding.

I remember the name of the young girl my friends wanted to gangbang, even after twenty-five years, and I remember trying to have sex with her alone one night on the football field. I figured she was easy, at least, so maybe I could get lucky. I remember that it didn't work, or I didn't work. I couldn't keep it up at the age of fourteen or fifteen, not with a girl who still had her pants on and the two of us sliding down a muddy hill while cars went by with their radios blaring.

Although I resisted the brutish experience of the gang bang, I had still been affected profoundly by the socialization that teaches young boys that getting laid is what it takes to be a man and that women are just vehicles to that end. As a metaphor of male sexuality, the gang bang exemplifies the callous, selfish, violent, and ignoble assumptions men have not only about women but about their own sexuality.

### HAVING THE BALLS . . . OR NOT

> Just keeping a handhold and staying where you are . . . even that takes tons of balls.
>
> —Martin Amis, *Money*

Not unlike "cojones," this phrase equates a man's gonads with courage. "Balls," of course, is a euphemism for the testicles, and "ballsy," for example, means courageous (Spears, 18). According to Ayto and Simpson, this predominantly American phrase suggests "determination [and] (manly) power or strength" (11). Once again the euphemism reduces masculinity to the size (or existence) of a man's gonads (or, by extension, genitals), and courage becomes identified with virility, or strength and power. A man's mind or intelligence does not guide him to do what is right, and his heart (or compassion) does not lead him to take a risk; he has the balls.

*The American Heritage College Dictionary* refers to the "reckless[ness] or great presumptuousness" (104) of this kind of courage, and Wentworth and Flexner see this phrase as "an expression of incredulity, disappointment, [and] disgust" (17). Thus here too a certain ambiguity about what this phrase really means highlights men's confusion about masculinity. On the one hand, "having the balls" refers to what is assumed to be a positive male quality of being recklessly courageous, while on the other hand this term connotes bewilderment and abhorrence of manhood.

A man who has the balls to do something may indeed not have the brains not to do it. Cohn, in her essay on wars, wimps, and women, stresses this point in her discussion of the jargon of the U.S. defense community that was developed by men for whom "in their informal conversation it was not their rational analyses that dominated their response, but the fact that for them, the decision for war, the willingness to use force, is cast as a question of masculinity—not prudence, thoughtfulness, efficacy, 'rational' cost-benefit calculation, or morality, but masculinity" (236–37). "Having the balls" may be an antonym for having the intelligence, and thus masculinity emerges once again as stupid, oafish, and ultimately insensitive.

Women should be careful that they not become victims of the same characterization. Paul Beale points out that this "term can be used to describe a dominant woman in a home" (19), and Thorne suggests that even "in spite of the anatomical inconsistency . . . the [term] may now be applied to women" (24). In his personal history of the Salomon Brothers' demise on Wall Street, Michael Lewis provides an excellent example of this kind of transference. A "big swinging dick," the title reserved for those who sell hundreds of thousands of dollars' worth of bonds, is coveted by both men and women. Although this phrase may suggest a humorous image, as it did for Lewis, the desire to gain this appellation was not restricted to men: "Everyone wanted to be a Big Swinging Dick, even the women. Big Swinging Dickettes" (46).

The insidious power of language to determine meaning gains strength when it becomes part of the general discourse. When "having the brains" replaces "having the balls" or "big pulsing heart" replaces "big swinging dick," the possibility for intelligence and compassion to take the place of testosterone as the guide for many of our decisions may have emerged.

### PRICK

His nakedness and limp prick . . . were new properties of the changing room.

—Anthony Burgess, *M/F*

They have good jobs, big futures. And the pricks won't even do their service.

—Mario Puzo, *Fools Die*

As a slang term for the penis, "prick" has been in use since at least the sixteenth century and "was probably coined with the image of a thorn in mind, from the shape and the image of penetration evoked" (Thorne, 405). Like the phalanx of the ancient armies, the prick is an effective weapon to penetrate an enemy's fortress. In this case the fortress the prick wants to penetrate is either the vagina or the assertiveness of a female colleague.

Men fight women's attempts to gain equality. One of man's primary weapons is his penis: as a literal weapon to inflict rape or the metaphorical phallus that reminds women of who in contemporary society is entitled to privilege and power.

According to the *American Heritage College Dictionary,* "prick" means: "1. a. the act of piercing or pricking. b. the sensation of being pierced or pricked. 2. a. A persistent or sharply painful feeling of sorrow or remorse" (1085). By extension, then, in this term the penis becomes both something that pierces the woman (maybe, or especially, her hymen) and something that elicits the sensations of grief and regret. Like so many euphemisms for the penis, a "prick" is a weapon with which men inflict pain and even humiliation on a woman. In war, especially, the penis becomes a battering ram to penetrate (i.e., rape) a woman.

This ambivalence about the role of the penis in heterosexual relationships is apparent also when "prick" becomes a "term of contempt or abuse for a man; a fool or jerk" (Ayto and Simpson, 178). As "an oaf, an offensive male [or] a hard taskmaster" (Spears, 355), and as "a fool, [or] obnoxious [and] contemptible male" (Thorne, 405), a "prick" takes on the aura of contempt that men (and women) feel about male heterosexuality in general.

## PUSSY WHIPPED

> Some men are pussy whipped from the day they are born, some have it happen to them later in life, some never.
> —Judith Krantz, *Scruples*

Whereas the dominant discourse of war and conquest affirms men's superiority over women, in this term a reversal of power occurs that locates the source of dominion in the woman. The man who is "pussy whipped" is under the control of a woman and dependent upon being in her good graces to get sexual favors. Indeed, the definitions offered by all the dictionaries I used tend to emphasize the pejorative nature of this phrase and refer almost exclusively to the sexual power the wife or female has over the man. "Pussy whipped," according to these references, means the man will not do anything for fear of not getting sex from his wife or lover. In these definitions sexual "favors," or sexual pleasure, becomes a weapon a woman uses to control a man.

The phrase certainly lends itself to this kind of interpretation. Etymological evidence suggests a connection between "pussy whipped" and both "pistol whipped" (Thorne, 409) and "horse whipped" (Spears, 362); Beale believes that in the early twentieth century "pussy" was a synonym for the cat-o'-nine-tails. This association strengthens the link between "pussy whipped" and domination. To be whipped is to be punished or beaten, and when the vagina becomes the whip, this phrase becomes one more way in which men gain control over their situation with women. By naming the weapon used against them, and applying a derisive synonym to women's genitals, men can still hold women in contempt and maintain their sense of dominion. Indeed, "as a disparaging term for a woman" or a "vulgar slang [term for] the vulva" (*AHCD*, 1112) the term "pussy" allows men to insult the person who supposedly holds power over them and in that way assert a form of control over their personal lives.

Usually, though, the phrase "pussy whipped" is used by men about another man. A man would not characterize himself as being pussy whipped but rather would sneer at another man for allowing himself to be controlled in that manner. Not unlike "the social function of sexist jokes among the guys [which] control[s] the threat that individual men might form intimate emotional bonds with women and withdraw from the group" (Lyman, 158), phrases like "pussy whipped" help men to police masculinity to make sure that all men remain within the group of real men. Men who prefer to be outside that oppressive group still fear the power of the group to put them down as men, to question their masculinity.

In the larger context of men's unwillingness to give up power, a phrase like "pussy whipped" emerges as a way for men to protect themselves from any kind of power a woman might be supposed to have. In the discourse of manliness the only real power women possess lies in their sexual favors. A man has trouble acknowledging that he is in love with a woman or prefers her company. Love threatens male power; it makes men weak and puts them in a position in which they may no longer feel in control.

Ironically, a "pussy-whipped" man is under someone else's power. Indeed, most formal definitions see this term as synonymous with "henpecked." Chapman, for example, says this phrase describes a man who is "dominated by one's wife or female lover; obsequiously uxorious; henpecked" (344). "Henpecked" obscures the complexity of this phrase, however. Although "pussy whipped" may suggest henpecked, it is usually more specific to the sexual power a woman has over a man. Henpecked, according to the *American Heritage College Dictionary,* means "to dominate or nag (one's husband)" (633) and refers frequently to everything from taking out the garbage to not tracking in mud. Nagging is an important component of the definition. "Pussy whipped" does not mean or even imply nagging. Indeed, a man who is henpecked may not be pussy whipped at all because "pussy whipped" refers quite explicitly to the woman's sexual power. "Henpecked" as a synonym for "pussy whipped" ignores the latter's application to the newly married man who may prefer to be at home making love with his wife rather than to be at the bar hanging out with the guys (or playing softball, or participating in any number of other male bonding rituals). A man's use of such a debasing term as "pussy whipped" allows him to believe he is still in control. The irony of language is that it frequently tells us more about our fears and our doubts than most of us care to know.

## SHOOTING BLANKS

A reference to a man's inability to impregnate a woman, this phrase portrays male sexuality as reducible to a military or at least firearms-related experience. Combining the slang term "to shoot," meaning to ejaculate (Spears, 396), with another slang term, "shooter," a reference to a gun (Thorne, 458), the phrase "shooting blanks" figuratively diminishes sperm to a form of ammunition that cannot kill anyone.

The sterile man, one who cannot produce children, has no posterity, having no possibility of heirs. Without an heir a man cannot pass on his wealth or his accomplishments or his masculinity, for that matter. The sterile man, not unlike the impotent one, becomes less than a man solely because of his inability to perform sexually in the way that is expected of him. Without the production of sperm, as with the absence of an erection, a man borders on being a eunuch, an object of ridicule, half a man.

Considering that I was reminded of this phrase by a self-identified feminist colleague, the insidiousness of language becomes even more apparent. With the emphasis of feminism on how we refer to women, you would think those lessons would carry over to both genders. To reduce a man's reproductive capacity to an ability to fire his gun/penis effectively reinforces the pervasive idea that male sexuality is characterized by associations of inflicting harm on someone, in this case his wife and the potential mother of his children.

## SHORT-ARM INSPECTION

> Before you go to bed with a guy, give him a short arm. . . . You strip down his penis, you know, like you're masturbating him, and if there's a yellow fluid coming out like drippage, you know he's infected.
> —Mario Puzo, *Fools Die*

This reference to the penis originated in the armed services where it was a euphemism for a medical examination for symptoms of venereal disease. The use of the word "arm" "reflects the common notion of the penis as a limb" (Thorne, 459) but derives as well from the term "small arm," in the sense of a handgun. Wentworth and Flexner suggest that this phrase may be "based on the frequent inspection of the soldier's rifle or 'arm'" (471), and Beale speculates on "there being a 'pun on pistols'" (400).

As a sidearm or a pistol the penis evokes a weapon, and in the parlance of army basic training the relationship between male anatomy and permission to rape with impunity becomes even more apparent. As Adrienne Rich points out in her essay on the Vietnam war and sexual violence: "'This is my rifle, this is my gun [cock]; This is for killing, this is for fun' is not a piece of bizarre brainwashing invented by some infantry sergeant's fertile imagination; it is a recognition of the fact that when you strike the chord of sexuality in the patriarchal psyche, the chord of violence is likely to vibrate in response; and vice versa" ("Caryatid," 115).

Male power is once more at stake here. The suggestion that the penis resembles an arm, even a short arm, suggests an organ with a muscle that can be flexed and thus used as a club to bludgeon (or "cold cock") someone. In the army (or in the locker room) men are naked, and that exposure elicits comparison. Characterizing the penis as a short arm accentuates a man's insecurity about the size of his penis while at the same time provides a generalization that suggests equality and fraternity. This reduction gives a man a sense that he has a large enough penis because it is at least a short arm. As an arm, though, the penis remains an isolated part of the body, and the erogenous is limited once again to a singular organ. In this case the isolated organ is turned into a short muscular arm or a pistol empowered to wrest control and assert domination.

# 5    Sex as Exclusively Heterosexual

The terms heterosexual and homosexual apparently came into common use only in the first quarter of this century; before that time, if words are clues to concepts, people did not conceive of a social universe polarized into heteros and homos.
—Jonathan Ned Katz, *The Invention of Heterosexuality*

In [the] context [of] a private conversation among male friends it could be argued that to gossip, either about your sexual exploits with women or about the repulsiveness of gay men . . . is not just one way, but the most appropriate way to display heterosexual masculinity.
—Deborah Cameron, "Performing Gender Identity: Young Men's Talk and the Construction of Male Heterosexuality"

Today, one of the most obvious characteristics of masculinity is heterosexuality.
—Elisabeth Badinter, *XY: On Masculine Identity*

The hostility and the devaluation implicit in the usage of homophobic terms . . . occur by virtue of the assumed correctness of anything heterosexual.
—James Armstrong, "Homophobic Slang as Coercive Discourse among College Students"

Contrary to popular belief, the concept of heterosexuality is a fairly modern development. The current dominant, and assumed to be natural, distinction between homosexuals and heterosexuals had no significance until the twentieth century. According to Jonathan Ned Katz, whose book *The Invention of Heterosexuality* traces the historical evolution and changing definitions of "heterosexuality," the term "homosexual" was not invented until around 1868 while "the first use of 'heterosexual' listed in the *Oxford English Dictionary Supplement* dates to 1901" (10). Katz goes on to explain that these terms gained common usage only in the first quarter of the twentieth century and had no "operative existence in ancient Greece" (11).[1]

Originally, the concept of heterosexuality referred to a perversion, not to our common use of the term as a sexual relationship between a man and a woman and not to the focus on procreation that the term eventually acquired. The earliest known use of the word "heterosexual" in the United States occurs in an article by Dr. James G. Kiernan, published in a Chicago medical journal in May 1892, in which heterosexuality is referred to as a perversion and thus not equated with normal sex. Kiernan linked heterosexual to one of several 'abnormal manifestations of the sexual appetite'—in a list of 'sexual perversions proper'—in an article on 'Sexual Perversion'" (19–20). "Heterosexuality" as a perversion informs much of the early literature on sexuality. As late as 1923, for example, when the word "heterosexuality" made its debut in Merriam-Webster's authoritative *New International Dictionary,* it was defined as a medical term "meaning morbid sexual passion for one of the opposite sex." "Homosexuality" had been listed fourteen years earlier in 1909 when it was defined as a "morbid passion for someone of the same sex" (Katz, 92). The general assumption today—that homosexuality is the perversion and that heterosexuality is normal—defies historical evidence with its common emphasis on morbid passion and underlying assumption that all sexual desire is somehow diseased.

From its original characterization as a sexual perversion "heterosexuality" became identified with sexual reproduction, which eventually became a justification for sexual pleasure between the sexes. While it is certainly true that the Judeo-Christian tradition beginning with Leviticus sacralized reproductive sex in opposition to nonreproductive sex, only during the last few years of the nineteenth century and the first years of the twentieth did Freud and other medical men help establish what Katz refers to as "The Heterosexual Mystique—the idea of an essential, eternal, normal heterosexuality" (82). In fact, the first quarter of the twentieth century saw a consolidation of the concept of heterosexuality as normal.

Although heterosexuality as both normal and normative dominates our views about sexuality, as John D'Emilio and Estelle Freedman show in their history of sexuality in the United States, sexual meanings have a history associated with a range of human activities and values. Katz too makes the point that the word "heterosexual" "signifies one time-bound historical form . . . one specific way of organizing the sexes and their pleasures" (34) and goes on to identify several societies not organized around the heterosexual matrix. Ancient Greece provides one model, as does New England in the years 1607 to 1740. Greek society did not have such modern terms as "bisexual," "homosexual," and "heterosexual" to describe what Katz refers to as "freemen's problematic, pleasurable intimacies with

women and with boys" (34). The formative years of the United States saw
a sexuality dominated by the imperative to reproduce that was engendered
in an "operative constraint . . . between fruitfulness and barrenness, not
between different-sex and same-sex eroticism" (38). Katz cites other historical examples of American societies not organized according to our
heterosexual law. Overall, his research suggests that the overt distinction
between heterosexual and homosexual that appeared in 1892 did not
emerge out of the blue. As Katz makes clear, in the last quarter of the
nineteenth century, with the medicalizing of sexuality, a tradition emerged
in which the abnormal was equated with homosexuality and the normal
with heterosexuality.

When seen as compulsory or constructed, a matrix and/or invention,
heterosexuality emerges as a one-sided conception of gender relations
linked to a particular historical period and its economic and social
agenda.[2] Part of that agenda was to denigrate the feminine in order to
keep women in their place. As Sally Johnson demonstrates in her feminist
analysis of language and masculinity, "one important element in the construction of heterosexual masculinity will be the perpetual denial, subjugation and exclusion of the feminine—as symbolized by both women and
homosexual men" (22). Heterosexuality as the rule, both in law and as
acceptable behavior (such as speech, clothing, and appearance in general),
reinforces straight male privilege by acting on a variety of levels.

One important component of this ideological construction is masculine
identity itself. In providing a broad historical perspective on masculine
identity, Badinter asserts that "since the birth of the patriarchy, man has
always defined himself as a privileged human being, endowed with something *more,* unknown to women. He believes he has *more* strength, is *more*
intelligent, *more* courageous, *more* responsible, *more* creative, or *more* rational. And this *more* justifies his hierarchical relationship to women, or at
least to his own woman" (4).[3] Cultural examples of this characterization
abound in Western literature, but U.S. popular culture has played an even
greater role in strengthening our bifurcated ideas about gender. Television,
movies, and rock videos reinforce the distinction between the genders by
positing this polarity as based on commonsense assumptions, meanings,
and definitions. Indeed, in the seventy or so years from the introduction
of the term "heterosexual" in the 1890s to the progressive decade of the
1960s, both "heterosexual" and "homosexual" gained precedent in American popular culture: "constructing in time a sexual solid citizen and a
perverted unstable alien, a sensual insider and a lascivious outlaw, a hetero
center and a homo margin, a hetero majority and a homo minority. . . .
The term heterosexual manufactured a new sex-differentiated ideal of the
erotically correct, a norm that worked to affirm the superiority of men
over women and heterosexuals over homosexuals" (Katz, 112). The neces-

sity for men to define themselves as not feminine, as we have seen amply demonstrated, resides at the center of the heterosexual regime. Indeed, the only real man has to be the straight man. Consequently, men must never show any sign of such supposedly feminine traits as tenderness, passivity, or care giving, and a man should never find another man attractive. On the contrary, men must exhibit qualities considered as at the opposite pole to "the feminine," like a "preoccupation with being strong, independent, hard, cruel, polygamous, misogynous, and perverse" (Badinter, 46–47).

Although we have already examined at great length most of these learned male qualities, the occurrence of "perversion" in the masculine experience (defined here as the failure to conform to the heterosexual norm) is far more frequent than in the feminine, which raises important questions about what it means to be a man in Western society. So-called perversions in the form of fetishism, transvestism, and transsexualism affect far more men than women: transsexualism, indeed, "affects boys almost four times as often as girls" (Badinter, 39). Contrary to Badinter's essentialist explanation that this differentiation occurs because "nature [has] more difficulty differentiating the identity of the male than that of the female" (33–34), it seems more likely that this male proclivity results from the terror boys are raised to feel in becoming men and thus not female. Differences in rigidity of gender roles between men and women also might be partly responsible for differences in reaction to "perversion" or differences in the incidence of "perversion."

The other important question that must be posed here, of course, is why cross-gender identity must be conceived of as a perversion in the first place. I would argue that male perversion in the form of cruelty, misogyny, homophobia, rape, and violence in general appear to be the perversions in need of analysis. If more men felt comfortable wearing a dress or caring about someone else, we would all be much better off. Indeed, perversions of that form should be encouraged, not ridiculed or psychoanalyzed out of existence.

In their struggle to repress any feelings or qualities associated with the feminine, however, straight men assume a masculine identity "associated with possessing, taking, penetrating, dominating, and asserting oneself, if necessary, by force" (Badinter, 97). Chapter 4, on war and the metaphors of conquest, confirms this paradigm, illustrating the "prick's" fixation on penetration and the "cock of the walk's" obsession with domination.

Misogyny asserts itself once more in the form of homophobia, a behavior that reinforces the assumption that a real man is free of the taint of the feminine. In our modern society a real man prefers women exclusively, "as though possessing a woman reinforced the desired otherness by distancing the specter of identity: *to have* a woman in order not *to be* a woman. In the eyes of some, the very fact of not being homosexual is already an assurance of masculinity" (Badinter, 97). The discourse of male bonding reinforces the necessity to be unambiguous about one's heterosexual masculinity. Straight men remind their colleagues of their membership in the heterosexual club by disparaging other men with insults characterizing them as gay.

In addition, the seemingly apparent contradiction in Badinter's observation—between the latent hatred of women as inferior and their desirability as mates—is resolved in male heterosexual ideology and behavior with far more men identifying women as their best friends rather than men. A man feels more comfortable expressing his intimacy and commitment to a woman than to a man because, according to Michael Silverstein, "he can reveal himself and make himself emotionally dependent only on someone who is not a potential rival, but who, on the contrary, has been trained to be emotionally supportive of men rather than competitive with them, and to expect a position of dependency" (117).[4] For most men, the closest friend, the person they talk to about emotional and personal problems, is a woman. Men trust women to be caring, not to judge them, and certainly not to ridicule them about perceived weaknesses.

With the transition from an agrarian to industrial society at the end of the nineteenth century, men could no longer easily demonstrate their "real maleness" by toting that barge and lifting that bale when they were instead confined to an office. Men lost a tremendous amount of confidence in that societal transition, and with the emergence of the term "homosexuality" at the beginning of the twentieth century, male anxiety about masculinity became much more pronounced than previously. As heterosexual men began "to define themselves in opposition to all that was soft and womanlike" (Kimmel, *Manhood,* 100), the definition of the real man dwindled to qualities like hardness, competitiveness, unemotionality, and omnipotence. As a side-effect of this anxiety of resistance to a dreaded "otherness," however, men also began to experience such emotions as rage, fear, impotence, perversions, self-hatred, and the hatred of others. A defensive strategy was to develop "certain images and metaphors of women and the feminine" that would help shape their male identity by negating women. Men sought thereby to "assuag[e] their anxieties about masculinity" (Haste, 208). According to Badinter and others, men's fear of passivity and of the feminine are especially strong because "men's most powerful and deeply repressed desires" lie in the forbidden domain (54–55).[5]

Hatred of the homosexual man coincides with the male heterosexual's dread of the feminine. While homophobia expresses fear of one's own homosexual desires, it also replicates a fear and hatred of the feminine. For Badinter, "homophobia is the hatred of feminine qualities in men whereas misogyny is the hatred of feminine qualities in women" (115). By treating homosexuals as the other, straight men confirm their heterosexuality. This corroboration is especially important in all-male groups, where the expression of prejudices against gay men can garner the approval of others. Straight men use homophobic slang as a weapon to signal their true heterosexual masculinity. James Armstrong's study of coercive discourse among college students corroborates that those who use this language in public frequently are young heterosexual males: "Often in public interactions, people who might not think of openly attacking homosexuals use language that derogates homosexuality. . . . In some contexts this language asserts male (heterosexual) dominance by confirming presumed masculine values, while degrading presumed feminine gender attributes" (326–27).[6] Men lash out against all that is feminine in an effort to prove their legitimacy and superiority, and the male arsenal is replete with effective weapons, not least of which is the language they use. The discourse of homophobia, a set of phrases examined in this chapter, demonstrates some of the ways in which "language is an act that can be violent, exclusionary, and coercive" (Armstrong, 326). The loaded use of "lesbian" as an insult levied against women who refuse any particular man's advances is an excellent example of this kind of retribution.

Armstrong also observes that part of the power of homophobic slang is the way in which it renders gay men invisible, partly by coercing participants in the conversation, straight or gay, to adopt the same values or speak the same language. The discourse of male bonding excludes women and gay men as the enemy against whom straight men reinforce their fragile masculinity. Evidence for the fragility of this gender identity is reflected in how frequently disparaging remarks about gays (men or women) appear in everyday conversation. In this case, surely, the man doth protest too much.

## FAGGOT

> Austin had been given the keys to a luxurious, metal-and-velvet faggot's lair with enormous mirrors on the bedroom ceiling.
> —Richard Ford, *Women with Men*

In common American usage "faggot" refers to a gay man, a homosexual, but the derivations of the term and the contradictory observations about its origins and use are informative. To begin with, what "faggot" has in common with at least two other metaphors examined in this book ("wimp" and "wuss") is its early use as a synonym for a woman. According to Tony Thorne, "faggot" was used in seventeenth-century Britain to refer to "an unattractive or disreputable woman" (170), and *The Oxford English Dictionary* defines "faggot" as "a term of abuse or contempt applied to a woman" (20). The *Dictionary of American Regional English* identifies the origin of this term as coming from a British dialect in which "faggot [was] a term of abuse for a woman or a child [and was then] transferred to an effeminate or unmasculine man" (334).

The evolution from a derogatory term for a woman to a homosexual man is not a difficult one to follow. A gay man is, at best, half a man and certainly not a real man; in the dominant discourse he is as "low" as a woman, as reprehensible, and as weak. This characterization of the gay man as less than fully a man is reinforced when you consider that "faggot" has also been used to refer to "a person temporarily hired to supply a deficiency at the muster, or on the roll of a company or regiment; a dummy" (*OED*, 20). As a stand-in for a man, and in particular a soldier, a "faggot" was decidedly less than a complete man.

Today the youth who prefers to take on a role other than that of high school athlete risks similar denigration. Lefkowitz points out, for example, that at Glen Ridge High, male members of the high school band were seen as "worse than a nobody . . . and widely known as 'band fags,' even among many parents" (62). Mariah Nelson comments also on the use of the term "faggot" in her discussion of football speech where this "popular derogation . . . refers . . . to weakness, timidity, cowardice—and femininity" (87). Straight men, young or old, consistently police male behavior with the constant threat of being labeled too feminine.

"Faggot" may also derive from the word "fag," which refers to a first-year male student at a British private high school. There seems to be considerable debate about this association, though; Thorne maintains that "there is no discernible connection with the British public-school term meaning a junior boy performing servant duties" (170), and often sexual duties as well, whereas Harold Wentworth and Stuart Berg Flexner believe that "the use of the word, 'fag' = a boy servant or lackey has been common English schoolboy use since before 1830, and may be the origin of 'fag' = homosexual" (176). The connection between "fag" as a synonym for a cigarette and the word "faggot" should not be overlooked "since cigarettes were considered effeminate by cigar and pipe smokers when they were first introduced at the end of W.W.I" (Wentworth and Flexner, 176).

Literally, though, "faggot" means a bundle of sticks bound together. As we think about this term, we should remember that an emblem of power for the fascists was the faggot (from *fasces,* the Roman bundle of sticks); the bundle symbolized the collectivity of the nation. Although a direct correlation between this symbolic use of the *fasces* by fascism to today's use as a reference to gay men may not be a clear one, the *OED* emphasizes with respect to "faggot" the "special reference to the practice of burning heretics alive" (19). Homosexuals were victims of the Nazis' genocide program and continue to be a major target of skinheads and fundamentalist Christian and neofascist groups today. Historically, women as witches (heretics) and homosexuals (as in gay bashing) share the heritage of victimization at the hands of religious fanatics and political zealots. Even in the United States, land of the free and so forth, homosexual men, as "faggots," have been and continue to be victimized by heterosexual men troubled by living in a society that derogates homosexuality and who sometimes resort to the dogma of Christianity to defend their hostility. These men enact what is socially sanctioned in their experience, in their beliefs, and in their language.

An excellent example of this "heterosexual male confusion" and its resulting enmity can be found, according to Susan Faludi, at The Citadel, the infamous military academy in Charleston, South Carolina, that tried for years to exclude women from enrolling. In an article in the *New Yorker* Faludi describes the "Treehouse, a 'mixed' bar in Charleston, with an upstairs gay bar and nightly drag shows on the weekends" that is frequented by cadets who, according to one customer, "love faggots like me [and] go for the drag queens" ("Naked Citadel," 80–81). Faludi visited this bar to inquire about cadet violence against gay men, which she assumed was inevitable. Her findings, though, suggest a much different reality, one that warrants turning to her account:

> There are thousands of cadets, presumably, who have not dated drag queens, but in two visits to the Treehouse I could find only two drag queens, out of maybe a dozen, who did not tell me of dating a cadet— and that was only because these two found Citadel men "too emotional." Cadets can also occasionally be dangerous [my informant] told me. "You can get the ones who are violent. They think they want it, then afterwards they turn on you, like you made them do it." Nonetheless, a drag queen who called himself Holly had been happily involved with a cadet for three years now. Marissa, another drag queen, the reigning "Miss Treehouse, 1993–1994," had gone out with one cadet, broken up, and was now in the throes of a budding romance with another. A third drag queen, who asked to be identified as Tiffany, was known to be a favorite of cadets. (81)

As a haven of macho masculinity, The Citadel manifests many of the contradictions men experience in their lives, especially those centering on the meaning of manhood. Although straight men, trained to be soldiers and athletes, husbands and fathers, learn to internalize as masculinity that which is not femininity, Faludi's research exemplifies the ambivalence men feel about the burdens of such a restrictive masculinity and echo an observation made by James Baldwin in a 1971 discussion: "Straight guys invent faggots so they can sleep with them without becoming faggots themselves"

(Katz, 103).[7] Ironically, though, and what should be clear from my earlier discussion of "blow job" in chapter 2, who would know better how to perform fellatio than another man?

The use of the term "faggot" demonstrates clearly both the confusion surrounding the parameters of being a real man and the extent to which language is never neutral. "Faggot" is not just some word; it is a term with a violent history and a particular and hostile reference to gay men. These terms are not without effect on heterosexual men. To return to the study of college students in the particular scenarios Armstrong evaluates, he points out that "the use of the term faggot is generated by the association between caring about the well-being of children and being effeminate, in contrast to the manliness of speeding down a residential street (i.e., risk taking)" (331).

If gay men represent undesirable male sexuality and straight men embody the only acceptable male sexuality, all men become victims of the language passively adopted to describe "authentic" masculinity. This kind of language does not allow us to entertain the thought that there are alternate forms of masculinity to the heterosexual.

If men concentrate their energy on not being called a "faggot" or a "pansy," they ignore the more constructive enterprise of creating a new way to describe themselves. A language that neither denies our femininity nor derides men who have other than just traditional masculine traits or "normal" sexual proclivities would be liberating to us all.

## LETTING HIS LITTLE HEAD RULE HIS BIG HEAD

The phrases "letting his little head rule his big head," "thinking with his dick," and "being led around by his dick" lend an intelligence to the penis and suggest that it has a mind of its own.[8] The head of a penis (a metaphor in itself, of course) is smaller than the head in which the brain resides, but in the case of sexual desire the penis (or this small head) controls a man's behavior. Indeed, as Badinter observes, the penis, as a metonymy for the man, "is also his obsessive master. The part lays down the law to the whole since it defines the whole" (137). As metaphors for male sexuality, these terms reinforce once again the insistent assumption that men have an uncontrollable need for sex and that their genitals are preeminent in their relation to women.

The characterization of the penis as having a mind of its own is consistent with "the dualistic model of the rational head and the irrational body [and] allows for separation, so the rational mode, thinking, is dominant at certain times, the less rational mode of love and sexual feeling is appropriate at other times" (Haste, 168). The dichotomy between lust (i.e., physical passion) and love (i.e., emotional passion) in which only love is feminized echoes this distinction between the rational and the irrational. Although both feelings are irrational (lust and love), only emotion is feminized, and polarity is maintained. This metaphor, "letting his little head rule his big head," favors the irrational (love and sexual feeling) but also lust over love which, by being feminized, is removed from the discourse.

Men's ambivalence about their sexuality emerges in these metaphors where the omniscience of the penis provides a rationale for uncontrolled male desire. On the one hand, men always want to be in control of their passion—to be emotional flirts too closely with being feminine—while, on the other hand, men want an excuse for being out of control. Much like the drunk who blames his bad behavior on alcohol, the man who hands over his intelligence to his sexual organs can behave as a brute (or a rutting animal) without having to take responsibility for it.

### PANSY

This disparaging term for a homosexual male connotes, specifically, the passive partner in a homosexual couple: "especially [the] receiver," according to Spears (327), or the "one who plays the female role," according to Wentworth and Flexner (374). Consistent with this interpretation, this slang term refers more broadly to a weak or effeminate man (Spears, 327; Thorne, 382).

In the early part of the twentieth century, fear of feminization was a preoccupation of the American male, whether middle class or working class. In their efforts to prove that they were "men among men," these men frequently reassured themselves of their "regular guy" status with a preoccupation with the obverse; men felt in constant danger of being called something unmanly: a mollycoddle, a sissy, even a pansy (Kimmel, *Manhood,* 124).

Literally, though, as a hybridized garden plant, a pansy has rounded "velvety petals of various colors" (*AHCD,* 898); it is a popular annual or short-lived perennial obtained by hybridizing and selecting forms derived from viola tricolors crossed with various other species (Perry, 278). The etymological origins of the word date to Old French, however, and may come from *pensée,* meaning thought, or *penser,* to think (*OED,* 427); the *American Heritage Dictionary* suggests "pensive" as a synonym (898).[9]

In this broad linguistic context a pansy becomes a thoughtful, reflective, brightly colored, attractive man. These qualities (intelligence, sensitivity, beauty) are commonplace characterizations for women in our society, as is passivity. When a man uses his mind before he acts, feels concern for someone's plight, considers the consequences of his behavior, or pays attention to how he looks, he distances himself from the norm of male heterosexuality. Although some censure of color has relaxed in recent years, a well-dressed man, especially one wearing particular colors such as pink, purple, or a bright green or blue, would leave himself open to ridicule as a pansy. The restrictive nature of male fashion still helps police men's behavior however, constraining them from even flirting with what might easily be construed as gender transgression.

In their examination of the relationship between changes in fashion and our evolving ideas about masculinity and femininity, Claudia Kidwell and Valerie Steele caution the reader not to draw simplistic assumptions about "the complex processes of gender socialization [that make] it diffi-cult . . . to understand past and present changes" in fashion (plate 1). Hav-ing said that, though, the authors point out that in the 1950s, for example, "the male's dark business suit contrasts sharply with the colorful, curva-ceous female silhouette" (plate 1). A half-century later, not all that much has changed. After describing how women easily don garments based on traditional masculine forms and materials, Kidwell and Steele make clear that "men are much less likely to wear clothes drawn from feminine tradi-tion" (159). In U.S. society, at least, heterosexual masculinity has clear boundaries across which an individual male advances at risk of self-exile.

## PUSSY

> "I always thought you were a pussy," said Aaron. "Look at you. Big as a fucking house, but you're just a pussy. All fucking righteous now, aren't you? You weren't so righteous when we started this, were you? Now, you decide. We're going to kick some more ass, aren't we?"
> —Sherman Alexie, *Indian Killer*

Although used predominantly as a reference to the female genitals, and thus more accurately a metaphor women live by, "pussy" has two mean-ings as a slang term: as references both to the vulva and an effeminate male. The precise origin of its use as a reference to the female genitals remains inconclusive; Thorne believes "'pussy' or 'puss' was first recorded in the sexual sense in the 16th century" (409), whereas Spears (361) and Chapman (344) locate its origin in the 1800s. Not only are the origins of the term unclear, its meaning is somewhat confused: as a reference to the vulva, according to Thorne, "pussy" "derives from the resemblance of pubic hair to fur, perhaps reinforced by male notions of affection," but Thorne characterizes this word as "an unromantic male term used in the same indiscriminate manner as tail, ass, etc. In this generic sense, the term may be expressed as pussy, 'some pussy,' or occasionally 'a piece of pussy'" (409).

The suggestion of a connection between "pussy" and "male notions of affection" needs some discussion: does this affection refer to petting a cat or a dog, or does it mean skinning an animal for its pelt? And what difference does it make? The implication advances the idea that a woman's genitals should be seen as either a pet to be taken care of (not unlike the contemporary term "chick") or the skin of an animal to be valued. As a pet or as a pelt, this meaning reduces a woman both to her sexual organs (a recurrent theme, it seems, in heterosexual male notions of affection) and to a helpless animal in need of protection and looking after, in need of a husband.

This implication carries over to the use of "pussy" to refer to a weak or harmless man. A man who is not an aggressive or skilled athlete or not a ferocious warrior may find the epithet of "pussy" raining down upon him. Nelson describes the experience of Julie Croteau, the only woman to play baseball on a men's team through three years of college, before she resigned because of sexual harassment. For three years, though, Croteau watched and listened to some of the more horrendous ways men initiate other men and boys into the world of sports and masculinity. According to Nelson, Croteau "was horrified. Not so much by the 'you bat like a girl' remarks—she had become accustomed to such 'ordinary' sexism in Little League—but by how sexual the comments were, how vulgar. 'You pussy.' 'You cunt.' 'You whore'" (83). Male discourse relies on the denigration of women as a means to teach little boys how inferior and disgusting the female is. For after all, as Badinter quite accurately observes, "*a man's first duty is: not to be a woman*" (47).

The military is, of course, another powerful site of male bonding. Carol Cohn, in her essay on the discourse of war, observes firsthand the use of "pussy" to describe a weak or harmless man when she identifies this term as "another popular epithet, conjoining the imagery of harmless domesticated (read demasculinized) pets with contemptuous reference to women's genitals" (235). According to Cohn, a male civilian defense analyst who raises questions about the other side's casualties might be referred to as a "pussy" and thus learns rather quickly not to ask such a question: "Attention to and care for the living, suffering, and dying of human beings . . . is again banished from the discourse through the expedient means of gender-bashing" (235).

A man relegated to the status of a woman, or a "pussy," can then experience the same kind of violence women have to fear all their lives. The Citadel again provides an excellent example of this kind of retaliation. There, according to one cadet, "They called you a 'pussy all the time . . . or a fucking little girl. . . .' Virtually every taunt equated him with a woman. . . . The knobs even experienced a version of domestic violence. The upperclassmen . . . 'would go out and get drunk and they would come home and haze, and you just hoped they didn't come into your room'"

(Faludi, "Naked Citadel," 70). As in so many examples already discussed, any man who reveals himself as a gentle, timid, or harmless person (Chapman, 344) may become tainted by the feminine, and men must control the female no matter what form or incarnation it takes. The resultant violence against women and against gay men is the most blatant example of this heterosexual male fear. Were women to become subjects and not just sexual objects, and heterosexual men secure in their identities as men (whatever that might be), women and nonaggressive nurturing men might no longer have to harbor fears for their lives. Here too a language that described us as subjects, as whole people with minds and feet and kneecaps, rather than just holes and poles, could move us closer to an appreciation of ourselves and others as equals.

### SISSY (MAMA'S BOY)

> As early as four and five, boys learn what is expected of them as males and restrict themselves. . . . What this means in large part is not being like a girl, or, what is the same thing, not being a "sissy."
> —Marc Feigen Fasteau, *The Male Machine*

Yet one more synonym for "a cowardly, weak or effeminate boy or man," the term "sissy" also frequently connotes a homosexual man (Wentworth and Flexner, 478; Spears, 410; Chapman, 391). Obviously, an extension of the word "sis" and by derivation "sister," a "sissy" equates an effeminate man with a powerless woman (or girl, even), someone's (a man's) sister (or his mother). Understood in the larger context of the adage "boys don't cry" or men don't show their emotions, "sissy" can be understood in juxtaposition to the phrase "taking it like a man" (Seidler, 151).

Michael Kimmel traces the historical evolution of this term from its origin in the 1840s as an affectionate term for "sister." By the 1880s, however, "the term had become a derisive description for spineless boys and men and by 1900 had become clearly associated with effeminacy, cowardice, and lack of aggression" (*Manhood*, 100).

Calling a man a sissy as a means to question his masculinity has remained a powerful insult for well over one hundred years. A manhood "defined by courage, generosity, modesty, dignity and affect" can easily feel threatened by the specter of the sissy, with its connotations of weakness, dependency, and helplessness; from Rafford Pyke's diatribe against sissies in the 1902 issue of *Cosmopolitan* magazine to Thomas Wolfe's 1976 essay on "Honks and Wonks," the requirement that the American male be tough, muscular, aggressive, and hard has remained a singularly powerful one (Kimmel, *Manhood*, 122).

The similarity between the use of "sissy" (to reflect cowardice and weakness) and "mama's boy" (dependency) and that of "pansy" (flamboyant) and "pussy" (effeminacy) should be apparent. I have included "sissy" here because it represents another disparaging label for a man who challenges the traditional masculine role. Men who are not clearly masculine are womanish, and women, according to the male imagination, are subordinate. Thus the language of masculinity posits unequivocal distinctions, and anyone who steps outside those boundaries risks the fate of the servile and the inferior.

Ironically, though, in sibling relationships older sisters can wield a lot of power. "Sissy," then, exemplifies the use of language to enforce the notion that women are powerless and sisters weak, in contradiction to the reality that older, and even younger, sisters may be disconcertingly powerful. Language can reconfigure experience to conform to ideology. The ideology of masculinity relies on these unambiguous differentiations to remain in power. Once the delineation between master and slave becomes obscure, the ability to rule is threatened.

## STUD

> A notorious seducer; a ladies'-man; a cuckolder of the rich; in short, a stud.
>
> —Salman Rushdie, *Midnight's Children*

The word "stud" has several meanings, not all of which relate directly to male heterosexuality. A stud is the two-by-four in the wall that provides a framework to which Sheetrock is nailed, and a stud is "a small ornamental button mounted on a short post for insertion through an eyelet, as on a dress shirt" (*AHCD,* 1348). A stud also refers to that part of a pierced earring that goes through the ear lobe.

Clearly, though, as a metaphor for male heterosexuality, "stud" derives its meaning from a male horse used for breeding purposes. When a man is referred to as a "stud," it relates to two things: the desire to have sex with as many women as possible and, concomitantly, a sense of sexual prowess that attaches to him. Although "stud" no longer refers exclusively to heterosexual men, having currency in gay male discourse as well, I include it here because of its original and primary use, since at least the 1890s, as a reference to a "womanizer" (Ayto and Simpson, 249). In the discourse of heterosexual male bonding, "stud" designates a promiscuous straight man who has several female lovers.

Thorne provides the most extensive definition of the use of this slang term for a male: "a sexually active, powerful, potent male. Only slang when applied to men as opposed to (real) animals, the term often indicates a degree of approval or admiration, even if grudgingly. In black American street parlance the word was sometimes used in the late 1960s and 1970s simply to mean 'guy.' There seems to be no female equivalent that stresses sexual power rather than degeneracy" (499). Thorne raises several important points: the lack of a word used in a similar way to describe a woman, the implication of this term as a positive male characteristic, and one original use of this word (by blacks) to refer to a black man.

The closest comparable expression for a woman might be "slut," but even though it means promiscuous and having sexual prowess (the word "prowess" refers exclusively to men, however), "slut" is a pejorative term for a woman. Here, as in the epigraph to this section, the language reinforces the acceptability for a man to be sexually active and the rejection of a similar freedom for a woman.

As a positive male quality, the phenomenon of the stud was certainly a part of my own adolescent experience. Although I was never a "stud," not being large enough or masculine enough or athletic enough, I did seek male acceptance through my ability to have several girlfriends at the same time. That girls found me attractive and were willing to have sex with me gained me status in the world of young boys trying hard to establish themselves as acceptable males.

Where I grew up, young boys secured a position in the world of manhood in three ways: getting drunk, getting into fights, and getting laid. Boys as drinkers, as bullies/athletes, and as "ladies' men" were accepted into the fraternity of masculinity. I was no fighter, so I drank and screwed my way into deserving maleness. I have struggled against these early influences throughout my adult life, and I have my feminist female friends and lovers to thank for my partial liberation from these oppressive male roles. The image of the man as stud pervades our popular consciousness so deeply, though, that an individual man's struggle to jettison such a role remains a constant battle. Although many of us laugh at the absurdity of such a role model, and chuckle at how our physique compares to the guy in the Calvin Klein commercial, we still aspire to get the beautiful exotic babe and have sex with her until we drop (or she begs for mercy).

The exotic and the masculine are fused in the conjunction of the term "stud" and the black man. Ayto and Simpson echo Thorne's suggestion that "stud" was used originally to describe a black man, and both Chapman, and Wentworth and Flexner identify its origin in "1930s jive talk" (Chapman, 421) considered to be a "fairly common cool use" (Wentworth and Flexner, 526). Chapman also points to the attractiveness of the male who is called a stud, whereas Spears lists four characteristics associated with this term: "virility, stylishness, sex appeal, [and] sexual success with women" (428). Thus the word "stud," usually used by men in a friendly, congratulatory way to describe a pal who has several lovers or gets laid a lot, reverberates with sexist and even racist overtones.

Helen Haste, though, seems to suggest that the sexism of this term is minimal and certainly not misogynist when she observes that

> the macho stud figure is trapped in a particular image of sexuality—crude scoring, and performance—but he is not guilt-ridden. . . . Feminist ideas may challenge his simple world-view, but macho studs saw the benefits of the permissive society, and misinterpreted the message of feminism as an opportunity for even more free-and-easy sex. Such chauvinism is unthinking, sexist and exploitative, but it is fueled by at worst indifference and incomprehension towards women, not fear and hatred. (166)

Haste's suggestion that the macho stud is not motivated by fear and hatred of women seems problematic indeed. The language of sexual oppression creates victims, and while an argument can be made that men are also victims of their discourse, to ignore the extent to which women are its primary victims disregards the significance of how we talk about ourselves. The stud as an animal whose exclusive function is to breed with many females reduces men and women to animals who either fuck or are fucked. This kind of relationship rests on alienation at the very least, and most likely fear and hatred lie at the root of it.

This term refers not only to a stud horse that is free to just have sex without having to work but also derives from the white male fantasy about the sexual prodigiousness of the black man. According to this fantasy, all black men are studs if for no other reason than that, it is assumed, all black men have large penises. In his essay on the history of the penis, Toby Miller points to "the mythology surrounding penises of color" that "illustrate(s) white men's 'sexual inferiority,' a contradictory mass of feelings that combines an elevation of the phallus to omniscience, and a hatred of the black man for being the ultimate 'penis symbol'" (10).

The antagonism between the dark villain and the white hero is almost universal in Western culture. In his book, *White Hero Black Beast: Racism, Sexism, and the Mask of Masculinity,* Paul Hoch discusses this polarization at great length. According to Hoch, "The conflict between hero and beast becomes a struggle between two understandings of manhood: human versus animal, white versus black, spiritual versus carnal, soul versus flesh, higher versus lower, noble versus base" (45). These dichotomies result in "the achievement of manhood by the conquest of hero over beast [an achievement that] became the allegory for the struggle of civilization against barbarism, white Europe against the dark continent of Africa, West against East—and of the civilized consciousness over the dark, bestial sexual forces in its unconscious" (Hoch, 47). Hoch argues further that these dichotomies are at the heart of the "interracial competition for women" and that "the super-sexualised black stud, so dreaded by the racist, represents an unconscious projection of those aspects of his own sexuality which society has made taboo" (54).

The reduction of the black man to an animal whose dominant characteristic or quality is to breed highlights the ambivalence white men have about their sexuality. In their imagination many men want to be seen as a "stud" and wish that all they had to do all day was have sex, but at the same time they are doubtful of their ability to assume this role. Are their penises large enough, do they have enough stamina, can they perform well enough, are they really animal enough to take on this function? These are the questions concealed behind the simple label of "stud," questions men prefer not to confront as they hide behind an epithet that obscures more than it elucidates.

## STUDMUFFIN

The only dictionary reference to this fairly new metaphor for a man appears in Spears, who defines it simply as "a good-looking, sexually attractive male" (429). The combination of "stud" as a sexually active man and "muffin" as an edible treat seems to suggest a male who is both sexy and tasty. This comical term juxtaposes "stud" (power and sexuality) with "muffin" (cute and sweet) and in this way defuses the power aspect of the metaphor. It is an ironical metaphor that undercuts its own significance.

As a term coined and used by women (not men) to describe an attractive and youthful masculinity, studmuffin may say more about the current situation of female sexuality than it does about male sexuality: that women want to control the discourse of their sexuality as a way to define it for themselves.

Lesbians also use this metaphor to refer to an attractive, masculine-type, or butch, lesbian, but in this context "studmuffin" seems to uncritically reenact a dominant notion of masculinity while acknowledging the female. According to Kath Weston, whose book *Render Me, Gender Me* includes several references to the term "studmuffin": "If 'butch' brings to mind nothing more than a hackneyed picture of some truck-driving diesel dyke, you probably won't know what to make of the paradoxical figure of the studmuffin. As precious as she's butch, a studmuffin could be you (depending) or me at a moment when butch collides with femme" (4).[10] The paradox of such a term as "studmuffin" is significant, whether it refers to a man or a woman. Its power, however, may come from the seemingly passive and cute image it brings to mind.

The sound of this metaphor, the way its enunciation suggests its meaning, makes it effective. "Studmuffin" sounds almost poetic. It suggests an image of a powerfully built, slender, dark young man in tight jeans looking seductively into the camera. On the one hand, this image is a counterpart to the recurrent photograph of the female model in the Guess clothing commercials with that "Come fuck me" look; now we have a cultural icon of a man making the same suggestion. The studmuffin, as the sexually exploitable male body there for the woman's sexual pleasure, may be a step toward sexual liberation, and that it is a phrase owned almost exclusively by women certainly proposes such a reading. On the other hand, this metaphor highlights one of the great failures of the liberal feminist perspective. The view that women are just like men, that they can assume male roles and all will be well with the world, fails to attack the source of these roles or the implications of why contemporary dominant male roles emphasize certain qualities and denounce others.

As a metaphor that is synonymous with "boy toy," "studmuffin" reinforces the predominant notion of the male body as an erection, as a nonfeeling sexual machine. Does a studmuffin talk, does he cry or laugh or defer? Or does he sit there unmoving with a perennial hard-on, just waiting to be the stud who is eaten, the sexual plaything of the compulsorily heterosexual woman? Ironically, even though "studmuffin" originates as a female fantasy relying on what women say he wants, as a metaphor for masculinity it resonates with the great male heterosexual fantasy writ large: the man who wants to be used sexually by the beautiful, hungry, insatiable woman. Does he think beyond his penis, or does he see himself as the popular culture encourages most American men to see themselves: as one large, irresistible erection?

## WHISKEY DICK

This phrase underscores a man's ambivalent relationship with alcohol by alluding to him as being too drunk to get an erection. Spears, the only slang dictionary to include the term (of the six I use), defines "whisky dick" (British spelling) as: "an impotent penis due to too much alcohol" (476).

Among the limited options boys have available to them as a means to demonstrate their masculinity, getting drunk, getting laid, and getting into fights vie for their attention. The less athletic, more pusillanimous boys can still remain viable males in the eyes of their peers by drinking just as much as anyone else and being successful with the girls.

Hoch stresses the importance of alcohol consumption as "one of the most common ways of certifying one's manhood" in what are frequently all-male institutions "as a defense against the 'feminine' elements within" the male psyche (85). Kimmel echoes Hoch's observation when he views drinking as "a form of masculine resistance to feminization" (Kimmel,

*Manhood,* 124). One reason men get drunk, that is, is to assert their stereo-typically belligerent and imperious masculinity.

Hard drinking, then, becomes a badge of manhood while releasing a man's inhibitions about approaching a woman. Alcohol makes scared men brave, but too much alcohol makes drunk men impotent. It also makes them violent and aggressive; alcohol brings out the worst in men, ex-acerbating, as it does, their socialization to be bullies and warriors. Men use alcohol as an excuse for their worst behavior and then coin a phrase like "whiskey dick" to provide them with a rationalization for their weak-ness and their subsequent embarrassment.

The irony of such a phrase as "whiskey dick" arises from the confusion and inadequacy it reveals in men's relationship to women. Men are afraid of women, they fear rejection, and they fear love with its attendant loss of autonomy. "Whiskey dick" identifies a situation in which a man confirms his masculinity by his ability to consume large quantities of alcohol but experiences inferiority as a "real man" by describing his inability to obtain an erection. The tragedy such a metaphor conveys is men's bewilderment about the stress placed on the importance of the erection in the definition of what it means to be a man. If a man were to feel secure enough in his masculinity not to feel the need to get drunk, treated a woman as an equal and not as a target of conquest, and focused less on the role of his erect penis in making love, "whiskey dick" would disappear from the discourse of male bonding because men would no longer feel compelled to get drunk in order to have a conversation with a woman, much less seduce her.

# II    Beyond the Present

# 6 Insidious Humor and the Construction of Masculinity

> When a logonomic system allows a statement offensive to women to be read as "a joke," this signifies a particular structure of gender relations, one in which males are dominant as a group in relation to females but need to mask their hostility and aggression towards them.
> —Robert Hodge and Gunther Kress, *Social Semiotics*

> Joking reflects and partially compensates for our failings, dissatisfactions and self-alienation.
> —Christopher Wilson, *Jokes: Form, Content, Use, and Function*

> Formalised humour will generally fulfill an ideological function in supporting and maintaining existing social relations and dominant ways of perceiving social reality.
> —Chris Powell, "A Phenomenological Analysis of Humour in Society"

The title of this book, *Studs, Tools, and the Family Jewels,* frequently elicits laughter, a laughter related to embarrassment or shame. Some people smile, others smirk, some cough, some even blush, but all the people to whom I have told the title have at least chuckled, and many have rolled their eyes as if to say, "You can't talk about that in public, it's private, forbidden, and the domain of the select few." In this case the select few are men, and their discourse of sexuality gains power in direct proportion to their ability to control language. Humor empowers that control.

Humor has the potential to be liberating, though, and in my concluding remarks to this chapter I try to identify ways in which we can harness humor toward positive ends. Satire may be the best source for this liberating form of humor, and ridicule in the form of reverse victimization may also serve as a potent weapon. The problematics of any victimization must be considered, and at the end of the chapter I reflect upon the complications that result from this particular option. Primarily, though, I am interested in the power of humor to liberate us, just as I am convinced that new metaphors can change the way we think about ourselves as men.

Indeed, jokes and metaphors have much in common. Both rely on language as a means to provide incongruous comparisons, and both require an audience.[1] Puns may be the best example of the play on words endemic to both jokes and metaphors, but profanity provides another instance. Freud's work on humor, and in particular his analysis of profanity, brings together the disjunctive use of language with the necessity for there to be an audience. Freud observes that "a favourite definition of joking has long been the ability to find similarity between dissimilar things—that is, hidden similarities" (*Jokes,* 7). Much of one of his chapters, "The Technique of Jokes," examines "the process of condensation with substitution-formation" and "double meaning arising from the literal and metaphorical meanings of a word" (*Jokes,* 31, 39).

In his analysis of smut Freud recognizes the need for at least another man to be present in order for a joke to work and thus introduces an early and profound insight into the dynamics of male bonding. Although Freud views smut as prefatory to "a wooing speech" (117), and thus quite consistent with what he sees as the difference between men's and women's libidos (the former active and the latter passive), he recognizes that smut is sexually aggressive and can become "positively hostile and cruel" (117). When women resist smut, the "third person . . . acquires the greatest importance. . . . The onlooker, now the listener, becomes the person to whom the smut is addressed, and owing to this transformation it is already near to assuming the character of a joke" (118). The third person, the audience for this kind of harassment, must be a man.

Men bond around the sexual disparagement of women, and insidious humor empowers male bonding. The discourse of male heterosexuality can be quite funny. Humor distracts people from the real purpose of this language; it disarms them and thus fosters a subtle control over interpersonal relationships (both heterosexual and homosocial). In comparison to other, more heavy-handed methods of control, humor may be seen as comparatively benign. The sly treachery of male humor, and the extent to which it is frequently more dangerous than may at first glance seem evident, intensifies its force. However, the sense of playfulness attached to humor exacerbates its insidiousness. Michael Mulkay, the author of an important study of the nature and place of humor in modern society, maintains that "in the domain of humour men's control over and sexual domination of women is exceptionally stark and unrestricted" (141). Mulkay's point is in danger of generally being overlooked, however, because humor works best the more insidious men manage to make it. Indeed, I believe it is this balance between the stark and the subtle that characterizes much male humor and enhances its effectiveness.

I want to begin by sharing with you two incidents I recently witnessed that, I believe, show how men use humor insidiously in their ongoing attempt to control women by degrading them. The first occurred while I was out to dinner at a local restaurant some months ago. I overheard two men at a table nearby exchange some words with and about the young woman who was the hostess. One of the men (who might have known the young woman) asked her, jokingly, why she never agreed to go out to dinner with him. In an attempt to defuse the situation she responded by saying that she worked late, too late for dinner. He told her that he liked to eat late, to which she said something like, "Well, it's too late for me."

At this point, after she had left their table, the guy who had been conversing with (or harassing, depending upon how you look at it) the young woman, turned to his buddy and said, "It would never be too late to have her for dessert." His buddy laughed snidely, and the two of them continued to exchange what they considered to be humorous remarks about her desirability.

The second incident occurred in the lobby of a large hotel where two businessmen, dressed in suits of course, were sitting on a sofa waiting for another guy to show up. When he arrived, also dressed in a suit, he said to his friends: "Well, are you ready to go to the mall?" One of the other guys responded sarcastically, "Yeah, let's go spend the day shopping," and all three burst out laughing.

The second anecdote seems the most straightforward. Essentially, these men are laughing about their belief in the contrast between men's and women's roles: that women waste their time happily shopping all day, while men have to work hard at making difficult business decisions. Their insidious laughter characterizes the exchange as much as do their cultural assumptions. The laughter signals that all three men share the same presuppositions about their social and economic importance and, concomitantly, women's relative insignificance. By laughing together, the men bond around the degradation of women while sharing the belief that men and their work are consequential.

The first story is a bit more complicated though not much. These two men bond over the reference to the young woman as a sexual object. What makes the story a trifle more complex, though, is the suggestion that a man might want to give a woman pleasure through the act of cunnilingus (having her for dessert). By contrast, the tone of the remarks communicates the sense that what the man really wants to do is molest the young woman, to use her for his pleasure, to relegate her to a sexual body upon which (whom) he will exercise his right to make her his domain. Together the tone and the content make the source of the bonding both reductive and aggressive.

The lexicon of male bonding is by its nature predominantly aggressive;

it is mean and at times even terrorizing.[2] The use of humor enhances the effectiveness of male bonding. As D. E. Berlyne points out in his social psychological study of the relationship of laughter, humor, and play, by serving to express agreement and undermine the morale of those against which it is aimed, "humor acts as a means of control, [that] is used to . . . develop common attitudes, indicate safety or friendship" (811). That is, humor functions in a purposeful way to manipulate the outcome of the interchange among men and between men and women. Laughter, according to Christopher Wilson in his study of jokes, provides a consensus and expresses a shared sentiment that "evokes a sense of solidarity between group members and against the butt of humour" (214).

In the two anecdotes I have just described, the butts of the jokes and the victims of the humor are women. Men bond around certain assumptions about women (that they are stupid and that they are sexually available, to name just two), and in this bonding they gain approval by other men in the group.[3] This communal approbation empowers the group to "graduate to the more satisfying expression of direct disparagement" (Wilson, 227). When men move from the relatively confined exchange among themselves of dirty jokes to overt kinds of shared aggressive sexual badgering of women (or verbal rape), their disparagement of women becomes terrifying. Individual men can also use humor as a weapon against a lover or wife, but in either situation—the man alone or in a group—humor no longer remains "just a joke." It becomes threatening and violent, and much male humor actively and intentionally victimizes women. Here is but one example:

**q:**   What do you tell a woman who has two black eyes?
**a:**   Nothing, she's already been told twice.

Men can also be the butt of the jokes, and ironically the insidiousness of male humor empowers men to exert control over each other. In the restaurant scenario I described, for example, if the guy's friend had not laughed with him about the young woman's desirability, the friend's credibility as a "real" man would have been in question. Had there been three men at dinner, two might well have ganged up on the other one and ridiculed his treason to the group as evidence of his being a "faggot" or impotent or some other term that questioned his heterosexual masculinity. The two men would have laughed hilariously over their attack on the other guy and bonded around the implicit recognition that they, at least, were "real men."

This reciprocal policing of male behavior in turn allows men to dominate women by giving men a sense of their collective power (as a result, they present a unified front). If, as Wilson suggests, "joking reflects and partially compensates for our failings, dissatisfactions and self-alienation" (231), male humor must be seen as an effective form of retaliation. Male bonding, through the use of humor, allows men to use their sense of power in a way similar to that of the bully. Most men in U.S. society, while certainly privileged, have little real power. By elevating their group status, male bonding compensates for the fear of individual impotence that results from men's sense of powerlessness and alienation.

Relying for the most part on degradation and shame, most male humor hurts someone. Dirty jokes, for example, although usually too overt to be insidious, demonstrate the extent to which the male sense of humor victimizes women. Mulkay observes that

> dirty jokes depict the relationship between men and women in terms of a radical form of sexual, social, and linguistic domination of women by men. The very words used to refer to women endorse and exemplify this domination. . . . The domain of humour is a world where the male voice constantly triumphs over that of the female and where women are made to exist and act only as appendages to men's most basic sexual inclinations. (137)

Although, as Marcel Gutwirth points out, the joke must be seen as "preeminently a bonding narrative, a make-believe framework for the permissible expression of objectionable sentiments," jokes are not neutral or "just fun."[4] They reinforce a social agenda and, as Peter Lyman finds from his case study of what was supposed to be a humorous encounter between some fraternity brothers and sorority sisters, "the defense that jokes are play defines aggressive behavior as play" (158). Abuse and degradation between men are just part of the horseplay and backslapping that structures male behavior. Men need to keep their interaction with women frivolous, and "the joke provides a socially acceptable means to express aggression" (Wilson, 206). To wit:

**q:** Why do men speak to women?
**a:** Because they have a cunt.

As all of us have had occasion to observe, when feminists resist complicity with this aggression, they earn the reputation of humorlessness, a humorlessness that evokes fraternal laughter.[5]

Male bonding engenders power and control, and humor—insidious humor—intensifies that domination. From the commonly used response, "it's only a joke," to the commonly held belief that humor allows us to talk about otherwise socially unacceptable experiences, humor reinforces the inequality of the sexes that remains central to U.S. culture.[6] The male response, "it's only a joke," indicts the critic for lacking a sense of humor.

Powell, in his phenomenological analysis of humor, sees this rejoinder as being "concerned with the mitigation of social hostility or tension via the re-establishment of a joke framework" (102). The idea—prevalent in the studies of humor from Freud to Charlie Chaplin—that humor is an acceptable way to exchange information about sexual activities unmentionable in our society—ignores completely the nature of the information being transferred.[7] According to Wilson, for example, "sexual themes and obscenities that are unacceptable in serious conversation, are amusing when incorporated in jest and attributed to absent or fictional third parties" (187). Although Wilson goes on to observe that jokes among men usually "express and foster the particular values of the male group" (188), not enough has been said about the pervasiveness of male dominance in sexual humor and the role of humor in sustaining the status quo.

The by-now-famous joke attributed to Harvey Sacks about the three daughters whose mother spies on them on their wedding night provides a prime example of this kind of one-sided interpretation. In case you have not heard this joke, here is a quick overview: three sisters who are married on the same day return to their home with their new husbands to spend the wedding night. The mother listens at each bedroom door and the next morning over breakfast they have the following exchange:

**Mother:**   Sally, why were you crying so hard last night?
**Sally:**   Because it hurt so much.
**Mother:**   And Cindy why were you laughing so hysterically?
**Cindy:**   Because it tickled.
**Mother:**   And Susy why were you so quiet?
**Susy** (*hesitates*):   Well, Mother, you told me never to talk with my
   mouth full.

Granted, my rendition is a truncated version, but it provides enough of the joke to raise questions about "the exchange of information" interpretation of humor. The obvious question is, whose information and for what purpose is it being exchanged? At least two-thirds of this joke is about penis size, one of the great male obsessions. The husbands' penises are either too small (so it tickles) or too large (so it hurts). Maybe, though, the latent and truly subversive message in this joke is that a large penis may cause pain, not the unequaled pleasure *Playboy* magazine wants us to believe women are dying to experience, and that the small penis may produce joy because it tickles.

But the joke scarcely focuses on that information: it concentrates on fellatio as a source of shame, as it taps into the notion of the dumb blond. People who laugh at this joke do so because they are embarrassed for the woman who has to admit that she was performing oral sex on a man. Part of its humor also arises from the suggestion that the third daughter reports performing oral sex as if she didn't know she had.

Something none of the many and varied interpreters of this joke have pointed out is that throughout the entire joke the men remain silent: they are silent in bed the first night and they are silent at breakfast the next morning. One could infer from the story (again subversively) that they were all silent because, like Susy, they all had their mouths full. It seems more likely, though, that the men are silent because the predominant assumption about men, the information we have about them, tells us that men simply are silent when they make love. Men are not known to scream in orgasm or cry out with the pleasure of love making. They must remain in control, and one of the subtle messages of this joke is the underlying premise that men are both silent and in control when they have sex. Men's control often comes from evasion, avoidance, and absence (particularly in the aftermath of orgasm), and in this joke the men all but disappear.

The joke presupposes too that the outcome of sex for men is never in question. When men have sex, they are assumed to have pleasure, whereas women's orgasms are always experienced as problematic. This male anxiety about women's ability to enjoy sex pervades men's humor and acts as a defense mechanism against their fear of being a bad lover (or, worse yet, impotent). Thus another layer of this joke suggests that Susy's mouth is stuffed (she is silenced) by her subordination to male desire. This keeps her from expressing anything, much less a sexual message of her own.

Women's humor differs from men's humor, which may be a result of the fundamental difference between the way men and women experience the world. Unlike men's humor, which is frequently grounded in notions of competition, aggression, humiliation, and ridicule, women's humor usually lacks hostility and forgoes the necessity to belittle others as a means to enhance their own status. According to one anthropological study of humor and laughter, women do not express a need to "humiliate others either psychologically or physically," and women rarely engage in such common male forms of humor as "verbal duels, ritual insults . . . practical jokes and pranks" (Apte, 70). A shared feature of many cultures is women's mockery of men's pretensions to sexual prowess. Thus women's humor can scarcely be characterized as primarily conciliatory and gentle or concerned exclusively with the niceties of love and romance. This misreading of women's texts, according to Regina Barreca, relies on "the belief that women are actually incapable of producing the challenging, angry and subversive comedy that they do in fact write" (5).

At the same time that women's humor differs from men's, it differs also from feminist humor. Gloria Kaufman, editor of two collections of feminist humor and satire, provides a helpful distinction:

> In contrast to feminist humor, nonfeminist women's humor is frequently survival humor. It accepts a status quo regarded as inevitable. The empowerment derived from such humor is far less than that of revolutionary humor, which points toward change. . . . Feminist humor celebrates modes of power quite different from masculine societal norms. Indeed, it regularly satirizes as puerile or illogical the common equation of force and power. In the feminist view, the man with the gun, lacking persuasive power, lacking imagination, insecure in himself, is weak, not powerful. (viii–ix)

Nonfeminist women's humor still laughs about ugly women and fat women, women who shop too much, and women who are just dying to find the right man. Women's survival humor (e.g., the early Joan Rivers) relies on the social norm, what Adrienne Rich has referred to as "compulsory heterosexuality," and provides a means by which women can accommodate these oppressive expectations. Reactionary humor, whether presented by men or by women, perpetuates the notion of a natural sexual division in which men are and should be in power. Survival humor, from any oppressed group, allows these groups to remain disempowered by giving them a way to laugh at their own oppression. Frequently, this humor laughs at the oppressor as well, but that ridicule remains cathartic, not revolutionary. One example of this genre recently made the rounds in cyberspace:

> Eleven people were hanging onto a rope that came down from a helicopter. Ten were men and one was a woman. They all decided that one person should get off because if they didn't, the rope would break and everyone would die.
> No one could decide who should go, so finally the woman gave a really touching speech, saying how she would give up her life to save the others, because women were familiar with giving up things for their husbands and children, and giving in to men.
> All of the men started clapping.

In contrast to what Kaufman calls "mainstream masculinist attack humor," feminist humor seeks to empower people by presenting them with information. Intended to improve people, not damage them in some way, feminist humor "invites its 'victims' to change their behaviors and join the laughter" (ix). Brett Butler, the southern feminist comedian, relies on her origins for her repertoire of redneck jokes in her video called *Brett Butler: The Child Ain't Right*. Reflecting on her bubba first husband, she says that after that marriage was over, what she learned is, "You let one dog get away, you're going build a taller fence and put better food out." Which is not to suggest that feminist humor is passive and kindly: feminist humor can be hostile to men, certainly, and to patriarchy in general. Indeed, it can be said that when women's humor lacks open virulence, perhaps it still panders to male supremacy.

Like female humor, feminist humor tends to be less ego obsessed than men's. Feminist comedians tend to deal with such issues as sexism, homophobia, racism, and the homeless, not with how many times they got laid last night or how good they are in bed. By focusing on the world out there, much feminist humor reflects a stronger sense of security about themselves as women than women can express in another milieu. Marlo Thomas's famous line, "A man has to be Joe McCarthy to be called ruthless. All a woman has to do is put you on hold," and Erica Jong's, "Show me a woman who doesn't feel guilty and I'll show you a man," demonstrate a feminist humor concerned with the job site and the broader framework of gender socialization.

Whoopi Goldberg exemplifies a feminist humor concerned with social issues. In the character of Fontaine, a strung-out heroine addict, she explores class and gender through the greed of corporate America and the hypocrisy of fundamentalist Christian men opposed to women's freedom of choice. In an airport scene in the video *Whoopi Goldberg,* Fontaine/Whoopi tells us, "I passed this big dude walking around in a circle with a picket sign talking about stopping abortion, so I said, 'Motherfucker, when was the last time you was pregnant?' And he looks at me and says, 'I don't have to discuss that with you.' Because I have the answer to abortion, I said, 'Shoot off your dick.' I said, 'Take that tired piece of meat down to the ASPCA and let them put it to sleep.' And I feel better then because I know he put his money where his mouth is."

But women's sense of humor appears to differ materially from men's. According to one study designed to have male and female students identify their favorite dirty jokes, the male students preferred aggressive or sexual jokes, while females identified more jokes with "social or intellectual functions" (Ziv, 158). Frank MacHovec observes that in the realm of the dirty joke, forms of humor that deal with love and romance are by no means as widespread as jokes featuring "an explicit sexual content or direct association with sexual function" (148). That is, dirty jokes tend to focus on such male obsessions as physical endowment and sexual performance.

In fact, most dirty jokes are retailed among men, reinforcing the role this kind of humor plays in fostering a shared set of values. As a symbolic form of "verbal rape," men's humor in general, and the dirty joke in particular, frequently imply the availability of women for sexual pleasure. As Gershen Legman, who has written extensively on the dirty joke, puts it, men's humor relies on the reduction of "woman-as-vagina" (374) and exemplifies the "primacy of coitus" (236) that underlies almost all male humor: the tendency to degrade women's anatomy and blame women for precisely the promiscuity men impose upon them.[8]

This kind of disparagement, especially in the form of ridicule, represents one of the more prevalent forms of male humor. Wilson discusses
ridicule at great length in his chapter called "The Use of Abuse" and
points out that ridicule is "the prerogative of the powerful," not an option
for the weak and the oppressed. By supporting existing status and power,
ridicule reinforces the dynamics of male bonding: "The amusement evoked
by ridicule provides a shared sentiment that serves to cement feelings of
criticism or dislike within a group. The threat of becoming the target of
ridicule, and suffering the consequent feelings of isolation, will tend to
enforce conformity within a group" (Wilson, 213). Ironically, this particular kind of humor engenders yet one more configuration of men's violence
against themselves while forging a way for men to bond against women.
Misogynist and homophobic humor, while not always overt, certainly provides a potent weapon that men can use to protect themselves.

All-male groups and organizations manifest this kind of aggressive
behavior, and Peter Lyman's case study, "The Fraternal Bond as a Joking Relationship," elucidates the role of sexist jokes in male group bonding. Lyman's essay focuses on an incident in which an entire men's fraternity (forty-five men in all) broke into the dining room of a sorority house
during dinner, "surrounded the 30 women residents, and forced them to
watch while one pledge gave a speech on Freud's theory of penis envy as
another demonstrated various techniques of masturbation with a rubber
penis" (148). The women remained sitting at the table, passive and silent
for about ten minutes, until the graduate resident in charge of the house
walked in and demanded that the men leave. It was not until the men had
left that the women got angry. About this same time, the guy who made
the penis-envy speech returned and said, "That was funny to me. If that's
not funny to you I don't know what kind of sense of humor you have, but
I'm sorry."

Lyman explains that the penis-envy ritual had always been a successful
joke at this college and analyzes why it did not succeed that year. The
women thought the joke had failed not because of its subject but "because
of its emotional structure, the mixture of sexuality with aggression and the
atmosphere of sexual intimidation in the room that signified that the
women were the object of a joking relationship between the men" (149).
In contrast, the men "argued that the special male bond created by sexist
humor is a unique form of intimacy that justified the inconvenience caused
the women" (149). Clearly, the young women's consciousness had been
raised to the point where they were no longer willing or able to accept the
assumption that violence against women is okay.

Men's belief in and commitment to the sanctity of a male friendship
defined by the exclusion of women (and gay men) takes on a stark reality
in this assertion by young college-educated middle-class males. This in-

sight into male thinking contradicts the assumption that the discourse of male bonding is restricted to working-class lushes who hang out in the local bar or at amateur sporting events. Abusive male discourse, in a variety of forms, cuts across class barriers. Men bond around a joyful assertion of the exclusion and abuse of women, and frequently that subjugation gains legitimacy as it becomes "funnier."[9]

As he uncovers the emotional dynamics of male friendships, Lyman finds that jokes are never just stories, humor is never neutral. Jokes, in particular, provide "a theater of domination in everyday life, and the success or failure of a joke marks the boundary within which power and aggression may be used in a relationship" (150). This shared aggression toward an outsider allows a group to overcome internal tension and affirm its solidarity. For men, sexist jokes against women help to maintain the gender domination prevalent in all domains of men's lives.

Lyman also sees the joking relationship that governs much male bonding as a response to men's fear of work and of women. Men's resentment about the constraints imposed upon them by, for example, marriage and corporate America suggests that "sexist jokes may function as a ritual suspension of the rules of responsibility for men, a withdrawal into a microworld in which anger about dependence upon work and women may be safely expressed" (157). Jokes about women and money conflate these two anxieties: shopping jokes and jokes about women spending a lot of money, handing over the paycheck to the wife jokes, alimony jokes, and jokes about women as gold diggers all represent this form of humor. This form of humor, once so prevalent in public comedic discourse, is now largely confined to private jokes and exchanges between men.

A further function of men's sexist jokes is to forestall the possibility that some men might form intimate emotional bonds with women and withdraw from the group of men. In their humor men split intimacy off from sexuality to create what Lyman calls an "instrumental sexuality" that they direct at women. This eroticized male bond, this "erotic of shared aggression" among men (158), is directed at women as a means for men to remain in control of a life that they experience as more and more complex. Robin Williams makes fun of this by riffing on alcoholism and male bonding in beer commercials, which always show "manly men doing manly things: you've just killed a small animal, and now it's time for a light beer." And as men continue to drink, "the next thing you know you've got your friend in a headlock going, 'I love you, you little fucker, I love you'" (*Robin Williams*).

One significant facet of the complexity men face is the emotional aspect of male experience. Long considered the realm of the female, this is an area in which many men feel powerless. (The feminist comedian Elayne Boosler [*Showtime*] plays off exactly this aspect of the male experience when she tells her audience emphatically that she knows what men want: "They want to be really close to someone who will leave them alone.") As outsiders to the emotional, and thus frequently overwhelmed by this human dimension, men fight back with ridicule and sarcasm. By deriding the emotional, men assert some kind of control over it, and this allows them to feel a little more secure about the legitimacy of what they believe to be an omnipotent masculinity.

Many men prefer to remain adolescents (a charge leveled against men for any number of reasons), and it is true that male humor often resonates with a sexuality frozen at the emotional level of the teenage boy. It may not be coincidental that adolescence is also the point in psychological development when "sexual jokes are more than just frequent" (Ziv, 17). Adolescent male sexuality abundantly reflects a consciousness about sex and sexuality fraught with fear, confusion, and shame. Many adult men retain this ignorance and insecurity about their sexuality and find in the cover of laughter a safe haven in a world beset with complication and emotional confusion. Teenage boys who make jokes about sex, and laugh at their lack of experience as a means of maintaining their position as virile heterosexual men, may be forgiven some of their sexist humor; they are but boys after all, and they will outgrow this stupidity. Adult men, on the other hand, for whom sexist humor becomes misogynist, homophobic, and violent (against anyone who is not clearly a heterosexual macho male), ought not be forgiven for giving vent to so pathetic and destructive a masculinity.

Can humor make a contribution to eradicating this kind of injurious male behavior, or is humor intrinsically conservative and oppressive? Does humor have to injure someone to make us laugh? Can there be a humor that does not require a victim? These are tough questions but ones that force us to think about the potential for humor to be a progressive force.

Theorists of humor from Henri Bergson to Charlie Chaplin have stressed the educational quality of humor and suggest that, in pointing out the absurdities of everyday life, humor can help to reform the world. Chaplin, according to Ziv, believed that comedy can "sharpen our sensitivity to the perversions of justice within the society in which we live" (40). Although Chaplin was far more concerned with class than with gender, clearly he saw humor as a means to transform society's abusive and reactionary tendencies. As does Robin Williams. Speaking of South Africa in the days of apartheid, he says, "Pretty soon Lester Maddox will have to go over there. He'll say, 'Mr. Botha, Mr. Botha, let me explain something to you. There are fourteen million blacks here and three million whites. Does the name Custer mean anything to you?'" (*Robin Williams*).

As I tried to demonstrate earlier in this chapter, the general assertion that humor functions as a source of valuable information is both problematic and self-serving. As Karl Marx points out in the third thesis on Feuerbach, we cannot ignore the issue of who educates the educator. In the case of humor (as is true for almost all education), the educator usually reflects the ranks of those in power. With humor the education derives overwhelmingly from the male point of view that reinforces the basic social assumption of women's inferiority.

Some contemporary theorists of humor remain skeptical about the potential for humor to become a form of effective resistance to the status quo of male power. Powell, for example, understands the problematic nature of the use of humor by the powerless to effect any real change. He claims that, ultimately, radical humor may amount to nothing but "a 'resigned' expression and 'cheerful' demonstration of the subordinate's very weakness" (103). But Powell's pessimism ignores some rather significant evidence that a radical, even transformative, humor already flourishes. The political cartoon, for example, has been a vital source of a radical humor (e.g., Herblock, Feiffer, Garry Trudeau, and Tom Toles, and certainly for feminist humor, Nicole Hollander, bulbul, and Etta Hulme). Indeed, the mere existence of women stand-ups of high quality and persuasiveness like Lily Tomlin, Kate Clinton, Whoopi Goldberg, Tracey Ullman, Rita Rudner, Ellen DeGeneres, Elayne Boosler, Brett Butler, and others represents a reformation of the humor scene that has begun to rob male misogyny of its monopoly on sexual humor.

Humor remains, if not the only weapon of the oppressed, certainly one of the more powerful sources of retaliation. Bertice Berry, a stand-up comic, sees "the common denominator of laughter [as a great source] of power" (Warren, *Revolutionary Laughter*, 25), and Kaufman believes that "feminist humor, insofar as it indicates (or inspires) change, is obviously concerned with the transfer of power from those who have it overwhelmingly to those who have too little" (viii).

With these caveats in place, humor in general, and satire in particular, have been and continue to be potent vehicles for political consciousness raising. Comedy can take issue with the status quo and pour out ridicule on prejudice: Moliere's *School for Wives*, Fielding's *Tom Jones*, and even, in its way, Wilde's *The Importance of Being Earnest*.[10] Today a satire of masculinity that raises men's consciousness about the ludicrous inadequacy of their beliefs about women would certainly be a step in the right direction. David Mamet's scathing satire of men's roles in *Sexual Perversity in Chicago* represents one attempt to expose men's more hostile behavior toward women, even if the play is at times too heavy-handed and certainly not very funny. But satire can be funny, and when it succeeds it disempowers those who assume a position of superiority. Kate Clinton, the well-known lesbian feminist comedian, points out that "there is a window of vulnerability that opens up when people are laughing. They let down their guard and new ideas can come in" (Warren, *Revolutionary Laughter*, 54).

Satires of masculinity that allow men to laugh at themselves, and in that way learn about the glaring contradictions in their relationships with women, could raise men's consciousness and change their behavior. These satires by men are disappointingly few, although Dave Barry and some of the work of Garrison Keillor represent a promising trend.

Ridicule may provide a further potent weapon against male domination. Although ridicule is almost always the prerogative of the powerful, it might also be used sympathetically, not just punitively. Wilson alludes to a "forgiving ridicule" that a group might use "as an alternative to more extreme sanctions." The ridicule would "mark and criticize the social offense without being severely punitive to the offender" (Wilson, 206–7). A humor that excoriates men for their sexist and homophobic behavior would simply ostracize the jokers. Brett Butler quotes Pat Robertson as saying, "AIDS is God's way of controlling the homosexual population." Adds Butler: "Like, right, they reproduce like bunnies" (*Brett Butler*). But women cannot do it alone. Here men must take an active role in ridiculing their male buddies.

Some feminist humor already relies on ridicule. Butler, star of the now defunct TV sitcom *Grace under Fire,* acknowledges that she is "comfortable with humor that often makes others uncomfortable." She remarks on how guys watch fishing shows as if both narrative and suspense are involved. Two guys in a boat, repeatedly casting and reeling in, turn to each other and say, "'It don't get no better than this.' Apparently they've never seen a nipple up close before" (*Brett Butler*). Joy Behar sees "a dick joke [as] a beautiful thing" (Warren, *Revolutionary Laughter,* 39, 15). If more humor ridiculed the male fixation on sexual performance as a race to the finish line, and men's conviction that more is better in all aspects of their lives, men might well begin to rethink some of their assumptions about themselves as men. One example of this kind of "progressive ridicule" is evident as a recurrent theme in much contemporary feminist humor about the absence of men from and their ignorance of women's experiences of orgasm.[11] This kind of critique, couched in a humorous mode, might suggest to men the desirability of slowing down and making love in a way that is attentive to their partners' needs.

In fact, a humorous theme that identifies men's ignorance of the male orgasm would be a major contribution to men's sexual liberation. More humor about the ways men oppress themselves might contribute to men's becoming more cognizant of the ways in which they abuse their own sexuality. A male humor that laughs at power, its institutionalization, and its myths would help all of us to move beyond self-hatred and alienation. Robin Williams's famous line—"God gave man a brain and he gave man a penis . . . and, unfortunately, only enough blood to run one system at a time"—exemplifies this kind of humor.

Although some seem to suggest that this alternative humor is the responsibility of the women's movement, I believe that the creation of a radical humor has to be the responsibility of men as well.[12] Unfortunately, men's contribution to a humor of liberation does not so far appear to be forthcoming. With the exception of Robin Williams, Billy Crystal, Eric Bagosian, Sinbad, Alan Alda, and maybe Steve Martin, it remains difficult to think of many mainstream male comics whose comedy does not succumb to sexism, racism, or homophobia (or all three).[13] The popularity of such sexist and homophobic comedy presented by entertainers like Eddie Murphy, Howard Stern, and Andrew Dice Clay suggests that the appeal of these kinds of jokes is still quite widespread.

So long as humor remains predominantly male humor, a humor of aggression and victimization, a humor of the oppressor, progressive social change will be hampered. Feminist humor represents a clear alternative to a masculine humor of injury and exploitation. We need more humor like George Carlin's and Dick Gregory's that ridicules those in power and exposes the evils of American society: a humor that extends beyond the individual inconveniences of middle-class existence and reveals how capitalism, patriarchy, and religious fundamentalism work together to perpetuate sexism, racism, and homophobia. We need a humor expressed in public discourse and mirrored in private discourse that focuses on the complicity of these institutions in the advocacy of greed and individualism as basic human values, a humor that illuminates how crime, drug addiction, and the homeless are products of this society, not aberrations. We need a humor that exposes how, in the United States, more minority men are either in prison or in the army than have jobs. We need a humor that shows how violence against women and gay men continues as unabated underpinnings of this society.

In this way humor can transcend the insidious and become overt; humor can express the evils of American society and the contradictions that produce these social ills. The most enduring works of American humor have done just that (e.g., Twain, Parker, Vonnegut).[14] A humor that asks us to think about the powerful and not blame the weak and disenfranchised, a humor of sexual and social liberation, would focus our attention on growth and change, not a celebration of the "normal" and "natural."

It is possible that humor can only oppress and victimize and injure and that the task of sexual and social liberation may be beyond humor's reach. Maybe humor can serve only as an activity for us to critique and through that critique better understand where we are in relation to social change and progress. But it is also possible that humor can do more, that humor can build, and create, and take us somewhere we have never been before.

I want to believe that humor is a potent political weapon against the status quo in all its manifestations. I want to believe that if we ridicule enough men in enough bars, we will change the way they think about women and about themselves; I want to believe that one great wave of satire of male heterosexuality might bring down the patriarchy. But I don't want to be naive. I will settle, therefore, for a humor that reaches out to those who are victims, rather than just continuing to make new ones.

# 7 From Theory to Practice
## New Metaphors of Masculinity

> In the search for new definitions of masculinity and femininity the first task is to challenge received wisdom, received symbols and the metaphors which explain and justify the traditional patterns.
> —Helen Haste, *The Sexual Metaphor*

> To stand outside of heterosexual ideology and to develop an alternative way that male-female relationships could exist is an incredibly creative act.
> —Jonathan Ned Katz, *The Invention of Heterosexuality*

> Metaphor, deliberately invoked, intensifies language's characteristic activity, and involves, quite literally, the creation of "new" reality.
> —Terence Hawkes, *Metaphor*

Part of the motivation behind this project is the assumption that if we understand the sources of these terms, their history, and the complexity of their meanings, we will begin to comprehend the insidiousness of their usage. Within this broad critical context we can begin to re-create the language with which we discuss our sexuality and our identities as men.

While the development of progressive forms of humor might constitute one major contribution to changing men's roles, the creation of new metaphors could have positive consequences as well. As should be clear by now, language, and discourse in particular, do not exist in a vacuum. In order to invent an original discourse of male sexuality we need to revise some of the fundamental social experiences constructing manhood. If we were to reconceptualize our situation with work, for example, an oppositional vision of masculinity could emerge. A ubiquitous metaphor for masculinity other than the machine would also introduce a different conception of manhood.

Male sexuality is not separate from men's experience as human beings, and in a society where competition, greed, and being on top dominate the way we relate to the world around us, these governing social values are the source of the metaphors we create about our lives and the lives of others. New metaphors require broad new cultural experiences, and the way one conceives of work affects profoundly the range of alternatives we can identify for our lives as men. Kai Erikson poses a provocative question when he asks, "Are we ready to move into a world where the way one plays, the way one consumes, the way one volunteers or helps out or raises children can supply identity and a feeling of usefulness?" (12). Men spend a large proportion of their waking hours at work, and that encounter structures their vision of themselves as men. Erikson suggests a new conception of manhood derived from a unique understanding of work.

In their efforts to revitalize work into a more humane and cooperative experience, men can affect who they are as men. Out of these new circumstances can emerge different metaphors for their involvement with work. The juxtaposition of craftsmanship and the artisan to the alienating experience of work as routinized drudgery alters our conception of work. A sense of work that involves creativity and play, and one with a strong commitment to cooperation, would change radically the construction of American manhood. If men were taught to help each other build the better mouse trap rather than destroy each other on the way up the corporate ladder, our view of manhood would be altered radically. While some progress has been made in this direction, especially since the influence of the counterculture of the 1960s, a dominant competitiveness still informs much behavior in American society. Sadly, this kind of behavior is not restricted to men, though they do seem to be strongly affected by a desire to win and to be a success. There are exceptions, however: the growing number of young men choosing to work at home and be househusbands, who are truly active as care givers to the children, or the artisan master-carpenter, suggest movement toward a new conception of masculinity as opposed to victory at any cost.

These are not new ideas, of course. In the early 1950s the American sociologist C. Wright Mills articulated a notion of work centered around play and craft: "The simple self-expression of play and the creation of ulterior value of work are combined in work-as-craftsmanship. The craftsman or artist expresses himself at the same time and in the same act as he creates value. His work is a poem in action. He is at work and at play in the same act" (12). When work becomes creative, satisfying, and playful, men will be better prepared to see their sexuality as an artistic, creative activity and approach "sexual ability" as a craft rather than as a product.

An emphasis on cooperation rather than competition can help us restructure all the ways we conceptualize social roles, whether as men or as women. A society based on cooperation could jettison the heterosexual/homosexual division, for example, because there would no longer be a need for heteros to stand above homosexuals "in a social hierarchy of superior and inferior pleasures" (Katz, 187). That is, a society built on equality among all genders and all races, a society based on cooperation among all its citizens, would be a society capable of true tolerance and authentic liberation.

A discourse of masculinity suffused with metaphors of concern for the whole person as a subject possessing qualities of quiescence and calm, sensuality, beauty, and care would engender a very different conception of manhood and of male heterosexuality from the one examined in this book. This is not to suggest, as Ellen Willis warns against in her discussion of pornography and erotica, a view of sex that is sentimental and goody-goody or that love making should be restricted to being "beautiful, romantic, soft, nice and devoid of messiness, vulgarity, impulses to power, or indeed aggression of any sort . . . [or that] the emphasis should be on relationship not (yuck) organs" (224). What I am proposing, though, is the necessity for men to think about love and sexual pleasure in ways that are not exclusively possessive, controlling, dominating, and alienating.

Central to this project of reimagining masculinity lies the realization that much of our social reality is understood in metaphorical terms, and "since our conception of the physical world is partly metaphorical, metaphor plays a very significant role in determining what is real for us" (Lakoff and Johnson, 146). Although changing the metaphors we live by is a monumental task, in order to create new metaphors we must do no less than seize the language. We must write our own poetic discourse of masculinity and create new and positive speech to describe our lives as men.

Although the terms examined here represent only part of the discourse of male bonding, they are a powerful component of it nonetheless. Male hatred is obvious in this language, a language that pervades the way men relate to women, to other men, and even to themselves. Men poeticize their sexual activities as a way to cover guilt and to hide fear. In the metaphors analyzed in this book men strive to conceal their desire, their passion, and thus their vulnerability as they objectify their sexuality as a way to control it. This form of "masculine poetry" derives from certain assumptions about manhood and male desire, which expose a deep ambivalence about male heterosexuality.

Indeed, several tropes examined here have double meanings, characterizing male heterosexuality in a positive (or at least powerful) light while having negative connotations. Most notably, "dick," "prick," and "cock of the walk" exemplify this confusion, but metaphors possessing an economic subtext also reduce masculinity to a regressive common denominator. When love has a "bottom line" and gonads are equated with expensive gems, male heterosexuality turns into a cost-effective experience in need of a tally sheet and maybe even insurance. The overwhelming emphasis on performance and the portrayal of the penis as a mechanical device, whether tool or weapon or machine in need of manipulation and repair, reduces masculinity to values of hardness, power, and control.

Men are victims of this heteronormative discourse of masculinity, a discourse that acts as a policing action wherein men control the behavior of other men and reduce male conduct to a homogeneous behavior. This situation raises the questions of how (or why) men who adopt this language and rely on this misogynist discourse continue to create relationships with women and what effect this language has on those relationships.

Fitzgerald points out that "men who feel that they have to be different from both women and homosexual men construct an oppositional identity, an identity based on negative (opposite) poles, rather than positive ones" (112). He ponders the costs and benefits of this kind of "a 'view of sexual self' . . . so negatively formulated" (121). Michael Kimmel sees this male behavior as men viewing themselves as "martyrs for the male role." He suggests that only when men come to understand the extent of the negative consequences of relying on an oppositional identity for their sense of self will personal change for men become possible.[1]

Our refusal to be complicit in any form of misogyny would be a powerful form of resistance to the regime of male bonding and the practical manifestations of this discourse. But we cannot be naive about how difficult this task will be. As Lefkowitz makes clear in his study of the suburban gang rape in Glen Ridge, parents, teachers, social workers, ministers, and law enforcement agencies can easily conspire around a code of silence that allows them to believe that insensitive and even cruel behavior by boys against girls does not exist. This denial is not unique to one New Jersey suburb, however. According to Lefkowitz, "Schools across the country just didn't think the everyday treatment of girls by boys was a serious issue that merited discussion among faculty and students" (79). This conspiracy of silence haunts us all.

One strategy for opposition to these kinds of destructive portrayals is to confront our friends about the phrases they use when referring to women and to men. This may force us to refuse to bond with sexist, and in this case, misandric language. Many of us have become sensitive to racist jokes and some of us even refuse to give our consent to those who tell them. We do not laugh at racist jokes even though our resistance to this kind of humor may make us appear to be antisocial.

I confess that I find it more difficult to not bond with sexist humor than to reject racist humor, but that probably says something about me and about where the "nonsexist movement" is historically. Remembering that feminists who have over the years refused to laugh at misogynist jokes have earned the appellation of humorless may empower me to join this defiant contingent. Maybe by identifying how our language oppresses me as a man, maybe by seeing myself as a victim of this discourse, I will be more eager to defend myself against this particular tyranny. Although, as Carol Cohn points out, "to have the strength of character and courage to transgress the strictures of both professional and gender codes and to associate yourself with a lower status is very difficult" (231), this kind of confrontation is certainly one place to begin.

Another potent area of confrontation is the political arena and in particular the legal field. As Frank Mort asserts, "The law must remain a central arena for struggle and contestation over sexuality" (49). All of us need to be vigilant in opposing any legislative attempts to control sexuality in general and, in this day and age, especially legislation aimed at homosexuals and at women's bodies. We should not be naive about the significance of new repressive legislation, and we should be active in our support of laws that provide equal rights to all, regardless of sexual preference, race, religion, gender, or age. Political struggle is crucial, and we should not underestimate the importance of even small changes. If we wish in all seriousness to get the government out of the bedroom, at the top of our list of human rights should be abortion rights, the rights of single parents, women's rights in general, and the right of gay couples to marry and share benefits such as health, retirement, and insurance.

The task this book sets forth, however, culminates in the necessity of identifying different metaphors that describe masculinity in a positive way. Badinter urges us to "sing the praises of masculine virtues . . . [such as]: self-control, the desire to surpass oneself, a love of risk and challenge, and resistance to oppression" (184), and even Pat Califia, the guru of lesbian sadomasochism, has some nice things to say about masculinity. After providing such necessary qualifying remarks as "men are not my favorite critters," and pointing out that "straight men can be crude, violent, hateful, misogynist and insensitive," Califia praises the fact that men "*do* things":

> They go out in the world and work. They make things. They compete with one another without getting bitchy. And when they want to, they can cooperate on teams or in packs to play games or hunt. Men take it for granted that they have to protect their stuff. They are capable of being caretakers. And when ugly and scary things start to happen, men know they have to get off their asses and go meet fire with fire. They are physically brave in a way most women can't imagine. (96)

While it is certainly reassuring that not all male characteristics are reprehensible, men's ability to be brave, to win wars, and to succeed at competitiveness all come back to their obsession with power. So even despite Califia's kind words (which buy in to some traditional stereotypes), as Fitzgerald points out, "it is difficult to break the cultural pressure to make our lives as males fit the metaphors that give the imagery of power to our existence" (117). Men need to establish specific metaphors that provide a new vision of masculinity.

If a new conception of work can change the way men conceive of themselves as social beings, the river as an alternative to the machine metaphor might affect the way we imagine ourselves as men. I conceive of the river not in its Huck Finn motif as a source of escape from responsibility but as a fluid, sustaining, vital image of masculinity. In place of the metaphor of the machine, the river provides an organic, exciting, moving, and changing conception of manhood. With its flowing channels, plunging waterfalls, and deep ravines, the river suggests a masculinity that is dynamic, forceful, and receptive. The languid marshlands and the plummeting whirlpools, racing currents, and serene bays allude to a sexuality based on periods of both activity and rest. The flowing, surging, rippling river with its islands, beaches, and sandbars presents an image of manhood associated with vitality, subtlety, and complication, that is, a masculinity that appreciates the dynamic in life, the give and take, the complexities, dangers, and satisfactions.

The river introduces the heron as an alternative to the woodpecker as a metaphor for the erect penis. Although I am convinced that the new discourse of masculinity has to de-emphasize the penis altogether, and certainly the erect penis as the site of male sexuality, we cannot deny that a male erection is one source of pleasure.

The quiet gracefulness of the heron as it lifts off the ground and soars into the sky presents an image of a penis that arises slowly and calmly, not abruptly and with a vengeance. In her short story, "A White Heron," Sarah Orne Jewett describes this bird as "a single floating feather [that] grows larger and rises . . . with [a] steady sweep of wing and outstretched slender neck and crested head" (678). A penis that soars quietly like a feather and then glides softly before landing on the wet shoreline to blend into the marshland suggests a gentle, indistinct presence.

The otter, another inhabitant of the river, provides an alternative metaphor to such dominant male labels as jock and stud. As a graceful, furry, and lustrous animal that plays and swims and frolics, the otter suggests a masculinity intent on joyful exuberance.

Seamus Heaney captures many of these qualities in his poem, "The Otter," where he describes a "fine swimmer's back and shoulders / surfacing and surfacing again." As the lover sits on shore, "dry-throated on the warm stones," he or she experiences the "the slow loadening / When I hold you now / We are close and deep / As the atmosphere on water." With its "palpable, lithe / Otter of memory / In the pool of the moment," this beautiful and graceful animal turns to swim on its back, "Each silent, thigh shaking kick / Re-tilting the light / Heaving the cool at your neck." The otter moves suddenly "intent as ever / Heavy and frisky in your freshened pelt." As a strong, muscular swimmer who dives under water only to surface with the intensity of love and passion, the otter represents a playful winsome lover who is both supple and sincere. As it splashes around in the river, it reminds its lover on shore of its beauty and its sensitivity.

As a metaphor for masculinity, the otter appears also in Kerry Greenwood's short story, "Salmancis," where the male lover is described in the following way: "Sleek as an otter, with green eyes like chips of emerald, strong fingers, a sweet mouth. His kisses are deep. I can feel his eyelashes flutter as he opens his eyes against my breasts" (65). Here the otter possesses a silken smoothness not unlike the penis itself, and its eyes are beautiful and transfixing. The strength of its hold is matched by the intensity of its affection, and its touch is sensual and exciting. The otter gives masculinity a playful enthusiasm matched by a soft richness.

Water in general and the moist in particular offer another source of masculine imagery. A masculinity that celebrates the moist as a nice place to be, as a source of life and pleasure, suggests a manhood derived from pliancy and appeasement. The river reminds us that what is moist is beautiful, powerful, and gentle. While it is true that you can drown in a river, it is also true that you can float and swim and dive below the surface. As metaphors for male heterosexuality, these activities offer a conception of manhood more diverse, playful, and sensitive to the other than the ones with which we are most familiar. Indeed, the soft and the moist suggest the penis after ejaculation when male tumescence is disempowered, and the penis is at rest. This tranquil moment, when the man is both worn out and satisfied, produces a peaceful image of masculinity.

In everyday language the juxtaposition of flaccid to erect dominates and limits the way we can think about male sexuality. Metaphors that deemphasize the necessity for the penis to be rigid are a welcome source of liberation from that lie. These two conceptions of the penis do not have equal status, however. The flaccid penis equates with impotence while the "hard-on" symbolizes male sexuality or potency with all that term connotes. When "cooked spaghetti" becomes an acceptable metaphor for the penis and replaces such phrases as "hard-on" and "dick," we will have made progress in reconstituting the way we think about male sexuality.

Words like "quaggy," "flabby," "droopy," "limpy," "weary," "puny," "slumpy," and "silky" (a new seven [or eight] dwarfs) can replace "prick," "dick," "pecker," "hard-on," and "tool." "Quaggy" has little poetic resonance, and related as it is to "quagmire," it means, literally, "like a marsh, soggy" (*AHCD*, 1012). When, however, the penis can be accepted as soft and wet, and even irrelevant to sexual pleasure, men and women will be able to enjoy love making in a more subtle, more tactile, more polymorphous way. An emphasis on the silky softness of the penis (even when hard), a consideration of its condition when droopy and limp, as having the same importance as when turgid, would refocus the way we talk about one aspect of male sexuality.

A reliance on the experience of touch, as in "I was touched last night" instead of "I got laid last night," suggests a more positive way of conceiving the experience of making love. To touch or "the touch," expresses what is sensuous and erotic in the experience, in contrast to the jabbing, the poking, and the driving forward of "getting a nut off."

In her nationwide study of female sexuality, Shere Hite found that one of the most basic changes women would welcome in physical relations "involves valuing touching and closeness just for their own sakes—rather than only as a prelude to intercourse or orgasm" (553). Women are not alone in this preference. According to Badinter, in a recent survey of men a majority reported that "they wanted to be warmer, gentler, and more loving, and that they despised aggressivity, competition, and sexual 'conquests'" (143).

The moment when two bodies come together—as orgasm, yes, but through touch as well—identifies a different source of pleasure. When your skin brushes gently across another's, and when your body caresses ever so lightly your lover's body, that is a wonderful, exciting, and delightful sensation. The emphasis on tactile sensitivity that the word "touch" suggests offers the basis for a positive discourse of sexual experience. To fondle or stroke your lover stresses a delicate intimacy quite different from penetration and urgency.

"Melt" as an alternative conception of making love also counters the notion of penetration that pervades our thinking about heterosexual pleasure while focusing on the mutuality of the experience. Although as a slang term "melt" is a synonym for ejaculation (Spears, 285–86), "to melt" literally means "to change from a solid to a liquid state, generally by heat; to dissolve, to disintegrate . . . [and] to merge gradually . . . soften; make or become gentle and tender" (*Webster's,* 917). In this conception "melt" becomes a term emphasizing a mutual coming together, an embrace, and a commingling.

Another potential avenue for changing the way we talk about ourselves might be derived from different flower metaphors. We all know about "pansy" and its homophobic use, but maybe we should look at other flowers as metaphors for masculinity. Ginu Kamani, in her short story "Swollen Tide," refers to the erect penis as a flower when she describes the following scene: "Plainly visible for all to see was the rigid straining organ of a newborn male, so milky translucent on Omi's dark skin, so pure and innocent between her rounded feminine thighs that it could be mistaken for a flower" (122). This beautiful story of Shiva, the Hindu god of creation and destruction, depicts the annual rebirthing of its lingam, or phallus. This miracle, dislodged from "orange petals" (121), provides a metaphor of androgyny while suggesting "a manifestation of power and love" (122).

In our own rather mundane world, among the subgroups of wildflowers identified by the Audubon Society (Niering and Olmstead), "elongated clusters" provide the best source for metaphors of erection. "He had such a wonderful blazing star" might provide a transitional metaphor for men who are still a bit reluctant to cavalierly jettison the erection fixation. Then we could introduce the metaphor of the common mullein or the nodding trillium as a step toward ridiculing the necessity to always have an erection and, more positively, toward emphasizing the beauty of the flaccid penis. My own favorite alternative metaphors might go something like this: "His downy false foxglove was so gentle and soft I hardly knew it was there," or "He has such a wild lupine (with its blue and red veins) that I was transfixed by its beauty."

Another option might be to "liberate" the pansy metaphor. We could silk-screen a t-shirt that says something like: "We are all pansies."

How much, though, do you know about the pansy? Pansies are richly colored annuals that serve as a border along sidewalks or in front of a home. They are short stocky flowers, and they are fairly hardy. This is not a bad metaphor for masculinity, when you stop to think about it. Maybe the t-shirt should read: "You should be so lucky as to be a pansy," or "You think you're a pansy? Prove it."[2]

The point, of course, is that we often speak without really knowing what we mean. We need to look beyond the given and ascertain what would work better, how to speak more accurately and more positively. Men have to assume the responsibility for re-creating the language of masculinity. The discourse of heterosexuality pervades our society and our culture in such a way as to make it difficult for the victims, women and men, to transcend it easily. We must be vigilant and critical if we are to invent a truly new language of male sexuality.

In order to do this "men need a kind of courage that is only exhibited by those who have no doubts at all about their manhood—and that is the courage to assert their humanity" (Komisar, 142). Men need to see themselves as sensuous caring human beings, and to facilitate that consciousness we need to do no less than to seize the language.

Indeed, the politics of everyday speech suggest that we can change our language and that we can imagine new metaphors. We can reimagine masculinity by creating a new way to describe manhood and to live as men. Men must, as Paul Smith recommends, write "our imaginary" (37). This new image of masculinity cannot be ahistorical or, as in the case of Robert Bly and his compatriots, transhistorical. The metaphors of the warrior and the king are reactionary. They rely on retrograde images of masculinity and move us backward rather than forward.[3]

We should not underestimate the power of metaphor to help us imagine a new masculinity. In place of the warrior, the machine, and the businessman/husband, metaphors of the gardener, the artisan, the guide can help move men beyond the current belief in the importance of competition, aggression, and rigidity as central to the masculine experience. Men can share a vision of masculinity informed by equality, not rivalry, caring about other human beings, not subordinating as many people as possible. When these assumptions inform male heterosexual behavior, a masculinity different from today's notion of manhood, which is structured around assumptions of superiority and conquest, can emerge. A discourse of male–male relationships that does not exclude women and is not concerned with bonding at all will further our struggle against the irrationality of unquestioning submission to misogyny and homophobia. A discourse of affinity, compassion, and cooperation will allow men to create a masculinity based on love, not war, a masculinity of hope, not despair, a masculinity of sharing and caring and tenderness.

# Notes
# References

# Notes

### Introduction

1. Although the subtitle of my book echoes that of Lakoff and Johnson, I do not follow their methodology closely at all. Their approach to metaphor relies on quite specific linguistic mappings from an identified, explicitly language-linked Source Domain to an explicitly language-linked Target Domain. The metaphors I examine are categorized more loosely by the domains of experience from which they are drawn or to which they most centrally relate. Thus the book is in no way intended as a contribution to cognitive linguistics.

In tracing the metaphors to their original domains, I try to elucidate their implications for our understanding of ourselves as men. In a sense, this represents an analysis of key metaphors, and the domains to which I assign these metaphors, especially sports, work, and war, are the key metaphor domains of masculinity in American English.

2. I wish to thank James Armstrong for pointing out the necessity to clarify my position on the relationship between discourse and cultural behavior. He provided this and other helpful insights in his thorough and critical reader's report.

3. Hawkes points out that for Landar, language "expresses . . . the manner in which society as a whole represents the facts of experience" (81).

4. See de Beauvoir, *The Second Sex,* where she examines a variety of ways in which women have been complicit in their oppression. Bourdieu also makes the point that "the language of authority never governs without the collaboration of those it governs, with the help of the social mechanisms capable of producing this complicity, based on misrecognition, which is the basis of all authority" (113).

5. See Lakoff and Johnson, p. ix, and Carol Cohn, p. 230.

6. The *Dictionary of American Regional English* maintains that this term is a common reference to female genitalia, especially in the American South: "It seems that 'cock' also has mixed references, depending on the region. At a point roughly the same as the Mason-Dixon Line, there is a division in meaning. . . . . Missouri is a border state in which both meanings are used" (Cassidy, 707).

7. Which is to say, the metaphors included in this book come from my memory of the language used by men as I was growing up. That is, I did not go through slang dictionaries to find phrases to analyze. This language has been part of my maturation as a man, not the result of a research project or a keyword search.

8. For an insightful look at gay men's English that focuses on the linguistic practices underlying gay men's conversations, see Leap. This text is helpful too as

a reference to other studies of gay language that have centered on vocabulary, word history, and folklore.

One question implicit in my book is, "What are the metaphors women live by?" Although I believe men should focus their attention on the ways in which they are affected negatively by a patriarchal society, this analysis should not be a monologue. Men still have a lot to learn about how their discourse oppresses women, and insights into particular metaphors aimed at women would help us to move beyond that kind of language.

Among the metaphors used to talk about women, especially in their relationship to men, are the following: "bitch," "broad," "cock teaser," "cunt," "gold digger," "maidenhead," "nymphomaniac," "slut," "tomboy," and "wife." This list is in no way exhaustive, but it provides a sense of how language constructs interpersonal relationships in another closely related context. For a comprehensive study of the "vocabulary of culture and patriarchal society" that focuses on the language of women's oppression, see J. Mills, and for an analysis of women in contemporary slang, see Sutton. For insights about lesbian discourse see Moonwoman-Baird and Queen.

Lines of cross-over from the discourse I examine and other ethnic groups might also be a rich area for analysis. How this discourse influences or is translated into rap music, for example, could provide insights into the depth and breadth of male bonding. Though nothing has been written specifically about this subject, for those interested in such concerns I recommend Costello and Wallace, and Rose.

Other cultural variations among different definitions of masculinity could broaden our understanding of the discourse of masculinity. For assistance with this particular topic, the reader should examine Brandes, Cornwall and Lindisfarne, and Gilmore. In the Cornwall and Lindisfarne book, I recommend Shire's essay on Zimbabwe in particular.

9. Before the early 1960s, with the publication of Black's *Models and Metaphors*, the significance of metaphor as a literary device had been all but ignored. Although its centrality to any poetics was made clear as early as Aristotle, and despite the crucial role metaphor played in the poetic vision of the Romantics, critics in the modern period have demonstrated an interest in it only relatively recently.

Since the early 1970s, however, metaphor has assumed far greater prestige as an important literary concern. Several provocative essays have been written, and books exclusively on metaphor have been published (e.g., Black, Booth, Bred, Cohen, Cooper, Culler, Eco, Embler, Frye, Lakoff and Johnson, Ricoeur, Ruegs, and S. Sacks, among others). For the most part this critical work focuses on literary metaphors while ignoring the metaphorical nature of everyday speech. At the same time much of the debate about metaphor centers on its significance in a wide range of tropes, most notably its relationship to metonymy, synecdoche, and irony (see White, in particular). In addition, analyses of the social construction of metaphors have come predominantly from anthropologists (e.g., Crocker, Fernandez, Quinn, and Sapir). All these thinkers recognize the importance of context for interpreting language.

10. See Fiedler's *Love and Death in the American Novel* (1960). Fiedler's classic study of representations of manhood in American literature has spawned many other studies. Millet's important critique of men and masculinity in literature,

*Sexual Politics,* has to be mentioned, and the first volume of Gilbert and Gubar's trilogy, *No Man's Land,* should not be ignored. For a collection of essays on the literary construction of masculinities, see my anthology, *Fictions of Masculinity: Crossing Cultures, Crossing Sexualities.*

11. Clearly, animals as a "source domain" for metaphor have an important place in cognition, and their appearance in metaphors for masculinity is not accidental. I have tried, though, within the themes I use, to examine the relationship of the metaphor to its animalistic connections.

12. See, for example, Faludi (*Backlash*), Gibson, and Nelson.

13. See Ayto and Simpson, Beale, Chapman, Spears, Thorne, and Wentworth and Flexner, in particular, although the *American Heritage College Dictionary* was also helpful.

### 1. Sex as Machine

1. Feminists today discuss the emergence of the "third wave" of American feminism. Profeminist men may wish to consider the American men's movement to be at least in its second wave. Michael Kimmel and Thomas E. Mosmiller's book, *Against the Tide: Profeminist Men in the United States, 1776–1990: A Documentary History,* makes a powerful case for the existence of a first wave of men conscious of and sympathetic to feminism long before the 1960s and 1970s. Many men associated with the profeminist men's movement may wish to distance themselves from the "I'm okay, you're okay" mentality pervading much of the writings from the early years of what I would refer to as the second wave of profeminist males (1960s to the present). Those ideas, and even Robert Bly's reactionary explorations, have to be seen as part of the evolution of men's thinking about the social construction of masculinity. Recently, profeminist men, both American and others (certainly British and Australian), have stopped apologizing for their involvement in the struggle for feminism, however, and the ways in which feminism radically elucidates the male experience.

Continued study of how men's positive engagement with feminism spans at least two centuries and constitutes a rich tradition will provide the profeminist men's movement with a sense of its positive contribution. *Against the Tide,* after all, focuses on American men and thus does not attempt to include many earlier (and later) European profeminist men (e.g., Condorcet, John Stuart Mill, William Godwin, Friedrich Engels, Havelock Ellis, and others). At a time when the loudest men tend to be right-wing demagogues, a heritage of profeminist men should be celebrated, not denied.

2. In her 1994 book, *The Sexual Metaphor,* Helen Haste traces "the equation of mechanism with masculinity [to] the Aristotelian definition of the soul" as well as "the Platonic view of knowledge being gained through the communion of equals" (74). For Plato, only men can be equals.

3. For more on this see Chang's *The Tao of Love and Sex.*

4. The stories by Kamani, Torr, Warden, Wertheim, and Yolen provide some excellent examples, as do the poems by Lifshin, especially "Years Later Lorena Thinks of the Penis She Had for a Day."

5. See, for example, Gilbert and Gubar's *The Madwoman in the Attic,* which

begins by posing the question, "Is a pen a metaphorical penis?" (3) and goes on rather quickly to suggest that "male sexuality . . . is not just analogically but actually the essence of literary power. The poet's pen is in some sense (even more than figuratively) a penis" (4).

6. Another metaphor, "whiskey dick," highlights this situation as a reference to a man's inability to get an erection because he has consumed too much alcohol. See the separate section on this metaphor in chapter 5.

7. Mumford observes: "In still another way did the institutions of the Church perhaps prepare the way for the machine: in their contempt for the body. Now respect for the body and its organs is deep in all the classic cultures of the past. . . . This affirmative sense of the body never disappeared, even during the several triumphs of Christianity. . . . But the systematic teachings of the Church were directed against the body and its culture: if on one hand it was a temple of the Holy Ghost, it was also vile and sinful by nature: the flesh tended to corruption, and to achieve pious ends of life one must mortify it and subdue it, lessening its appetites by fasting and abstention" (35–36).

For another, much more sophisticated and comprehensive analysis of this tradition, see Elaine Pagels.

8. Fasteau reinforces this observation when he characterizes "the posture that men often assume toward women, at least as they describe it to other men, [as tending] to be one of uninvolved mastery." Fasteau cites such phrases as "a cool bitch," a "groovy chick," and a "great piece of ass" as terms that "convey detachment, a relationship based on standardized assessment of a woman's assets rather than one's own feelings for her as a person" (61).

9. Although the Diagram Group's book, *Man's Body: An Owner's Manual,* was published in 1976, not much has changed since then. A recent book by Gilbaugh, *Men's Private Parts,* uses the subtitle, *An Owner's Manual.*

10. Frequently, men's health is more the responsibility of women (wife, lover, mother) than their own. Dr. Sarah Brewer's book, *The Complete Book of Men's Health,* exemplifies this situation with its tag line on the cover: "The Essential Guide of Men and Women." When was the last time you saw a book on women's health that was suggested as reading for men? Women are supposed to take responsibility for their health and their man's health, whereas men ignore their health and everyone else's. The myth of masculinity entails not only strength and potency but invincibility, sometimes to the point of insentience (literally and metaphorically).

11. Brewer takes the Kinsey report's analogy one step further and makes a not-so-subtle connection in her chapter called "Sex as Work/Business," when she maintains that "eventually, nature will take control and sperm past their sell-by date will be discharged via a nocturnal emission (wet dream)" (57).

12. Although Kinsey, Pomeroy, and Martin do not suggest it, a correlation may exist between the academic field in which one earns a doctoral degree and the frequency of wet dreams. Do doctoral degrees in English or psychology cause the greater number of nocturnal emissions? Are the experiences of political scientists or physicists, or philosophers or economists paradigmatic? This could be a rich field of study, indeed.

13. Kinsey, Pomeroy, and Martin find, for example, that "in the male, noctur-nal emissions or wet dreams are generally accepted as a usual part of the sexual picture" (518), and go on to assert, *in 1948,* that "by nearly all moral philosophies, nocturnal emissions provide the one form of sexual outlet for which the individual is least responsible" (527). Further, they maintain, "the condemnation of nocturnal emissions has not been great" (527).

Although wet dreams do not account for a large portion of men's orgasms, according to Kinsey, Pomeroy, and Martin, "a high percentage of males experience nocturnal emissions at some time in their lives" (519). Specifically, they find that wet dreams are most frequent before marriage and that "in all social groups, noc-turnal emissions are primarily an outlet of younger adolescent and older teen-age boys" (523). The incidence of wet dreams declines significantly "after age thirty and are largely out of the picture after age forty" (523).

14. Ellis, for example, suggests the following causal relationships: "Physical, mental, or emotional excitement, alcohol taken before retiring, position in bed (as lying on the back), the state of the bladder, sometimes the mere fact of being in a strange bed, and to some extent apparently by the existence of monthly and yearly rhythms" (117).

One explanation, seemingly popular at midcentury, maintained that "the nerve centers that control ejaculation are in the lower spinal cord, and [that] . . . sleeping on one's back . . . may increase the frequencies of emission" (Kinsey, Pomeroy, and Martin, 528). Other influences believed to affect the incidence of wet dreams ranged from tight clothing to a warm bed, but Kinsey hastens to point out that none of these relationships has been scientifically established.

### 2. Sex as Work and Labor

1. For a much more extensive history of work, see Tilgher, *Homo Faber: Work through the Ages,* and for a brief overview see De Grazia, *Of Time, Work, and Leisure.*

2. Here too I wish to thank James Armstrong for his helpful suggestions about how best to tighten my arguments about work in this chapter. While any remaining weaknesses are solely my responsibility, Professor Armstrong's critique helped me strengthen my position.

3. For a fuller discussion of this aspect of manhood, see Gould. This belief is matched by the convention that women are gold diggers and devourers of male substance.

4. See Tannen's book, *You Just Don't Understand,* for an extensive analysis of "conversational style differences between men and women" (14).

5. The relationship between ejaculating sperm and spending one's resources has been examined carefully by Barker-Benfield in his study of male attitudes to-ward women and sexuality in nineteenth-century America. In his book *The Hor-rors of the Half-Known Life,* he points out that "men believed their expenditure of sperm had to be governed according to an economic principle," a principle he refers to as "the 'spermatic economy'" (181).

6. For more on this see Reynaud, p. 43.

7. For instruction regarding this approach to male sexuality, see Chang's *The Tao of Love and Sex.*

8. See Lewis's observation that "to this day the phrase brings to my mind the image of an elephant's trunk swaying from side to side. Swish. Swash. Nothing in the jungle got in the way of the Big Swinging Dick" (46).

9. As a metaphor for women's anatomy, "plumbing" devalues it by suggesting the lower bodily functions of defecation and urination.

10. For more on love and sex as commodities that are reduced to the power of money to buy, see Marx's *Economic and Philosophical Manuscripts:* "That which is for me through the medium of money—that for which I can pay (i.e., which money can buy)—that I am, the possessor of the money. . . . What I am and am capable of is by no means determined by my individuality. I am ugly, but I can buy for myself the most beautiful of women. Therefore, I am not ugly, for the effect of ugliness—its deterrent power—is nullified by money" (167).

With this insight in mind, it becomes clear that the term "getting laid" is not just a harmless phrase. When we conceptualize an activity as intimate as sexual intercourse in such reified language, we reduce love and passion to that which can be bought and sold. In this discourse all love making becomes prostitution, a point several feminists have made over the past century (cf. de Beauvoir, Dworkin, Goldman, and Rubin, to name just four).

11. For more on men as victims see Goldberg, although there are many others.

12. For other examples and men's writing on this subject, see Kimmel and Mosmiller, pp. 323–34.

13. In an essay centered around poignant rhetorical questions about male heterosexuality, Stoltenberg addresses the significance of the male gaze in its reduction of the female body to an object of his possession and control. One paragraph in particular addresses what is no doubt the predominant heterosexual male experience with jerking off: "When with one hand a man is paging through a magazine, a magazine containing photographs of naked and nearly naked bodies, bodies posed with their genitals concealed and bodies posed with their genitals showing, bodies posed with props and with other bodies, bodies posed with their faces looking at the camera and not looking at the camera, bodies posed by a photographer to look available, accessible, takeable, in color and in black and white, and with his other hand is masturbating, and he is searching from picture to picture, searching from body to body, from part of body to part of body, from pose to pose, rhythmically stroking and squeezing and straining, seeking some coalescence of the flesh he is looking at and the sensations in his own, imagining his body and one of the bodies attached, joined tenderly or forcefully, and he masturbates until he is finished, and when he is done he is done looking, and he stores them away until next time, the magazines, the pictures, the bodies, the parts of bodies, what does that mean?" (42)

14. For more on Corn Flakes as breakfast saltpeter, see Kimmel's *Manhood in America,* where he suggests, "Corn Flakes, for example, were designed by J. H. Kellogg as a massive anaphrodisiac to temper and eventually reduce sexual ardor in American men" (129). For a humorous novel about Kellogg and the antisex movement, see T. Coraghessan Boyle's *The Road to Wellville.*

### 3. Sex as Sport

1. For two helpful general histories of sports that examine all four of these areas, see Mandell's cultural history of sports and Gorn and Goldstein on American sports. For an extensive analysis of the relationship between sports and work that "characterize[s] modern sports not as the heroic alternative to industrial-capitalist society but rather its mirror image," see Rigauer (ix). Focusing on "the achievement principle" in both sports and in work, Rigauer traces the ways in which "achievement has become a socially sanctioned model of behavior related to high productivity, economic competition, material rewards, vocational practice, and social mobility" (15). The literature on sports and misogyny is too copious to list here, but I suggest the work done by Messner and Sabo as a place to start, especially in light of the general theme examined in this book. For a smart, critical, insightful examination of one of the more overt examples of the male athlete's fear and hatred of women, I highly recommend Disch and Kane's essay on Lisa Olson's sexual harassment by members of the New England Patriots football team.

2. Sporting events in which animals are pitted against each other to fight to the death (e.g., cock fights and dog fights with pit bulls) also demonstrate the low regard with which many men view nature, and contribute to their sense of superiority over nature.

3. For more on locker-room exchanges as a source of shared male power see Disch and Kane, and Curry.

4. For a more recent example of how these feelings of superiority on the part of high school football players can turn into horrendous violence against women, see Lefkowitz's book on the gang rape of a retarded girl in Glen Ridge, New Jersey, where high school athletes violated the young woman with a broomstick and a baseball bat.

5. At about this same time "a new group of impatient, anti-genteel, sexually charged epithets . . . became popular," say Gorn and Goldstein (168–69), who credit the examples they cite to the author John Higham: "sissy," "pussyfoot," "cold feet," and "stuffed shirt."

6. I say more about this in the next chapter, "Sex as War and Conquest," but I suggest here that provocative insights into the language of the military-industrial complex as a masculine discourse can be found in Cohn's essay on "War, Wimps, and Women."

7. Fasteau observes that "sports is . . . one of the few things men feel they are allowed to become emotional about" (110), and Gorn and Goldstein maintain that "along with the ceremonies and conduct of war, sports in the public arena are the only place in which men are expected or permitted to express vulnerable emotions" (208).

8. Miller cites Pronger's notion of the "paradoxical play of masculinity" as developed in his important study of "the social construction of the myths of gender, sexuality, and athletics as they appear in contemporary North American and Northern European middle-class culture" (Pronger, 7). Focusing on "an interpretation of gay and athletic experience," Pronger uses sport as "a vehicle for explor-

ing the meaning of homosexuality [and] . . . more broadly, sex and gender in our culture generally" (ix).

9. For more on sex as a contest, see Komisar (138).

## 4. Sex as War and Conquest

1. As a freelance journalist, and not a professionally trained military historian, Ehrenreich brings a fresh perspective to the study of war that elicits unique insights into both why war began and why it persists. It is not necessary to agree with her thesis—that war originated as a response to humankind's experience as prey to large, ferocious animals, and that that experience is written in the roots of our memory—to appreciate her assertion that war continues because war is a self-perpetuating phenomenon; we fight wars because we have always fought wars.

2. Ehrenreich qualifies this observation, however, and reinforces her overall thesis when she points out that "man-the-hunter no doubt invented war; at least he invented the weapons of war. But for the tendency to sacralize violence—to ritualize the slaughter of animals and bring 'religious' feelings to war—we have to go back further, to a time when 'man' was an object of prey" (57).

3. Ehrenreich reinforces this point in her chapter "The Rough Male Sport" in a subsection entitled "Masculinity and War," where she observes how war is seen to have been "an inevitable outgrowth of male aggressiveness, with the weaponry, the thrust of spears and missiles, the piercing and explosions, all mimicking the phallic side of sex" (125).

4. For an excellent analysis of the role of women in (and around) war, see Elshtain.

5. Including gay men on a list with other supposedly dubious "real men," especially in the context of the armed services, is complicated by the history of gay men in the military. On the one hand, a tacit acknowledgment exists that gays (both men and women) constitute a major presence in the military and that they perform heroically. And yet at the same time an overt attempt to deny their contribution, and in many cases to expel them, dominates much of their experience.

6. Of course, the branch of the contemporary men's movement established by Robert Bly and his Jungian followers, a fairly conservative one as it turns out, endorses initiation of young boys into manhood through rituals constructed in an all-male weekend escape into the wilderness. Re-creating such male roles as warrior, king, and father-knows-best, these initiation rites both reinforce traditional male roles and seek to assuage men's anger at women for undermining their privilege. Even Gibson, in an otherwise fairly radical critique of the rise of paramilitary groups as attesting to a cultural need of many American men to wrest control of their lives from foreigners, women, and government bureaucrats, endorses the necessity to create new initiation ceremonies for young men (305). For Gibson these ceremonies create new kinds of adventures for boys (307–8) while endorsing new myths (306) and excluding women (307).

7. For an extensive analysis of how often and why adolescent and college-aged male athletes, especially those on football and wrestling teams, perpetrate crimes against women, see Lefkowitz.

8. The phrase "pelvic congestion" is a pseudomedical term describing a wom-

an's condition of being sexually stimulated for awhile and not getting release. But when was the last time you heard someone say "Oh, yeah, she was out with a new guy last night and got a terrible case of pelvic congestion"?

9. In addition to the women who taught me to shut up and listen, I want to acknowledge an important essay in my personal and political evolution: Bob Lamm's "Learning from Women" (1976). If you have not read this short essay, I urge you to do so.

10. This caveat echoes the same concerns U.S. feminists had during the 1980s and 1990s with the "purity" wing of the women's movement and the contemporary debate about pornography and erotica. Any suggestion of control of female sexuality has to be scrutinized carefully, as historically it has been used to deny female desire or to depict women as uncontrollable sexual monsters.

11. Fasteau reinforces this point when he observes that "the fastest way to provoke a demonstration of [macho] masculinity is to suggest that it is lacking, that its pretenders are 'faggots'" (154).

12. For a well-documented, thoughtful, and radical examination of another gang rape, this one in New Jersey, see Lefkowitz. And for yet one more example, this time in California and perpetrated by a group of adolescent boys who called themselves the Spur Posse, see Nelson.

13. Obermiller's article summarizes the findings of Edward Laumann, John Gagnon, Robert T. Michaels, and Stuart Michaels, published in a pair of books: *The Social Organization of Sexuality: Sexual Practices in the United States* (University of Chicago Press), and *Sex in America* (Warner). The former, according to Obermiller, "is written for social scientists, counselors and health professionals, while [the latter] . . . a collaboration with *New York Times* science writer Gina Kolata, is intended for a more general audience" (34).

### 5. Sex as Exclusively Heterosexual

1. I rely heavily on Katz's book for the introduction to this chapter as his study is both exhaustive and succinct. I want to acknowledge his important work here and recommend it to any reader interested in the subtle dynamics of how our ideas about homosexuality and heterosexuality have taken on many and varied definitions throughout the history of Western civilization.

2. The conception of heterosexuality as compulsory was introduced by Adrienne Rich in a 1983 essay; seeing it as a matrix comes from Judith Butler; Janet Halley describes its construction; and, as stated in note 1, Katz traces it as an invention. For Rich, heterosexuality needs to be seen as a political institution that encompasses "violent strictures [that are] . . . necessary to enforce women's total emotional, erotic loyalty and subservience to men. . . . These forces range from literal physical enslavement to the distorting of possible options" (182–83). Butler builds on Rich's conception of compulsory heterosexuality while focusing her attention on phallogocentrism, or how "language constructs the categories of sex" (ix). Butler's work introduces a subversive potential that can "enable a critical challenge to [the dominant] masculinist sexual economy" (x). I also want to mention the work of Gayle Rubin, whose early essay, "The Traffic in Women," is an important text on heterosexuality as an oppressive ideology, and I recommend

again Katz's book, which provides an excellent introductory overview of some of the more important classical works in the critical engagement with heterosexuality (e.g., Ti-Grace Atkinson and the Radicalesbians).

3. Badinter's book is not unproblematic, however. Her reliance on a couple of founding texts from the American men's movement gives the book the sense of being a survey rather than an important original contribution to the critical engagement with masculinity. In addition, her belief that "the problem of masculinity is less acute in France than elsewhere" (5) remains highly debatable. Even with these qualifications, though, Badinter's book is well worth reading for its insights into some subtleties surrounding the creation of manhood in contemporary society.

4. For a collection of interviews with men exploring "what men derive from their male friendships . . . what men admire in their friends, what they want from friendships, what stands in their way of making friends, or simply how widely they vary in their relationships with other men" (vii), see Maas. And for a critique of Maas's book see my 1989 review essay.

5. In addition to Badinter, see Hoch and Reynaud, to name just a few who make this point.

6. The methodology that relies on surveys of college students by the professor or by students or by a combination of the two seems to be gaining in popularity. For other examples see Cameron and Eble.

7. For Baldwin, according to Katz, "The macho men—truck drivers, cops, football players—these people are far more complex than they want to realize. That's why I call them infantile. They have needs which, for them, are inexpressible. They don't dare look into the mirror. And that is why they need faggots. . . . I think it is very important for the male homosexual to recognize that he is a sexual target for other men, and that is why he is despised, and why he is called a faggot. He is called a faggot because other males need him" (104).

8. I dedicate this section to Bill Clinton, who seems to exemplify this condition.

9. In modern French *pensée* means "pansy," the flower.

10. Through a critical engagement with interviews of lesbians from a variety of class and racial backgrounds, Weston problematizes the recurrent dichotomy between "fluff" (femme) and "stud" (butch). Pointing to the common problem lesbians face "by taking 'the' heterosexual male as her object of imitation" (81), Weston suggests that "'like a man' occupies a key position in the meager vocabulary available for talking about gender and power. It is a phrase thrown around all too lightly, never designed to bear the weight of complex negotiations or to cover such a multitude of situations" (80).

### 6. Insidious Humor and the Construction of Masculinity

1. Michael Mulkay, in his study of the nature and place of humor in modern society, observes the ways in which men use "analogues and metaphors . . . to make fun of women's bodies" (148). Ted Cohen's point about the necessity for there to be a community in which metaphors work remains pertinent, of course.

2. Lyman, in a case study of male humor gone awry in a fraternity-sorority exchange, a study I rely on later in this chapter, makes the point that when, as men

often do in their humor, they "combine sexuality and force it [is] terrifying to women" (152). While "terrifying" may be too strong a word, women can be scared by this kind of humor, and they certainly are disgusted and even repulsed by it.

3. Mulkay observes that "a male-centered conception of sexuality" dominates men's jokes along with "the notion of female stupidity which features widely in men's jokes about women" (150). Apte suggests that "according to a folk belief in American culture that is shared by both men and women, women cannot tell stories or jokes correctly" (75). Perhaps this has to do with an unshared notion of what is funny.

4. Professor Gutwirth shared this insight with me in a personal communication. Anyone interested in laughter and the comic would do well to read his book, *Laughing Matter: An Essay on the Comic.*

5. See Frances Gray, especially her introduction, for a detailed critique of the belief that "women have no sense of humor" (3), as well as some of the techniques used "to shut women out of the comic arena altogether" (8).

6. Apte provides some background for men's dominance of the public domain of humor in his anthropological study of humor and laughter: "Humor fairly reliably indicates the inequality of the sexes. Although women are no less capable of developing and appreciating humor than men, women have been denied similar opportunities for publicly engaging in humor. Because modesty, passivity, and virtue are associated with ideal womanhood, women have been confined to the private domain, with many constraints imposed upon them" (18). While Apte's study is fifteen years old and some things have changed, the fundamental truth he describes remains pretty much the same.

For an excellent example of this kind of restraint upon women see Mulkay's summation of James Spradley and Brenda Mann's, *The Cocktail Waitress,* an enlightening case study of the interaction between bartenders and female servers at a particular bar.

7. The idea that humor provides a much-needed medium for sexual education resonates with the suggestion that pornography is an important source of sexual information. If dirty jokes and pornography are the basis of men's sexual education, that might explain why so many of them are reportedly such lousy lovers.

8. Legman provides many critical insights into the use of the dirty joke as a means of social control. He points out, for example, that "under the mask of humor, our society allows infinite aggressions, by everyone and against everyone" (9). Regarding what he refers to as "the male approach," Legman maintains that "one fact strikingly evident in any collection of modern sexual folklore, whether jokes, limericks, ballads, printed novelties, or whatnot, is that this material has all been created by men, and there is no place in it for women except as the butt" (217). While there may have been changes in the past twenty-five years, the bulk of folk humor overwhelmingly retains the residue of this tradition. Unfortunately, Legman's insightfulness is often marred by his acute homophobia.

9. While slapstick may be one component of this "humor," victimization is certainly another aspect. Men laugh at women, whites laugh at blacks, straight people laugh at gays as a way to make clear their difference (and assumed superiority), but what makes violence funny at all remains an issue central to the question of what humor really is.

10. Here too I wish to thank Marcel Gutwirth for this observation.

11. A joke I heard recently exemplifies this theme:

A little girl comes running into the kitchen after school and asks her mother, "Mommy, Mommy, what's an orgasm?"

The mother thinks for a moment and then says, "I don't know, dear, ask your father."

There are many more of these kinds of jokes, all of which point to men's ignorance of the female orgasm.

12. One example of this kind of assertion comes from Michael Mulkay, who proposes the necessity for "the development of an 'alternative humour' [as] an important task to be faced by the women's movement" (150). In Mulkay's defense, though, his general work on humor supports an alternative view of humor that emphasizes its victimization of women. Although I doubt that Mulkay would oppose men's involvement in the development of an alternative humor, his statement does de-emphasize the need for men to be involved.

13. Not much radical humor by men exists. *King, Warrior, Magician, Weenie,* Peter Sinclair's collection of contemporary men's humor, promised to fill at least part of this void (not that one collection can do that much work, of course) but falls far short of the mark. Its failure as a collection of supposedly feminist humor by men may indeed be foreshadowed by its title. As an obvious reference to Robert Bly's reactionary mythopoetic men's movement, the source of Sinclair's humorous collection is clearly limited from the onset. Sinclair's book is published by the Crossing Press, the same house that puts out several collections of feminist humor edited by Roz Warren; one would think that a book of men's humor would live up to the same standard. Sadly, Sinclair's collection tells us more about the status of men's humor than we may wish to know.

14. For this insight I wish to thank Nancy Walker, who provided it in a personal communication. Anyone interested in women's humor and American culture should see her pioneering work, *A Very Serious Thing.* Also, those doing work in humor and American literature should see Neil Schmitz's smart and lucid study, *Of Huck and Alice.*

## 7. From Theory to Practice: New Metaphors of Masculinity

1. For further discussion of the masculine self based primarily on opposition, see Fitzgerald, and Kimmel's essay on rethinking masculinity in his anthology, *Changing Men.*

2. The t-shirt presents a powerful means to distribute alternative metaphors. For a sampling of progressive slogans already available on t-shirts, see Roz Warren's *Glibquips: Funny Words by Funny Women.* Women have used this forum to respond to at least one metaphor they live by: "I'm not a bitch, I'm THE bitch."

Other pertinent examples are "Okay, the joke is over—show me your real penis!" and "I don't sleep with men who've named their dicks."

3. For further discussion of Bly's reactionary position, see Murphy (review of *Iron John*) and Kimmel (*Politics of Manhood*).

# References

*American Heritage College Dictionary.* 3d ed. Boston: Houghton Mifflin, 1993.

Apte, Mahadev L. *Humor and Laughter: An Anthropological Approach.* Ithaca, N.Y.: Cornell University Press, 1985.

Arendt, Hannah. *The Human Condition.* Chicago: University of Chicago Press, 1958.

Armstrong, James D. "Homophobic Slang as Coercive Discourse among College Students." In Livia and Hall, eds., 326–34.

Avenoso, Karen. "Amongst Friends." *Mirabella,* March 1995, pp. 102–6.

Ayto, John, and John Simpson. *The Oxford Dictionary of Modern Slang.* New York: Oxford University Press, 1992.

Badinter, Elisabeth. *XY: On Masculine Identity.* New York: Columbia University Press, 1995.

Baldwin, James. *Another Country.* New York: Dell, 1960.

Barker-Benfield, G. J. *The Horrors of the Half-Known Life: Male Attitudes toward Women and Sexuality in Nineteenth-Century America.* New York: Harper and Row, 1976.

Barreca, Regina. "Making Trouble: An Introduction." In Regina Barreca, ed., *New Perspectives on Women and Comedy,* 1–11. Philadelphia: Gordon and Breach, 1992.

Barthes, Roland. *A Lover's Discourse: Fragments.* Trans. Richard Howard. New York: Hill and Wang, 1978.

Beale, Paul, ed. *Concise Dictionary of Slang and Unconventional English: From a Dictionary of Slang and Unconventional English by Eric Partridge.* New York: Macmillan, 1989.

Beauvoir, Simone de. *The Second Sex.* New York: Bantam, 1952.

Berlyne, D. E. "Laughter, Humor, and Play." In Gardner Lindzey and Elliott Aronson, eds., *The Handbook of Social Psychology.* Vol. 3. Reading, Mass.: Addison-Wesley, 1968.

Best, Fred, ed. Introduction to *The Future of Work.* Englewood Cliffs, N.J.: Prentice-Hall, 1973.

Black, Max. *Models and Metaphors: Studies in Language and Philosophy.* Ithaca, N.Y.: Cornell University Press, 1962.

Booth, Wayne. "Afterthoughts on Metaphor: Ten Literal 'Theses.'" In Sheldon Sacks, ed., 173–74.

Booth, Wayne. "Metaphor as Rhetoric: The Problem of Evaluation." In Sheldon Sacks, ed., 47–70.

Bordo, Susan. "Pills and Power Tools." *Men and Masculinities* 1, no. 1 (July 1998): 87–90.

Boston Women's Health Book Collective. *The New Our Bodies, Ourselves: A Book by and for Women.* New York: Simon and Schuster, 1984.

Bourdieu, Pierre. *Language and Symbolic Power.* Cambridge, Mass.: Harvard University Press, 1991.

Boyle, T. Coraghessan. *The Road to Wellville.* New York: Viking Penguin, 1993.

Brandes, Stanley. *Metaphors of Masculinity: Sex and Status in Andalusian Folklore.* Philadelphia: University of Pennsylvania Press, 1980.

Bred, Hugh. "Metonymy." *Poetics Today* 5, no. 1 (1984): 45–58.

*Brett Butler: The Child Ain't Right.* Produced by Courtney B. Conte and directed by Gary Halverson. 26 minutes. Carsey-Werner Productions. Videocassette, 1995.

Brewer, Sarah. *The Complete Book of Men's Health.* San Francisco: Thorsons, 1995.

Bryant, Clifton D., ed. *The Social Dimensions of Work.* Englewood, N.J.: Prentice-Hall, 1972.

Burg, B. R. "Nocturnal Emissions and Masturbatory Frequency Relationships: A Nineteenth-Century Account." *Journal of Sex Research* 24 (1988): 216–20.

Butler, Judith. *Gender Trouble: Feminism and the Subversion of Identity.* New York: Routledge, 1990.

Califia, Pat. "Dildo Envy and Other Phallic Adventures." In Giles, ed., 90–109.

Cameron, Deborah. "Performing Gender Identity: Young Men's Talk and the Construction of Male Heterosexuality." In Johnson and Meinhof, eds., 47–64.

Cassidy, Frederic. *Dictionary of American Regional English.* Vol. 1. Cambridge, Mass.: Harvard University Press, 1985.

Chang, Jolan. *The Tao of Love and Sex.* New York: Viking, 1993.

Chapman, Robert L. *New Dictionary of American Slang.* New York: Harper and Row, 1986.

Christian, Harry. *The Making of Antisexist Men.* New York: Routledge, 1994.

Clausewitz, Carl von. *On War.* 1832. Reprint, New York: Penguin, 1983.

Cohen, Ted. "Metaphor and the Cultivation of Intimacy." In Sheldon Sacks, ed., 1–10.

Cohn, Carol. "Wars, Wimps, and Women: Talking Gender and Thinking War." In Miriam Cooke and Angela Woolacott, eds., *Gendering War Talk,* 227–46. Princeton, N.J.: Princeton University Press, 1993.

*The Compact Edition of the Oxford English Dictionary.* 2 vols. Oxford, U.K.: Clarendon Press, 1971.

Connell, Robert. *Masculinities.* Berkeley: University of California Press, 1995.

Cooper, David. *Metaphor.* Oxford, U.K.: Basil Blackwell, 1986.

Cornwall, Andrea, and Nancy Lindisfarne, eds. *Dislocating Masculinity: Comparative Ethnographies.* New York: Routledge, 1994.

Costello, Mark, and David Foster Wallace. *Signifying Rappers: Rap and Race in the Urban Present.* Hopewell, N.J.: Ecco, 1990.

Creeley, Robert. *For Love: Poems, 1950–1960.* New York: Scribner's, 1962.

Crocker, J. Christopher. "The Social Functions of Rhetorical Forms." In Sapir and Crocker, eds., 33–66.

Culler, Jonathan. *The Pursuit of Signs: Semiotics, Literature, Deconstruction.* Ithaca, N.Y.: Cornell University Press, 1981.

Curry, Timothy Jon. "Fraternal Bonding in the Locker Room: A Profeminist Analysis of Talk about Competition and Women." *Sociology of Sport Journal* 8, no. 2 (1991): 119–35.

Davidson, Donald. "What Metaphors Mean." In Sheldon Sacks, ed., 29–46.

De Grazia, Sebastian. *Of Time, Work, and Leisure.* New York: Vintage, 1962.

D'Emilio, John, and Estelle B. Freedman. *Intimate Matters: A History of Sexuality in America.* New York: Harper and Row, 1988.

Diagram Group. *Man's Body: An Owner's Manual.* New York: Bantam, 1976.

Disch, Lisa, and Mary Jo Kane. "When a Looker Is Really a Bitch: Lisa Olson, Sport, and the Heterosexual Matrix." *Signs* 21, no. 2 (1996): 278–308.

Dworkin, Andrea. *Pornography: Men Possessing Women.* New York: Perigree, 1981.

Dyer, Gwynne. *War.* New York: Crown, 1985.

Eble, Connie. *Slang and Sociality: In-group Language among College Students.* Chapel Hill: University of North Carolina Press, 1996.

Eco, Umberto. "The Scandal of Metaphor." *Poetics Today* 4, no. 2 (1983): 217–58.

Ehrenreich, Barbara. *Blood Rites: Origins and History of the Passions of War.* New York: Holt, 1997.

Ellis, Havelock. *Studies in the Psychology of Sex.* Vol. 1. 1913. Reprint, Philadelphia: Davis, 1931.

Elshtain, Jean Bethke. *Women and War.* New York: Basic, 1987.

Embler, Weller. *Metaphor and Meaning.* DeLand, Fla: Everett/Edwards, 1966.

Erikson, Kai. Introduction to Kai Erikson and Steven Peter Vallas, eds., *The Nature of Work: Sociological Perspectives,* 1–18. New Haven, Conn.: Yale University Press, 1990.

Erikson, Kai. "On Work and Alienation." In Kai Erikson and Steven Peter Vallas, eds., *The Nature of Work: Sociological Perspectives,* 19–35. New Haven, Conn.: Yale University Press, 1990.

Faludi, Susan. *Backlash: The Undeclared War against American Women.* New York: Anchor Doubleday, 1991.

Faludi, Susan. "The Naked Citadel." *New Yorker,* September 5, 1994, pp. 62–81.

Fairclough, Norman. *Language and Power.* London: Longman, 1989.

Fanon, Franz. *Black Skin, White Masks.* New York: Grove, 1967.

Fasteau, Marc Feigen. *The Male Machine.* New York: Dell, 1975.

Fernandez, James W., ed. *Beyond Metaphor: The Theory of Tropes in Anthropology.* Stanford, Calif.: Stanford University Press, 1991.

Fiedler, Leslie. *Love and Death in the American Novel.* New York: Stein and Day, 1960.

Fitzgerald, Thomas K. *Metaphors of Identity: A Culture-Communication Dialogue.* Albany: State University of New York Press, 1993.

Ford, Richard. *Women with Men.* New York: Knopf, 1997.

Freud, Sigmund. *The Interpretation of Dreams.* 1899. Reprint, New York: Avon, 1965.

Freud, Sigmund. *Jokes and Their Relation to the Unconscious.* 1905. Reprint, New York: Norton, 1960.

Frye, Northrop. "The Expanding World of Metaphor." In Robert D. Denham, ed., *Myth and Metaphor: Selected Essays, 1974–1988,* 108–23. Charlottesville: University Press of Virginia, 1990.

Fuller, J. F. C. *A Military History of the Western World: From the Earliest Times to the Battle of Lepanto.* Vol. 1. New York: Da Capo, 1954.

Gallie, W. B. *Understanding War.* New York: Routledge, 1991.

Gay Left Collective. *Homosexuality: Power and Politics.* London: Allison and Busby, 1980.

Gibson, James William. *Warrior Dreams: Violence and Manhood in Post-Vietnam America.* New York: Hill and Wang, 1994.

Gilbaugh, James H., Jr. *Men's Private Parts: An Owner's Manual.* New York: Crown, 1993.

Gilbert, Sandra M., and Susan Gubar. *The Mad Woman in the Attic: The Woman Writer and the Nineteenth-Century Literary Imagination.* New Haven, Conn.: Yale University Press, 1979.

Gilbert, Sandra M., and Susan Gubar. *No Man's Land: The Place of the Woman Writer in the Twentieth Century.* Vol. 1. New Haven, Conn.: Yale University Press, 1988.

Giles, Fiona, ed. *Dick for a Day: What Would You Do If You Had One?* New York: Villard, 1997.

Gilmore, David. *Manhood in the Making: Cultural Concepts of Masculinity.* New Haven, Conn.: Yale University Press, 1990.

Goldberg, Herb. *The Hazards of Being Male: Surviving the Myth of Male Privilege.* New York: New American Library, 1976.

Goldman, Emma. *Red Emma Speaks: Selected Writings and Speeches.* Ed. Kate Shulman. New York: Vintage, 1972.

Gorn, Elliott J., and Warren Goldstein. *A Brief History of American Sports.* New York: Hill and Wang, 1993.

Gould, Robert E. "Measuring Masculinity by the Size of a Paycheck." In Pleck and Sawyer, eds., 96–99.

Gray, Frances. *Women and Laughter.* Charlottesville: University Press of Virginia, 1994.

Greenwood, Kerry. "Salmancis." In Giles, ed., 65–72.

Guttmann, Allen. *The Erotic in Sports.* New York: Columbia University Press, 1996.

Gutwirth, Marcel. *Laughing Matter: An Essay on the Comic.* Ithaca, N.Y.: Cornell University Press, 1993.

Hall, G. S. *Adolescence, Its Psychology, and Its Relations to Physiology, Anthropology, Sociology, Sex, Crime, Religion, and Education.* New York: Appleton, 1905.

Halley, Janet E. "The Construction of Heterosexuality." In Michael Warner, ed., *Fear of a Queer Planet: Queer Politics and Social Theory,* 82–102. Minneapolis: University of Minnesota Press, 1993.

Hargreaves, John. *Sport, Power, and Culture: A Social and Historical Analysis of Popular Sports in Britain.* New York: St. Martin's Press, 1986.

Haste, Helen. *The Sexual Metaphor: Men, Women, and the Thinking That Makes the Difference.* Cambridge, Mass.: Harvard University Press, 1994.

Hawkes, Terence. *Metaphor.* New York: Routledge, 1972.

Heaney, Seamus. "The Otter." *Field Work.* New York: Farrar, Straus, Giroux, 1979.

Hirschfeld, Magnus. *Sexual Anomalies: The Origins, Nature, and Treatment of Sexual Disorders.* New York: Emerson, 1948.

Hite, Shere. *The Hite Report: A Nationwide Study of Female Sexuality.* New York: Dell, 1976.

Hite, Shere. *The Hite Report on Male Sexuality.* New York: Dell, 1981.

Hoch, Paul. *White Hero Black Beast: Racism, Sexism, and the Mask of Masculinity.* London: Pluto, 1979.

Holman, C. Hugh, and William Harmon. *A Handbook to Literature.* New York: Macmillan, 1986.

Jewett, Sarah Orne. *Novels and Stories.* New York: Library of America, 1994.

Johnson, Sally. "Theorizing Language and Masculinity: A Feminist Perspective." In Johnson and Meinhof, eds., 8–26.

Johnson, Sally, and Ulrike Meinhof, eds. *Language and Masculinity.* London: Blackwell, 1997.

Joyce, Patrick, ed. Introduction to *The Historical Meanings of Work,* 1–30. New York: Cambridge University Press, 1987.

Kamani, Ginu. "Swollen Tide." In Giles, ed., 112–23.

Katz, Jonathan Ned. *The Invention of Heterosexuality.* New York: Dutton, 1995.

Kaufman, Gloria. *In Stitches: A Patchwork of Feminist Humor and Satire.* Bloomington: Indiana University Press, 1991.

Keegan, John. *A History of Warfare.* New York: Vintage, 1993.

Kidwell, Claudia Brush, and Valerie Steele. *Men and Women: Dressing the Part.* Washington, D.C.: Smithsonian Institution Press, 1989.

Kimmel, Michael S. *Manhood in America: A Cultural History.* New York: Free Press, 1996.

Kimmel, Michael S., ed. *Changing Men: New Directions in Research on Men and Masculinity.* Newbury Park, Calif.: Sage, 1987.

Kimmel, Michael S., ed. *The Politics of Manhood: Profeminist Men Respond to the Mythopoetic Men's Movement (and the Mythopoetic Leaders' Answer).* Philadelphia: Temple University Press, 1995.

Kimmel, Michael S., and Thomas E. Mosmiller, eds. *Against the Tide: Profeminist Men in the United States, 1776–1990: A Documentary History.* Boston: Beacon, 1992.

Kinsey, Alfred, Wardell B. Pomeroy, and Clyde E. Martin, eds. *Sexual Behavior in the Human Male.* Philadelphia: Saunders, 1948.

Komisar, Lucy. "Violence and the Masculine Mystique." In Sabo and Runfola, eds., 131–42.

Lakoff, George, and Mark Johnson. *Metaphors We Live By.* Chicago: University of Chicago Press, 1980.

Lamm, Bob. "Learning from Women." In John Snodgrass, ed., *For Men against Sexism,* 49–56. Albion, Calif.: Times Change Press, 1977.

Landar, Herbert. *Language and Culture.* New York: Oxford University Press, 1966.

Laumann, Edward, John Gagnon, Robert Michaels, and Stuart Michaels. *Sex in America.* New York: Warner, 1994.

Laumann, Edward, John Gagnon, Robert Michaels, and Stuart Michaels. *The So-*

*cial Organization of Sexuality: Sexual Practices in the United States*. Chicago: University of Chicago Press, 1994.

Lawrence, D. H. *Lady Chatterley's Lover*. 1928. Reprint, New York: Grove, 1962.

Leap, William L. *Word's Out: Gay Men's English*. Minneapolis: University of Minnesota Press, 1996.

Lefkowitz, Bernard. *Our Guys: The Glen Ridge Rape and the Secret Life of the Perfect Suburb*. Berkeley: University of California Press, 1997.

Legman, Gershen. *The Rationale of the Dirty Joke*. Vols. 1 and 2. New York: Grove, 1968, 1975.

Lewis, Michael. *Liar's Poker: Rising through the Wreckage on Wall Street*. New York: Penguin, 1990.

Lifshin, Lyn. "Years Later Lorena Thinks of the Penis She Had for a Day." In Giles, ed., 74–75.

Livia, Anna, and Kira Hall, eds. *Queerly Phrased: Language, Gender, and Sexuality*. New York: Oxford University Press, 1997.

Louis, Adrian C. *Skins*. New York: Crown, 1995.

Lyman, Peter. "The Fraternal Bond as a Joking Relationship: A Case Study of Sexist Jokes in Male Group Bonding." In Kimmel, ed., *Changing Men*, 148–63.

Maas, James. *Speaking of Friends: The Variety of Man-to-Man Relationships*. Berkeley, Calif.: Shameless Hussy Press, 1985.

MacHovec, Frank. *Humor: Theory, History, Applications*. Springfield, Ill.: Charles Thomas, 1988.

Mamet, David. *Sexual Perversity in Chicago and the Duck Variations*. New York: Grove, 1978.

Mandell, Richard. *Sport: A Cultural History*. New York: Columbia University Press, 1984.

Marx, Karl. *The Economic and Philosophical Manuscripts of 1844*. Ed. Dirk J. Struik. New York: International, 1964.

Marx, Karl. "Theses on Feuerbach." In Karl Marx and Friedrich Engels, *Selected Works*, vol. 1, 13–15. Moscow: Progress, 1969.

Mead, Walter Russell. "Comment: Mutually Assured Stupidity." *New Yorker*, March 11, 1996, pp. 9–10.

Messner, Michael. *Power at Play: Sports and the Problem of Masculinity*. Boston: Beacon, 1992.

Messner, Michael, and Don Sabo, eds. *Sport, Men, and the Gender Order: Critical Feminist Perspectives*. Champaign, Ill.: Human Kinetics Books, 1990.

Miller, Toby. "A Short History of the Penis." *Social Text* 13, no. 2 (1995): 1–26.

Millet, Kate. *Sexual Politics*. New York: Ballantine, 1969.

Mills, C. Wright. "The Meaning of Work throughout History." In Best, ed., 6–13.

Mills, Jane. *Womanwords: A Vocabulary of Culture and Patriarchal Society*. London: Virago, 1991.

Mills, Sara. *Discourse*. London: Routledge, 1997.

Moonwoman-Baird, Birch. "Toward the Study of Lesbian Speech." In Livia and Hall, eds., 202–13.

Morgan, David. *Discovering Men*. New York: Routledge, 1992.

Mort, Frank. "Sexuality: Regulation and Contestation." In Gay Left Collective, 38–51.

Mulkay, Michael. *On Humour: Its Nature and Its Place in Modern Society.* London: Polity, 1988.

Mumford, Lewis. *Technics and Civilization.* New York: Harcourt Brace, 1947.

Murphy, Peter F. Review of *Iron John: A Book about Men* by Robert Bly. *Changing Men,* no. 23 (fall–winter 1991): 51.

Murphy, Peter F. "Toward a Feminist Masculinity: A Review Essay." *Feminist Studies* 15, no. 2 (summer 1989): 351–61.

Murphy, Peter F., ed. *Fictions of Masculinity: Crossing Cultures, Crossing Sexualities.* New York: New York University Press, 1994.

Nelson, Mariah Burton. *The Stronger Women Get, the More Men Like Football: Sexism and the American Culture of Sports.* New York: Harcourt Brace, 1994.

Niering, William A., and Nancy C. Olmstead. *The Audubon Society Field Guide to North American Wildflowers: Eastern Region.* New York: Knopf, 1979.

Nordheimer, Jon. "Some Couples May Find Viagra a Home Wrecker." *New York Times,* May 10, 1998, sect. 9, p. 2.

Obermiller, Tim Andrew. "Sex by the Numbers." *University of Chicago Magazine,* October 1994, pp. 34–37.

O'Connell, Robert L. *Ride of the Second Horseman: The Birth and Death of War.* New York: Oxford University Press, 1995.

Pagels, Elaine. *Adam, Eve, and the Serpent.* New York: Vintage, 1989.

Perry, Frances, ed. *Simon and Schuster's Complete Guide to Plants and Flowers.* New York: Simon and Schuster, 1974.

Pleck, Joseph, and Jack Sawyer, eds. *Men and Masculinity.* Englewood Cliffs, N.J.: Prentice-Hall, 1974.

Powell, Chris. "A Phenomenological Analysis of Humour in Society." In Chris Powell, ed., *Humour in Society: Resistance and Control,* 86–105. London: Macmillan, 1988.

Pronger, Brian. *The Arena of Masculinity: Sports, Homosexuality and the Meaning of Sex.* New York: St. Martin's, 1990.

Queen, Robin M. "'I Don't Speak Spritch': Locating Lesbian Language." In Livia and Hall, eds., 233–56.

Quinn, Naomi. "The Cultural Basis of Metaphor." In Fernandez, ed., 56–93.

Reynaud, Emmanuel. *Holy Virility: The Social Construction of Masculinity.* London: Pluto, 1983.

Rich, Adrienne. "Compulsory Heterosexuality and Lesbian Existence." In Ann Snitow, Christine Stansell, and Sharon Thompson, eds., *Powers of Desire: The Politics of Sexuality,* 177–205. New York: Monthly Review Press, 1983.

Rich, Adrienne. *On Lies, Secrets, and Silence: Selected Prose, 1966–1978.* New York: Norton, 1979.

Ricoeur, Paul. *The Rule of Metaphor: Multidisciplinary Studies of the Creation of Meaning in Language.* Toronto: University of Toronto Press, 1977.

Rigauer, Bero. *Sport and Work.* New York: Columbia University Press, 1981.

*Robin Williams: An Evening at the Met.* Produced by David Steinberg and coproduced by Vic Kaplan. Directed by Bruce Cowers. 65 minutes. Mr. Happy Productions. Videocassette, 1986.

Rose, Tricia. *Black Noise: Rap Music and Black Culture in Contemporary America.* Hanover, N.H.: Wesleyan University Press, 1994.

Rubin, Gayle. "The Traffic in Women: Notes on the 'Political Economy' of Sex." In Rayna R. Reiter, ed., *Toward an Anthropology of Women,* 157–210. New York: Monthly Review Press, 1975.

Ruegs, Maria. "Metaphor and Metonymy: The Logic of Structuralist Rhetoric." *Glyph* 6 (1979): 141–57.

Russo, Richard. *Straight Man.* New York: Vintage, 1997.

Sabo, Don, and Ross Runfola, eds. *Jock: Sports and Male Identity.* Englewood Cliffs, N.J.: Prentice-Hall, 1980.

Sacks, Harvey. "Some Technical Considerations of a Dirty Joke." In Jim Schenken, ed., *Studies in the Organization of Conversational Interaction,* 249–69. New York: Academic, 1978.

Sacks, Sheldon, ed. *On Metaphor.* Chicago: University of Chicago Press, 1978.

Sapir, J. David. "The Anatomy of Metaphor." In Sapir and Crocker, eds., 3–32.

Sapir, J. David, and J. Christopher Crocker, eds. *The Social Uses of Metaphor: Essays on the Anthropology of Rhetoric.* Philadelphia: University of Pennsylvania Press, 1977.

Scheman, Naomi. *Engenderings: Constructions of Knowledge, Authority, and Privilege.* New York: Routledge, 1993.

Schmitz, Neil. *Of Huck and Alice: Humorous Writing in American Literature.* Minneapolis: University of Minneapolis Press, 1983.

Seidler, Victor. *Rediscovering Masculinity: Reason, Language, and Sexuality.* New York: Routledge, 1989.

Shire, Chenjerai. "Men Don't Go to the Moon: Language, Space, and Masculinities." In Cornwall and Lindisfarne, eds., 147–58.

*Showtime Comedy Superstars—Elayne Boosler: Live Nude Girls.* Produced by Cara Tapper, Steve White, and Barry Bernardi. Directed by Juliana Lavin. 59 minutes. Paramount. Videocassette, 1995.

Silverstein, Michael. "The History of a Short, Unsuccessful Academic Career." In Pleck and Sawyer, eds., 107–23.

Sinclair, Peter, ed. *King, Warrior, Magician, Weenie: Contemporary Men's Humor.* Freedom, Calif.: Crossing Press, 1993.

Singer, Natalia Rachel. "Journey to Justice." *Ms.,* November–December 1994, pp. 29–40.

Smith, Paul. "Men in Feminism: Men and Feminist Theory." In Alice Jardine and Paul Smith, eds., *Men in Feminism,* 33–40. New York: Methuen, 1987.

Spears, Richard A. *Slang and Euphemism: A Dictionary of Oaths, Curses, Insults, Ethnic Slurs, Sexual Slang and Metaphor, Drug Talk, College Lingo, and Related Matters.* New York: Signet, 1982.

Spradley, James, and Brenda Mann. *The Cocktail Waitress: Woman's Work in a Man's World.* New York: McGraw Hill, 1975.

Stoltenberg, John. *Refusing to Be a Man: Essays on Sex and Justice.* Portland, Ore.: Breitenbush Books, 1989.

Sutton, Laurel A. "Bitches and Shankly Hobags: The Place of Women in Contemporary Slang." In Kira Hall and Mary Bucholtz, eds., *Gender Articulated: Language and the Socially Constructed Self,* 279–96. New York: Routledge, 1995.

Tannen, Deborah. *You Just Don't Understand: Women and Men in Conversation.* New York: Ballantine, 1990.

Thorne, Tony. *The Dictionary of Contemporary Slang.* New York: Pantheon, 1990.

Tilgher, Adriano. *Homo Faber: Work through the Ages.* 1931. Reprint, Chicago: Regenery, 1958.

Torr, Diane. "How to Be a Great Guy." In Giles, ed., 249–51.

Trimberger, Ellen Kay. "Feminism, Men, and Modern Love: Greenwich Village, 1900–1925." In Ann Snitow, Christine Stansell, and Sharon Thompson, eds., *Powers of Desire: The Politics of Sexuality,* 131–52. New York: Monthly Review Press, 1983.

Trujillo, Nick. "Machines, Missiles, and Men: Images of the Male Body on ABC's *Monday Night Football.*" *Sociology of Sport Journal* 12, no. 4 (1995): 403–23.

Walker, Nancy. *A Very Serious Thing: Women's Humor and American Culture.* Minneapolis: University of Minnesota Press, 1990.

Warden, Tricia. "Shhhhh." In Giles, ed., 142–49.

Warren, Roz, ed. *The Best Contemporary Women's Humor.* Freedom, Calif.: Crossing Press, 1994.

Warren, Roz, ed. *Glibquips: Funny Words by Funny Women.* Freedom, Calif.: Crossing Press, 1994.

Warren, Roz, ed. *Revolutionary Laughter: The World of Women Comics.* Freedom, Calif.: Crossing Press, 1995.

Warren, Roz, ed. *Women's Glibber: State-of-the-Art Women's Humor.* Freedom, Calif.: Crossing Press, 1992.

*Webster's New World Dictionary of the American Language.* New York: World Publishing, 1968.

Weeks, Jeffrey. "Capitalism and the Organization of Sex." In Gay Left Collective, 11–20.

Wentworth, Harold, and Stuart Berg Flexner, eds. *Dictionary of American Slang.* New York: Crowell, 1960.

Wertheim, Margaret. "The Pricks in Physics: A Historical Fantasy." In Giles, ed., 153–60.

Weston, Kath. *Render Me, Gender Me: Lesbians Talk Sex, Class, Color, Nation, Studmuffins.* New York: Columbia University Press, 1997.

White, Hayden. *Metahistory: The Historical Imagination in Nineteenth-Century Europe.* Baltimore, Md.: Johns Hopkins University Press, 1973.

*Whoopi Goldberg.* Produced by Whoop, Inc., in association with Broadway Video and DIR Broadcasting. Directed by Thomas Schlamme. 75 minutes. Based on an original HBO presentation. Videocassette. 1986.

Williams, Raymond. *Keywords: A Vocabulary of Culture and Society.* London: Oxford University Press, 1976.

Willis, Ellen. *Beginning to See the Light: Pieces of a Decade.* New York: Knopf, 1981.

Wilson, Christopher. *Jokes: Form, Content, Use, and Function.* New York: Academic, 1979.

Yolen, Jane. "Dick W. and His Pussy; or Tess and Her Adequate Dick." In Giles, ed., 162–66.

Zhou, Xiao. "Virginity and Premarital Sex in Contemporary China." *Feminist Studies* 15, no. 2 (summer 1989): 279–88.

Ziv, Avner. *Personality and Sense of Humor.* New York: Springer, 1984.